French Romantics on Progress:
Human and Aesthetic

José Porrúa Turanzas, S.A.
EDICIONES

Director General:
JOSÉ PORRÚA VENERO

Sub-Director General:
ENRIQUE PORRÚA VENERO

Director:
CONSTANTINO GARCÍA GARVÍA

Asesor literario:
BRUNO M. DAMIANI

stuóia humanitatis

Directed by
BRUNO M. DAMIANI
The Catholic University of America

ELWOOD HARTMAN

French Romantics on Progress:

Human and Aesthetic

studia humanitatis

Publisher and distributor
José Porrúa Turanzas, S.A.
Cea Bermúdez, 10 - Madrid-3
España

Distributor for U.S.A.
Studia Humanitatis
1383 Kersey Lane
Potomac, Maryland 20854

Printed in the United States of America
Impreso en Los Estados Unidos

Cea Bermúdez, 10 - Madrid-3
Ediciones José Porrúa Turanzas, S.A.

to Polly and Alex

Contents

Preface

Critics of the arts frequently find themselves divided into opposing groups, those who revere the masterpieces of the past, particularly of classical times, and disdain more recent creations, and those who, although acknowledging the contributions of other cultural epochs, feel that the present is producing equal and occasionally superior works of art. The two factions can be labeled "ancients" and "moderns" in the terminology of the seventeenth and eighteenth-century French literary quarrel.

The Quarrel of the Ancients and Moderns is an eternal one. Greeks and Romans expressed aesthetic preferences in terms of progress and decadence. Europeans have always measured themselves against men of antiquity and judged if their works have improved or degenerated. Recent artists and writers debate the direction that their disciplines seem to be following, with the traditionalists pessimistically announcing a decline from past standards, and the avant-garde optimistically promising the attainment of greater heights of achievement.

In most contemporary settings the Quarrel is now manifested in the rivalry of the cinema with traditional stage representations and/or the printed text as an art medium. In literature concern over the "death" of the novel and the relative worth of its heirs—the anti- and the new- (and even the anti-anti- or new-new-) novel—is evident. In music proponents of computer compositions and synthesizers speak glowingly of the rich new horizons opened for their art, while the unconvinced embrace more fervently Beethoven or Brahms, to them the tried and true. Defenders of the super-realism of pop art versus abstractionism represent but another aspect of the multifaceted Quarrel.

The Quarrel interpreted more broadly than as simply an artistic debate has also been eternal. The theory of progress has vied with that of decadence as the explanation of man's history. Since time immemorial believers in the myth of the Golden Age have decried man's decline since the destruction of the earthly paradise. Although they admit a possible increase in knowledge, i.e. information, they view contemporary man as possessing less moral fibre, less originality, less talent than his predecessors. They are the proponents of decadence. Those who favor the theory of progress describe the human race instead as climbing from darkness to light. They await the millennium when man will shed his cocoon of ignorance, prejudice, and cultural limitations to emerge in a perfected state.

This work is concerned with the theories of progress, both human and aesthetic, mainly literary, of several of the most renowned French writers of the first half of the nineteenth century. To illustrate their debt to past quarrelers and to emphasize their originality, an introduction of a historical nature treats the development of the idea of progress and its counterpart, decadence, from its inception through the French Revolution. Special emphasis is given to the seventeenth and eighteenth centuries in France, the epoch of the famous *Querelle des Anciens et des Modernes*, when the most intense debate on literary progress took place.

Eleven authors serve as a sounding board. Chosen for their preeminence in the field of letters, they represent Romanticism from its birth through its decline. Mme de Staël, whose dual nature as Romantic precursor and vestigial Classicist qualified her as a transitional figure between two ages, begins the discussion. Sainte-Beuve, whose advantageous position as post-Romantic historian and critic enabled him to assess the merits of that movement, ends it. Within these end points the ideas of poets—Hugo, Vigny, Lamartine, Musset, Gautier, and Baudelaire—and of novelists—Chateaubriand, Stendhal, and Balzac—are studied. In the varied approach to the question of progress taken by these writers one sees the reiteration of ageless arguments and the formulation of original theses reflective of the peculiar personality of each debater. Their theories have been extracted from manifestoes, prefaces, and polemical writings on the one hand, and from imaginative works of prose and poetry on the other, with particular attention being paid to the attitude of each author first toward mankind and then toward literature and the writer and the interrelation of the two to provide insights into his or her optimism or pessimism.

It is hoped that in reviewing the fortunes of the doctrine of progress over so many centuries generally and in detail in the early nineteenth in France, its application to literature will be recognized as a possibility, if not a fact. An effort will be made to dispel the prejudice that progress implies a blind awe of the new and total neglect of the old. Thus a compromise is sought in the Quarrel of the Ancients and Moderns. The extreme positions of both sides are abandoned in search of a more moderate position that recognizes advances in quality in the new while continuing to cherish the merits of the old. It must be admitted that few facts, in the scientific sense, are supplied in these debates. Art is the kingdom of opinion. Nevertheless, with the advantage of hindsight, we of the twentieth century are capable of determining which opinions have had an enduring influence and which have evaporated as mere personal prejudices.

Many books have served as an aid in the preparation of this study. Most, however, have concerned themselves with the idea of human rather than artistic progress. While French historians and critics have scrupulously investigated the period of the Quarrel, no one to my knowledge has extended his perspective to include the Romantic Era. Hippolyte Rigault, author of the definitive history of the *Querelle*, proposed such a project but unfortunately did not complete it.

The time period studied here is necessarily limited, and the investigation of succeeding literary epochs would doubtless prove worthwhile. Nevertheless, the first half of the nineteenth century in France has special significance, for it more fully bore the impact of the philosophy of the Enlightenment, founded on a belief in progress, and it esteemed itself a second artistic renaissance, to many more glorious than the first. Within such an atmosphere, the discussion of progress, human and literary, was most intense.

Acknowledgments

The various debts of gratitude owed for the completion of this study are both of long duration and numerous. Only a few can be acknowledged, and among these are: Professor Robert Greer Cohn, who first suggested this topic to me as a graduate student at Stanford University; Professors Raymond Giraud, John C. Lapp, and Leo Weinstein, under whose guidance it was then developed into a dissertation; Mme Florence Chu, Stanford Libraries, and Monsieur Fernand Tramier, Bibliothèque de Versailles, who aided in the research; Professor Robert T. Denommé, University of Virginia, who has been instrumental in its conversion into a book; and here at Washington State University, Associate Provost Thomas L. Kennedy, Executive Vice President and Provost Albert C. Yates, and Dean Lois De Fleur of Humanities and Social Sciences who have continuously provided funds essential to its completion. Overriding any other debt, however, is incontestably that owed to Pollyann Young Hartman, my wife, for her perpetual encouragement and support.

Chapter One

Introduction

The French Romantics form but part of the long series of debaters on the question of progress. From earliest antiquity to the present intellectuals have been fascinated by the idea that man and his accomplishments have improved with the passage of time.

Indeed by the beginning of the nineteenth the theory of progress had been widely discussed in France, particularly during the preceding two centuries, when proponents of progress claimed its permeation into all human endeavors, including the arts. Thus, the Romantics' discussion of the idea was scarcely unique, for it continued an age-old debate. Nevertheless, a note of originality was added as each author reconsidered the issues from his peculiar point of view as an artist in a post-revolutionary age. Sustained by the belief that his era was a second and more glorious artistic renaissance, but shaken by the experience of the recent political upheaval, the French Romantics found the issue of man and art's progress to be a pertinent one.

By investigating the origins of the concept of progress and the evolution of the idea from classical antiquity through the period of the French Revolution, a background can be reconstructed against which the Romantic debate can be set. Thus, both continuity and evolution in the nineteenth-century discussion will become evident. It should always be remembered that while a quarrel between ancients and moderns has always existed, it has also been ever changing.

Beginning with a definition of progress, we will then attempt to analyze the complex and multiple nature of the concept. Of the many kinds of progress, only two, human and artistic (sometimes plastic but mainly literary), are singled out for discussion. Statements of artists, philosophers and theoreticians are reviewed chronologically to determine pre-Romantic thought.

Definition and Analysis

To progress literally means to move forward, coming from the Latin root words *pro* and *gradi*, the latter being the present infinitive to the verb *gradior*, meaning "to step." In French *progresser* has as a definition *marcher en avant*.

Progress implies improvement, presuming that to move forward one advances from a less perfect state to a more perfect one. Thus, the term is commonly used in reference to humanity and the arts. One speaks of the progress of civilization or of the progress of poetry, meaning its improvement. One of the many examples of such usage is Fénelon's statement: "Je suis charmé des progrès qu'un petit nombre d'auteurs a donnés à notre poésie."[1]

When extended into the realm of philosophy the idea of progress is often expressed by the term *perfectibility*, meaning man's continuous march toward perfection and happiness. Although seriously questioned today, the idea of perfectibility was more commonly accepted as little as one hundred years ago. One finds in the *Dictionnaire Larousse* of the 1860's the following confirmation:

> L'Humanité est perfectible et elle va incessamment du moins bien au mieux, de l'ignorance à la science, de la barbarie à la civilisation

---

[1] E. Littré. "Progrès," *Dictionnaire de la langue française*. (Paris: s.d.)

. . . . Dans le domaine de l'intelligence, la loi de perfectibilité se manifeste si visiblement que personne n'oserait la méconnaître. Les faits parlent. L'homme s'élance des ténèbres de la nuit pour s'élever graduellement à la lumière. L'intelligence s'éveille. L'esprit d'observation se révèle. La science fait des premières conquêtes, les arts s'inventent, grossiers d'abord, plus raffinés ensuite, et chaque génération qui passe lègue à la génération suivante le patrimoine commun enrichi et agrandi.[2]

In actuality the lexicographer's assurance of man's progress has not always been shared by others. Along with those who believe in progress are those who believe in decadence. They view history as a diminishing progression in which each succeeding stage is always inferior to the one which came before. They long for the lost perfection of a Golden Age or *paradis perdu*. Voltaire took such pessimists to task in his mocking poem "Le Mondain":

Regrettera qui veut le bon vieux temps,
Et l'âge d'or et le règne d'Astrée, . . .
Moi, je rends grâce à la nature sage,
Qui, pour mon bien, m'a fait naître en cet âge.

The division of opinion is age-old, reflective of a fundamental difference in human nature, Rigault has suggested:

Deux esprits se partagent le monde, l'esprit ancien et l'esprit nouveau, tous deux légitimes, car ils correspondent à deux besoins réels de l'humanité, la tradition et le progrès. La tradition, on ne la respecte pas toujours, mais on ne doute pas de son existence; c'est un ensemble d'idées admises et de faits accomplis, et l'on ne peut nier ni le passé ni l'histoire. Le progrès, on en conteste souvent la réalité; on le prend pour un rêve, parce que c'est à la fois un jugement porté sur le passé, discutable comme tous les jugements, et une espérance dans l'avenir que l'avenir peut tromper, comme toutes les espérances.[3]

Rigault's analysis reaches to the root of the problem. Progress, like beauty, is often in the eye of the beholder. On the other

---

[2] Pierre Larousse. "Progrès," *Le Grand Dictionnaire universel du XIXème siècle.* (Paris: Administration du G.D.U., 1866)
[3] Hippolyte Rigault. *Histoire de la querelle des anciens et des modernes.* (Paris: Librairie de L. Hachette et Cie, 1856), p. 1.

hand, decadence is also a subjective phenomenon. Tradition alone comes closest to objective reality.

Rigault, who believed in progress for religious reasons, reflects a prevailing attitude among the moderns of nineteenth-century France. His twentieth-century American counterpart, represented by Professor J. B. Bury, whose work *The Idea of Progress* is now a classic, is equally convinced, if for different reasons. Bury flatly states that man continuously improves. He calls this belief the animating and controlling idea of Western thought.[4]

Up to this point we have been considering the concept of progress in most general terms. Sharpening our focus a bit, let us differentiate the kinds of progress. There are intellectual, scientific, and material progress. Because these three produce tangible results they are less disputed. The more controversial kinds are social, moral and artistic progress. Social progress seems more hoped for than achieved. The idea of moral progress is almost unthinkable today. The horror of two world wars has terminated the optimism such a belief would require. Aesthetic progress in general suffers almost the same abandonment as moral progress. Although the results of progress in art can be as tangible as those of scientific progress, in matters of technique, for example, there are also the aspects of taste, quality, and genius, which are more elusive and undemonstrable. In addition, one always has preferences in the distant past that innovations or perfections of more recent works in no way diminish.

In the realm of art, the debaters again fall into two categories. The more optimistic among the moderns are those who see not only an advance in technique but also in overall aesthetic quality. One such modern is Thomas Munro, who in his *Evolution in the Arts and Other Theories of Culture History* maintains that the concept of progress when defined broadly can be applied to the arts. He argues that man will accept the term progress in an artistic context if it is rid of prophetic overtones.

---

[4] *The Idea of Progress, an Inquiry into its Origin and Growth.* (London: Macmillan and Co., Ltd., 1920), p. vii.

Munro's position is that progress in art is possible, but not inevitable, and has been sporadic, not continuous.[5] The more pessimistic on the side of the ancients believe that art was created in a perfect form long ago, mysteriously, inexplicably. Since the beginning of art history, this initial perfection has been equaled but never surpassed. Sir Herbert Read among contemporary ancients best represents this position:

> If we take the art of drawing as a convenient testing-ground of aesthetic sensibility, then we can affirm that at no intervening state has the original quality of art been surpassed by any subsequent phase of art or by any individual artist. Some of the painters of Greek vases, some of the medieval illuminators of manuscripts, the great painters of the Renaissance, certain painters of the nineteenth century—all these have perhaps reached the level of aesthetic quality present in the cave paintings at Lascaux or Altamira, but they have not exceeded that original standard.[6]

The optimists and pessimists both agree that in the matter of technique there has been artistic progress. The discovery of chiaroscuro along with the development of perspective in painting is generally recognized as progress. The progress of non-artistic endeavors which have beneficially influenced creativity is frequently acknowledged by both sides—for example, scientific advances which have improved architecture, intellectual progress which has provided larger audiences for works of art, a more cultivated and demanding group of appreciators. The general advance of civilization, optimists maintain, has also improved the quality of art, by more greatly stimulating the creative genius.

Perhaps the greatest stumbling block to the acceptance of the concept of progress in the arts is the idea that progress implies a kind of annihilation, a relegation of past accomplishments to history. In science, for example, the latest knowledge replaces preceding information, proving it wrong or insuf-

---

[5] (Cleveland: The Cleveland Museum of Art, 1963), p. 177. Cf. "Do the Arts Progress?" *The Journal of Aesthetics and Art Criticism.* Vol. XIV, No. 2, (Dec. 1955).

[6] "Art and the Evolution of Consciousness," *JAAC.* Vol. XIII, No. 2, (Dec. 1954), p. 143.

ficient. In art, the newest work, even if superior, does not replace its predecessors, but must stand alongside them. Some insist that because progress by replacement does not occur in the arts, there can be no progress, only evolution, i.e. change. Bénac sums up this commonly held point of view:

Il ne faut pas confondre le progrès dans la pensée avec le progrès esthétique. Sans doute les modernes disent quelque chose de plus que les écrivains du passé, mais cela n'annule pas, comme pour la science, ce que ceux-ci ont dit. Car le message du passé garde une valeur permanente, que le présent peut même renouveler et enrichir et, surtout, il a été exprimé d'une manière unique et irremplaçable. Chaque civilisation, même si elle est en progrès sur la précédente (ce qui n'est pas toujours le cas), ne crée pas, dans les lettres et les arts, une beauté supérieure, mais une beauté qualitativement différente, oeuvre d'un génie individuel original.[7]

Bénac is supported by Brunetière and many others. Still some contest this view, believing there is progress by addition. Modern artists are superior to their predecessors, because they have the advantage of building upon a richer background. More recent art is not only different, but superior, Javarry among others has proclaimed:

Or, nous pensons que si en effet les idées d'une époque plus avancée pouvaient être amenées par des efforts . . . à un point de netteté et d'harmonie tel qu'elles puissent donner matière à des oeuvres d'un goût aussi irréprochables et d'une inspiration aussi élevée, ces idées étant plus riches et plus profondes, le résultat devrait être supérieur; et c'est en ce sens qu'on peut préférer les grands écrivains du siècle de Louis XIV à ceux de l'antiquité et que Voltaire . . . semble trouver un progrès d'Homère à Virgile, de Virgile au Tasse, en ce que, à l'égalité de mérite peut-être, la matière des oeuvres gagne en valeur, l'art lui-même se perfectionne.[8]

History of the Idea of Progress: Its Origins

Turning from the analysis of the problems involved in

[7] H. Bénac. *Guide pour la recherche des idées dans les dissertations et les études littéraires.* (Paris: Hachette, 1961), p. 273.
[8] A. Javarry. *De l'idée de progrès.* (Paris: Librairie philosophique de Ladrange, 1851), p. 111.

defining the concept of progress, in particular when it is applied to the arts, to the history of its evolution in form, one discovers almost as many variations of the doctrine as there were spokesmen. The subjective nature of the argument is constantly underlined.

Classical antiquity produces the first evidence of the concept of progress. It was poorly defined. There was no belief that mankind as a whole was improving. The idea of intellectual progress existed—Aristotle thought the moderns wiser—and the concept of decadence was known.

In fact, the theory of decadence enjoyed more support than that of progress. It was expressed by the myth of the Golden Age, a far-off time when men were larger and stronger, when there was no work, and man lived off nature. Crime, strife, and avarice were completely lacking. Man, devoid of knowledge, lived in simple ignorance, contented and good. He had no need for art or justice. Unoppressed by responsibility he needed no diversion.[9]

Prometheus' gift of fire (knowledge/the arts) to man signaled the end of the Golden Age according to mythology. With the awakening of knowledge in mortals, misfortune gained a foothold. Wisdom meant the knowledge of evil as well as good. Its price was the loss of happiness. It is interesting to note that according to the legend, the arts were then developed to enable man to forget his miserable state. Intellectual progress resulted both in artistic progress and moral decadence, a belief later to be repeated by Rousseau.

The Golden Age is a favorite theme among the poets of antiquity. Hesiod in the eighth century B.C. pictured man as experiencing continuous decline. He devised a theory that the world had passed through a series of ages, named for various metals, beginning with the most precious, gold, then moving to silver and lastly bronze. These three ages were then followed by a time of heroes, whose fall gave way to full-fledged decadence. Later poets condensed Hesiod's historical expla-

---

[9] F. J. Teggart and H. G. Hildebrand. *The Idea of Progress, A Collection of Readings.* (Berkeley: University of California Press, 1949), p. 5.

nation, naming four ages in the development of civilization, only those of the metals, followed directly by decadence. One also finds this version in Plato's *Politics* (ca. 360–348 B.C.) and Virgil's *Georgics* (37–30 B.C.) as well as in the writings of Ovid and Cicero.

An early and perhaps singular flirtation with a belief in progress is revealed by Thucydides in the fifth century B.C. He repudiated the idea of a Golden Age, having recognized the material progress of civilization, but he cautiously did not prophesy that such progress would continue into the future. (Teggart and Hildebrand, p. 6)

The Ionian philosophers in the fifth and sixth centuries B.C. also rejected Hesiod's theory of the Golden Age and embraced instead the concept of the Cycles of History. They viewed life as following a regular and inevitable pattern, and applying this to civilization, they saw mankind developing in terms of birth-to-death cycles. Plato supports this view when in the *Statesman* (ca. 360–348 B.C.) he speaks of the three ages of man and of the world—youth, virility, and old age. He thought the world mortal but refused to label its evolution from womb to tomb as either progress or decadence.

Plato extended his cautious attitude to the arts, declaring the various eras of art to be different but not superior or inferior to each other. In the *Laws* (ca. 360–348 B.C.) he illustrated his theory of the relativity of beauty with a reference to Egyptian art: "If one looks closely, one will find paintings and sculptures made 10,000 years ago . . . which are neither more nor less beautiful than those of today, and which have been created according to the same rules."[10]

In Roman antiquity the theories of progress and decadence were directly applied to the arts. The Quarrel of the Ancients and Moderns was in a way anticipated when partisans of Greek literature condemned Caesarian writers as upstarts and longed for the literary golden age. Later Seneca defended a new set of moderns against those preferring the

---

[10] Maurice Vauthier. "L'Idée du progrès," extrait de la *Revue de l'Université de Bruxelles*. No. IV (mai-juin-juillet 1926), p. 3.

8

days of Ciceronian eloquence. Pliny the Younger grew disgusted with the pro-ancients of his day and expressed contentment with the works of Virginius Romanus. In 81 A.D. Tacitus wrote the *Dialogue of the Orators* in which Messala, the pro-ancient, and Aper, the pro-modern, debate the merits of past and contemporary writers. Having pointed out the successes and failures of both groups, the combatants at last agree to a truce. Messala generally concludes that every man is both an ancient and a modern, for he can never be entirely free from the past. He also states that taste changes with time, but betraying a certain pessimism he adds that change is not necessarily corruption, while passing over the fact that change can also be improvement. Aper opts for relativity and declares there are no ancients or moderns. Both recognize the fortune of art to be heavily dependent on the health of political institutions and mores, an idea which will enjoy popularity among French authors of the eighteenth and nineteenth centuries. (Rigault, pp. 11–15)

Longing for the past was evidently a prevalent phenomenon in Roman times as revealed by the derivatives of the word *antique*. *Antiquus* was synonymous with *aestimandus* and *probus*. The comparative form *antiquior* could be replaced by *potior* or *melior*. The superlative *antiquissimus* was the equivalent of *optimus* or *carrus*.[11]

Leaping forward in time to the fifth century we find Saint Augustine refuting Plato's theory of the Cycles of History, while accepting some of his other beliefs. For man to be condemned continuously to repeat the past would mean that the good as well as the bad must recur. This would be impossible, Saint Augustine argued, for history is marked by the appearance of unique figures, such as Christ and Plato himself, who will have no equal no matter how long mankind endures. Saint Augustine believed instead that mankind developed in stages but did not repeat itself. Each man lived but once, each society enjoyed but one flourishing period. On this one-way

---

[11] Léon Maury. *Essai sur les origines de l'idée du progrès*. Thèse de théologie. (Nîmes: Imprimerie Clavel et Chastanier, 1890), p. 40.

path mankind matured as would an individual. It advanced by means of education from ignorance to knowledge and lastly to faith. Plato's analogy of mankind with an individual, repeated here, recurs in the writings of Pascal and Lamartine.

The concept of progress, as we have seen, was not a major issue in either classical antiquity or during the Middle Ages. Its formation was slow and limited with the counter-theory of decadence often proving the more popular. By the time of the Renaissance, however, Western man's attitude drastically altered. Instead of timid flirtation with the concept, one finds enthusiastic claims on its behalf presented by men who believed in progress because they were witnessing it.

The Idea of Progress in the Renaissance

It has been said that two principles governed the Renaissance mind: authority and progress. Scholasticism, the view that truth was to be found only in the assertions of ancient and learned authorities, vied with a new spirit, the scientific mind, which insisted upon proof by observation. The Renaissance man was conscious of the progress of the last few centuries. He was even more aware of the rapid changes occurring during his own times. His optimism bolstered by the success of his contemporaries, he became more willing to join the revolt against authority, which represented the past, in favor of freedom to examine and to experiment, expressing his trust in the future.[12]

Progress itself fitted nicely as a doctrine into the spirit of revolt of the times. It was naturalistic, humanistic philosophy, not at all supernatural or ascetic as were the medieval Christian doctrines. Progress encouraged a break with the past, for it required rejection of the Christian view that man must first suffer a mortal life in order to enjoy an immortal one. Utopia, it was decided, could be of this earth. Man was thought capable

---

[12] Hubert Gillot. *La Querelle des Anciens et des Modernes en France de la Défense et Illustration de la langue française aux Parallèles des anciens et des modernes.* (Paris: Librairie Ancienne Honoré Champion, 1914), p. 33.

of improving himself and his condition, perhaps indefinitely, unaided by Providence. The turning away from the divine to the human typified Renaissance thought.

Two early and audacious supporters of the doctrine of progress were Francis Bacon and Paracelsus. Bacon was particularly severe in his judgment of the past. In both the *Advancement of Learning* (1605) and the *Novum Organum* (1620) he protested against the cult of antiquity and ancient authorities. Modern men, he argued, were the true ancients, for living in an older world, they deserved reverence, not the children of the past.[13] Paracelsus was even more outspoken in his defense of modernity: "I address this book to those who think that new things are more valuable than old ones," he wrote, "simply because they are newer." (Javarry, p. 24)

In France Jean Bodin was among those who thought the ancient authorities to be fallible. In his *Methodus ad facilem historiarum cognitionem* of 1566 he scoffed at the myth of the Golden Age which he claimed was the product of poets' imagination, not historical fact. It prefigured seventeenth-century moderns by declaring that although the ancients had the merit of having invented many things, much was left to be done. The moderns must continue their work, extending the sphere of human accomplishments.[14] Bodin also believed in a flowering/fading concept of political history, a variation of the Greek theory of the Cycles of History. He compared the state to an organism which grew to perfection, then died. Bodin's image will be taken up by nineteenth-century poets to illustrate their concept of literary progress. Vigny and Lamartine in particular will describe the succession of literary movements as crops which mature, ripen and die, fertilizing the ground for succeeding artistic creation.

Cultural progress is attested by many French Renaissance writers. Etienne Dolet sings with enthusiasm of the new level of achievement in letters which his age enjoyed:

---

[13] Ferdinand Brunetière. *L'Evolution de la critique depuis la Renaissance jusqu'à nos jours.* (Paris: Librairie Hachette et Cie, 1890), p. 185.

[14] Jules Delvaille. *Essai sur l'histoire de l'idée de progrès jusqu'à la fin du XVIIIe siècle.* (Paris: Félix Alcan, éditeur, 1910), p. 135.

11

Les lettres s'épanouissent avec splendeur, heureuse et brillante floraison dont je m'applaudis pour elles! Les études littéraires sont cultivées avec des efforts si grands et si universels que, pour atteindre à la gloire des anciens, une seule condition nous manque, je veux dire l'antique liberté des esprits, et la perspective de la louange au début de la carrière des arts. . . . Néanmoins, les vices de notre époque n'ont pas rélégué si loin de l'Europe le progrès intellectuel qu'on ne rencontre sur tous les points des coeurs brûlants de ce noble amour. Ah! Sans doute elle a été sans trêve et sans merci, la lutte qui depuis un siècle se livre à la barbarie, et souvent la victime a chancelé, grâce aux forces prodigieuses dont disposaient les barbares. Mais, enfin, le succès a couronné la phalange du progrès.[15]

Dolet emphasized the contrast of his glorious epoch with the dark and ignorant past. Progress was a known fact to him, for never before, save in classical antiquity, had letters and the arts flourished as they did now. He did not place his own era above antiquity, but he certainly ranked it as equal.

The praise of cultural progress is even stronger in the famous Rabelaisian letter from Gargantua to Pantagruel, where father admonished son to study hard and to be worthy of his times. The present expansion of learning was without precedent, Gargantua suggested. In this respect the Renaissance surpassed antiquity.

Tout le monde est plein de gens savans, de precepteurs, très doctes, de librairies, très amples, qu'il m'est advis que, ny au temps de Platon, ny de Ciceron, ny de Papinian, n'estoit telle commodité d'estude qu'on y veoit maintenant, et ne se fauldra plus doresnavant trouver en place ny en compagnie, qui ne sera bien expoly en l'officine de Minerve.[16]

In one generation, Gargantua added, man has so progressed that now even brigands, adventurers, and stable boys are wiser than doctors or preachers of his youth. Rabelais limited his claims, however, to the advancement of learning. He did not pretend that the quality of art had improved.

Du Bellay, coming later in the Renaissance, betrayed less

_____

[15] Gillot, p. 31, quotation translated from Latin into French by Boulmier.
[16] Rabelais. *Pantagruel*. Ed. Pierre Jourda. (Paris: Editions Garnier frères, 1962), p. 259.

12

contentment with his age, for although progress had occurred, he felt that there was much more needed. The author of the *Deffence et illustration de la langue françoyse* (1549) was no less a modern than Rabelais. He prefigured the champion of modernity par excellence, Perrault, in proclaiming that nature is a constant force, producing men of the same calibre in the sixteenth century as in the times of ancient Greece and Rome. Du Bellay also proposed that scientific progress would have as a corollary literary advance. Unlike Rabelais, however, Du Bellay only foresaw the glorious day of cultural flowering rather than claiming that it had already arrived. To hasten its coming he suggested imitation of ancient writers as a means of improving literature.

Je confesse que les auteurs d'icelles [les anciens] nous ont surmontez en scavoir et facunde: ès queles choses leur a été bien facile de vaincre ceux qui ne repugnoint point. Mais que par longue et diligente immitation de ceux qui ont occupé les premiers ce que Nature n'ha pourtant denié aux autres, nous ne puissions leur succeder aussi bien en cela que nous avons deja fait en la plus grand' part de leurs ars mecaniques et quelquefois en leur monarchie, je ne le diray pas: car telle injure ne s'entendroit seulement contre les esprits des hommes, mais contre Dieu, qui a donné pour loy inviolable à toute chose crée de ne durer perpetuellement mais passer sans fin d'un etat en l'autre, etant la fin et corruption de l'un, le commencement et generation de l'autre.[17]

Du Bellay's remedy will prove popular not only in his own times but also in the seventeenth century. Resistance to imitation of ancient authors never disappears, however, and libertines will oppose classicists. Théophile de Viau will refuse Malherbe's rules; Perrault will denounce Boileau's veneration of antique models. The Renaissance spirit of revolt against authority, subdued for awhile because of lack of confidence, will be revived during the Quarrel and later under Romanticism. Imitation and innovation ceaselessly war against each other throughout French literary history.

---

[17] Du Bellay. *Deffence et illustration de la langue françoyse.* Ed. Henri Chamard. (Paris: Librairie Marcel Didier, 1948), pp. 56–57. Note Du Bellay's cyclical view of history.

13

The "ancient" side of Du Bellay's character which favored imitation is balanced by the "modern" one which complained that the time spent by contemporaries in learning Latin and Greek had prevented them from making greater progress in science. Because nature is a constant force the sixteenth century should in principle be capable of equaling classical antiquity in science and/or literature.

Et certes songeant beaucoup de foys, d'ou provient que les hommes de ce siecle generalement sont moins scavans en toutes Sciences, et de moindre prix que les Anciens, entre beaucoup de raysons, je treuve cete cy, que j'oseroy dire la principale: c'est l'etude des Langues Greque et Latine. Car si le tens que nous consumons à apprendre les dites Langues estoit employé à l'etude des Sciences, la Nature certes n'est point devenue si brehaigne, qu'elle n'enfentast de nostre tens des Platons et des Aristotes (p. 65)

Du Bellay is significant among his contemporaries for having noted man's tendency to belittle his own times. The influence of the myth of the Golden Age, although not specifically identified as such, is most evident among French men of letters, even in the nineteenth century. Du Bellay is but one of a long series of protestors against this wasteful longing. He prefers substituting respect for regret of the past.

Il ne fault point icy alleguer l'excellence de l'antiquite, et comme Homere se plaignoit que de son tens les cors estoient trop petiz, dire que les espris modernes ne sont à comparer aux anciens. L'architecture, l'art de navigaige, et autres inventions antiques, certainement sont admirables: non toutefois, si on regarde à la necessité mere des Ars, du tout si grandes, qu'on doyve estimer les Cieux et la Nature y avoir dependu toute leur vertu, vigueur et industrie. Je ne produiray pour temoings de ce que je dy l'imprimerie, seur des Muses et dixieme d'elles, et ceste non moins admirable que pernicieuse foudre d'artillerie, avecques tant d'autres non antiques inventions, qui montrent veritablement que par le long cours des siecles les espris des hommes ne sont point si abatardiz qu'on voudroit bien dire (pp. 52–54)

Even more cautious than those of Du Bellay are Montaigne's comments on progress. A sceptic, he proposed no theory of man's continued advance toward perfection nor did he favor modern authors over ancient ones. In Montaigne's

14

opinion the Renaissance's slow rate of scientific progress was in part due, as Du Bellay thought, to the amount of time contemporaries spent in learning ancient languages. Although knowledge of Latin and Greek authors was valuable, the price of attaining it seemed overly costly. Energy devoted to the memorization of paradigms could be better spent in creative activity, Montaigne suggested:

> C'est un bel et grand adgencement sans doubte que le grec et latin, mais on l'achete trop cher. . . . cette longueur que nous mettions à apprendre les langues qui ne leur [les anciens] coustoient rien, est la seule cause pourquoy nous ne pouvons arriver à la grandeur d'ame et de cognoissance des anciens Grecs et Romains.[18]

Montaigne generally did not believe man near perfection. Man was not rational enough, his institutions too imperfect, his scientific knowledge too doubtful to inspire faith in progress. If man is unsure of the physical world, which is "chose bien aultre que nous ne iugeons," ("Apologie de Raymond Sebond," II, 492) how can he know if he himself is moving toward progress or decadence? Such certainty would only be further deception.

> Il n'y a rien de seul et de rare, eu esgaard à nature, ouy bien eu esgaard à nostre cognoissance, qui est un miserable fondement de nos regles, et qui nous represente volontiers une tresfaulse image des choses. Comme vainement nous concluons auiourd'huy l'inclination et la decreptitude du monde, par les arguments que nous tirons de nostre propre foiblesse et decadence . . . ainsi vainement concluait cettuy-là [Lucrèce] sa naissance et ieunesse, par la vigueur qu'il veoyoit aux esprits de son temps, abondants en nouvelletez et inventions de divers arts ("Des Coches," III, 503)

In a limited way man may be capable of correcting himself through study; significant progress, however, can only be the result of divine intervention, i.e., grace.[19]

> [L'homme] s'eslevera, si Dieu luy preste extraordinairement la main; il s'eslevera, abandonnant et se laissant haulser et soublever

---

[18] Montaigne. "De l'institution des enfants," Essais. Ed. Charles Loudandre. Ed. variorum. (Paris: Bibliothèque Charpentier, s.d.), I, 242–243.
[19] "Le guain de nostre estude, c'est en estre devenu meilleur et plus sage." "De l'institution," I, 206.

15

par les moyens purement celestes. C'est à nostre foy chrestienne, non à [nostre] vertu stoïque, de pretendre à cette divine et miraculeuse metamorphose. ("Apologie," II, 550)

Montaigne's views on literary progress are no more sanguine. While showing pride in poetry's renascence, brought about in the main by Ronsard and Du Bellay, who "ont donné credit à nostre poësie françoyse" ("De l'institution," I, 238) and whom he found "gueres esloignez de la perfection ancienne" ("De la presomption," III, 97), Montaigne remained more impressed by the classics which seemed "plus pleins et plus roides" ("Des livres," II, 210) than by the timely creations of modern authors who had sacrificed all to novelty. ("Sur des vers de Virgile," III, 444)

A pervading influence on Renaissance aesthetic thought was Plato, rediscovered and popularized by Ficino and Marguerite de Navarre. Two theories contained in Platonism and its updated version, Petrarchism, particularly appealed to the members of the Pléiade, the concept of ideal archetypes and the belief that the poet, divinely inspired, was also a prophet. These ideas deserve special attention here because they will be reasserted in the nineteenth century.

Absolutes such as Goodness, Truth, Love, and Beauty, according to Platonic thought, exist in perfect form only in the celestial spheres, whereas on earth man views but pale and imperfect reflections of them. Human love poorly approximates the divine model as earthly beauty inadequately represents the ideal archetype. Although man can never capture the ideal while mortal, he can strive to attain it and by diligence come closer to perfection with time. While on the large scale man's progress may be inconsequential, on the shorter one it may be significant. Inspired by such limited hope Renaissance poets were willing to pursue with ardor elusive ideals. Du Bellay's dedication to the quest of the absolute is expressed in sonnet CXIII from the collection *Olive*, "Si nostre vie est moins qu'une journée":

Que songes-tu, mon ame emprisonnée?
Pourquoi te plaist l'obscur de notre jour,
Si pour voler en un plus cler sejour

16

Tu as au dos l'aele bien empanée? . . .
La, ô mon ame au plus hault ciel guidée!
Tu y pouras recognoistre l'Idée
De la beauté, qu'en ce monde j'adore.

In the nineteenth century the classicists will argue that beauty is absolute and was discovered and depicted in perfect form by the Greeks. The Romantics will counter that beauty is relative and defend themselves in Platonic terms, saying that since no earthly representation of beauty adequately depicts the ideal, each artist must strive to capture more of it than his predecessors. Thus, the hope that artistic progress is possible is maintained. Gautier most fully employs this argument against the disciples of Winckelmann, but the majority of Romantics generally agree that beauty is relative.

The second Platonic theory to gain popularity in both the Renaissance and the nineteenth century was that of the poet as a prophet. In both the *Ion* and *Phaedrus* (398–388 B.C.) Plato had spoken of poetic furor or madness which descends upon the inspired poet.[20] Under the spell, the poet comes into communication with the divine and his pronouncements are revered as prophecy. Ronsard, among others, shared this belief.

Car comme dit ce grand Platon, ce sage,
Quatre fureurs brulent notre courage,
Bacchus, Amour, les Muses, Apollon,
Qui dans nos coeurs laissent un aiguillon
Comme freslons et d'une ardeur secrete
Font soudain l'homme et Poëte et Prophete.[21]

The poet is thus distinguished from the mass of humanity as one of the elect of God and is given the responsibility of aiding his less favored brothers. Plato differentiated between poets who accepted their messianic mission to cultivate virtue in the citizenry and those who wasted their powers on the depiction

---

[20] R. V. Merrill and R. J. Clements. *Platonism in French Renaissance Poetry.* (New York: New York University Press, 1957), p. 123.

[21] Ronsard. *Oeuvres complètes.* (Paris: Lemerre, 1914–1918), V, 45.

17

of beauty alone. The social-minded he allowed in his republic, the aesthetes he banished.

In the nineteenth century Hugo, Vigny, and Lamartine will make much of the notion that the poet, semi-divine, is sent by God to direct his brothers from darkness to light, to lead mankind on the path of progress. Second generation Romantics, notably Gautier and Baudelaire, will rebel against the poet's double role and relieve him of the task of perfecting humanity. They will harbor the same resentment against Plato who "chassoit le poëte menteur/ Par les lois de sa république" as did Ronsard. (IV, 138)

Although the doctrine of progress, human and literary, is greatly developed during the sixteenth century, it is not pushed to its logical conclusion. Restrained by a sense of limitation in scientific achievement as well as by an excessive veneration of recently discovered classical authors, Renaissance intellectuals at best considered their age equal to antiquity but not superior. In the following century when scientific advance gains momentum, then writers will lose their timidity. Dissatisfied with equality, they will opt for superiority in all endeavors, including the arts.

The Seventeenth Century: The Quarrel of the Ancients and Moderns

A more concerted application of the concept of progress to the sphere of the arts occurs in mid-seventeenth century France with the outbreak of the Quarrel of the Ancients and Moderns. During the early years of the century, the forces for modernity became increasingly outspoken in their claims. Encouraged by the scientific, intellectual, and material progress of their age, the moderns conclude that the arts, in particular literature, are equally capable of advancing. Having witnessed the overthrow of the scientific giants of antiquity by modern men such as Bacon and Descartes, they seek the replacement of classical literary gods, particularly Homer and Virgil, by contemporary writers.

Greatly responsible for the aggressive tone of seventeenth-century moderns was Descartes, whose *Discours de la méthode* (1637) had revolutionized scientific thinking. His disdain of antiquity and tradition gave impetus to the growing spirit of revolt. Descartes had shown disgust for the then entrenched habit of first lauding the past before attempting to rival it. He felt no need for such reverence. Like Bacon, he argued that the world now being older, his contemporaries were the real ancients. If age were the basis for adoration, then let his colleagues adore themselves. By the passage of time and the accumulation of human experience, he thought, the moderns enjoyed the superior position of having a greater backlog of knowledge at their hands which would enable them to avoid the errors of the past. (Delvaille, pp. 183–185)

Descartes based his theory of progress on a belief in the orderliness of nature, which he, like Du Bellay, viewed as submitted to eternal laws, thus assuring the future of the continued appearance of great men. Because of the fixity of natural law, providential intervention, deemed necessary by Montaigne for man to progress, was dismissed as unnecessary. The French aesthetician Mustoxidi among others credits Descartes' theory with being the springboard of the Quarrel: "on a soutenu, avec beaucoup de bon sens, que la *querelle* . . . est la résultat de l'influence de l'esprit cartésien; effectivement les modernes triomphèrent à l'aide de l'idée cartésienne du progrès."[22]

Pascal appears equally Cartesian in his faith in progress. In an essay entitled "De l'autorité en matière de philosophie," a fragment not discovered until 1779 and then published by Bossut in his edition of the *Oeuvres de Pascal*, he maintained that knowledge is an ever-augmenting factor, passed intact from generation to generation. Mankind is an infinite being, Pascal explained, which progresses from age to age as does an individual. It begins in the ignorance of childhood, learns little by little, progresses through adulthood to old age. Through

---

[22] T. M. Mustoxidi. *Histoire de l'esthétique française: 1700–1900.* (Paris: Edouard Champion, 1920), p. 12.

books mankind possesses the wisdom of the past. Modern man, Pascal concluded, is the equivalent of an aged philosopher with full memory of past knowledge and virile youth with strength enough to add to human accomplishments.

De là vient que, par une prérogative particulière, non seulement chacun des hommes s'avance de jour en jour dans les sciences, mais que tous les hommes ensemble y font un continuel progrès; à mesure que l'univers vieillit, parce que la même chose arrive dans la succession des hommes que dans les âges différents d'un particulier. De sorte que toute la suite des hommes, pendant le cours de tant de siècles, doit être considérée comme un même homme qui subsiste toujours et qui apprend continuellement.[23]

The sciences—music and architecture included among them—alone show evidence of this kind of progress. Literature, the plastic arts, mores, laws, and politics do not submit to the same scheme, according to Pascal.

Guillaume Colletet, taking the opposite view from Pascal, claimed progress in the arts as well as in the sciences. In his "Discours à l'Académie" of 1636 he suggested that by virtue of greater wisdom the moderns were capable of surpassing the ancients in art. Almost Baudelaireian in his theory, Colletet felt that older civilizations possessed a special point of view unshared by younger times which enriched their aesthetic creations. In the graphic arts he cited Rubens as an example of this new richness, claiming him to be superior to all other painters. (Delvaille, p. 195) Pascal's hesitancy concerning artistic progress proves less popular a position in the seventeenth century than Colletet's endorsement of the concept. The Cartesian spirit of revolt against the past is no longer confined to the sciences.

The First Period of the Quarrel

In 1635 the Quarrel of the Ancients and Moderns officially began when Boisrobert, in a speech before the Academy,

---

[23] Pascal. *Oeuvres complètes.* Ed. Jacques Chevalier. Ed. de la Pléiade. (Paris: Gallimard, 1954), pp. 533–534.

criticized Homer for bad taste. He hoped that if this symbol of ancient literary greatness could be overthrown all other rivals of modern glory could be easily disposed of. Boisrobert's irreverence towards literary authority marks the transition of the concept of progress from a limited to an all-pervading debate. Following Boisrobert's initial attack, moderns for over a century will continue the struggle for supremacy over the past. Desmarets de Saint-Sorlin, a poet, was encouraged by Boisrobert's audacity and the academicians' enthusiasm for it. He went even further and criticized all ancient literary works for being pagan and thus out of place in modern, Christian times. In addition, he claimed that since Christianity is a superior religion to the pagan cults, it is also a better source of inspiration for artists. Desmarets' arguments concerning the advantages of a Christian literature are taken up in the nineteenth century by Chateaubriand, although the latter does not give him credit for them. Desmarets also believed nature to be a permanent force and agreed with Descartes that we are really the ancients and therefore wiser than the children of antiquity. He concluded that a modern who is wiser than an ancient and who has the benefit of superior inspiration will produce a better work of art. (Bury, pp. 81–82)

After Desmarets de Saint-Sorlin, Fontenelle appeared as the leading protagonist for the moderns. A scientific vulgariser and avid Cartesian, Fontenelle believed, like his mentor, that nature is a permanent force, which he colorfully characterized as a paste continuously moulded into new and varying shapes.[24] He played down the importance of the ancients' accomplishments, for he explained they had had the advantage of coming first into the world and thus enjoyed the opportunity to discover and invent. Had Fontenelle's contemporaries been born in the early years of civilization, they would have done the same, he argued. Fontenelle, like Pascal, thought of mankind as an individual constantly educated

---

[24] "La nature a entre les mains une certaine pâte, qui est toujours la même, qu'elle tourne et retourne sans cesse en mille façons et dont elle forme les animaux, les plantes, et les hommes." Quoted by Brunetière, p. 240.

21

throughout the centuries. He did not believe that mankind could grow old or senile, however, because nature was permanent. "Je suis obligé d'avouer que cet homme-là n'aurait pas de vieillesse . . . il serait toujours également capable des choses auxquelles sa jeunesse avait été propre, qu'il le serait de plus en plus des choses qui conviennent à l'âge de virilité."[25] Fontenelle believed in literary progress but in a restricted way. He distinguished between poetry and eloquence and the rest of literature. The former, dependent on the vivacity of the poet's imagination and not on reason, did not participate in the intellectual progress of mankind as did the latter. In imaginative literature the moderns could at best only hope to equal the ancients, he opined. This distinction prefigures the doctrine of Madame de Staël.

An interesting point is made by this author on the perspective of the Quarrel. Looking ahead towards posterity—Fontenelle, much like Stendhal, was quite concerned with future opinion of himself—he suggested that one day the moderns of seventeenth-century France would be lumped together with the Greeks and Romans as ancients. The interval between Greek antiquity and Louis XIV's France would seem smaller in time. This sort of change had already occurred in relation to the Greeks and Romans. To the Romans, the Greeks were the ancients and they the moderns. Now one scarcely distinguished between them. (Bury, pp. 101–108)

More audacious than either Desmarets de Saint-Sorlin or Fontenelle in his defense of modern literature was Charles Perrault. His polemics are contained in the epic poem "Le Siècle de Louis le Grand" (1687) and in his treatise *Les Parallèles des anciens et des modernes* (1688–92) which are to be noted in critical history as the first attempt to present a synthetic view of civilization at one given moment. According to Gillot, Perrault is unique in his effort to view all the arts and sciences and derive a general law from observing their development. (p. 527)

---

[25] Fontenelle. *L'Histoire des oracles.* Quoted by Brunetière, p. 200.

It was Perrault's idea that antiquity had gained its status of perfection because of its distance from the present. As with memories, the bad had faded away, leaving only the good and the pleasant. Were a true comparison possible of the merits of the two ages, Perrault was convinced modernity would be proven superior, a contention which he supported by using the same argument that the moderns were wiser than the ancients. Their increased knowledge was evident not only in scientific matters, he believed, but also in their insights into human problems. Because modern writers knew their subject, man, better, they were superior in all literary endeavors. Perrault did not make Fontenelle's distinction between poetic and unimaginative genres. Even poetry and eloquence enjoyed the benefits of progress, he contended. Poetry especially showed evidence of perfection because of the modern poet's increased knowledge of the soul. Poetry's function is to please the human heart, Perrault explained, and to do so the poet must know the heart. Progress occurs as the poet discovers new passions or new aspects of old ones, not previously treated in literature. Corneille had done this. He had added new reflections on ambition, vengeance, and jealousy not found in any of the ancients' works. (Bury, p. 86) In matters of form as well, poetry had progressed. The ancients did not have sonnets, rondeaux, ballades, or operas. The moderns had produced masterpieces in each of these forms.

Perrault also deserves study for his interest in the theory of beauty. He rejected the idea of an absolute beauty, for he could not agree that the ancients had definitively depicted the beautiful in their works. As in the case of poetry, aesthetic lacunae existed in all areas of the arts. Not only was the ancients' architecture limited, he stated, but their sculpture was also incomplete, their painting inadequate. In matters of technique as well the ancients were inferior to the moderns. They knew nothing of the laws of perspective nor of the use of chiaroscuro, technical advances which made modern painters' works superior. (Delvaille, p. 206)

Perrault's optimism was unqualified. He insisted that although progress in the arts appeared not to be continuous, it really was. Wars and other catastrophes may prevent a nation from cultivating the arts, such as was the case in the tenth century, he noted, but once the inhibiting force is removed, the arts spring forth with new vigor and continue their improvement. Progress is like a stream, Perrault illustrated, sometimes flowing above ground, sometimes below, but continuously moving forward.

The one qualification to Perrault's theory of artistic progress was his concession that genius does not progress from century to century but remains constant in keeping with the laws governing the permanence of nature—thus modern artists have no more talent than ancient ones. Perrault managed to give the moderns the lead, nevertheless, by adding that since both science and art consist of rules, the accumulation and the perfection of which depend on the passage of time, a man of genius in modern times, although innately no better than a good ancient, by his increased knowledge of the rules of art, would produce a superior work. He cited as proof of such progress the superiority of Virgil over Homer. (pp. 207–208) Perrault's thesis will be considered extreme by later students of progress who insist upon the separation of art and science when discussing the concept. Only Condorcet, in the late eighteenth century, continues Perrault's argument.

Perrault's doctrine, by virtue of its resistance to authority and its optimism, both Cartesian traits, prefigures the position of the Romantics. Certainly his *Parallèles* will have great influence upon both Mme de Staël and Chateaubriand who in a limited fashion imitate them. Fournel, a nineteenth-century historian of the Quarrel, recognized the Romantics' general indebtedness to him.

Ce que Descartes avait fait pour la philosophie, Perrault le fit pour la littérature: il introduisait le doute et le libre examen dans la place, avec moins d'autorité et un raisonnement plus faible, il est vrai, mais avec des résultats analogues. Son mérite fut de renverser l'idole de l'autorité pure, de la tradition absolue et tyrannique, de la convention s'imposant sans contrôle. C'est à lui que remonte la révolution romantique, qui devrait le compter parmi ses aïeux, plutôt que Ronsard, choisi un peu à contre sens, puisque c'est justement celui qui a poussé le plus loin le respect et l'imitation de l'antiquité. [26]

If Perrault is an ancestor of the Romantics, he is also the perpetrator of one of the crimes most detested by that group—the admission of the opinion of the man in the street in literary matters. Perrault, by appealing to public taste, which was then essentially aristocratic, opened the door to an invasion of everyman's taste, soon to be bourgeois. The Romantics, feeling themselves to be aristocratic by nature, resented the intrusion of the unlearned and uncultivated in the ethereal realms of the arts. The reaction of Art for Art's Sake was a natural defense.

The Quarrel continued for several years with Boileau heading the forces for antiquity. His most noted treatise was the "Réflections sur Longin" of 1693 in which he stated that all the ancients were not admirable, but there were a considerable number of exceptional writers among them. The respect they had gained did not come from their age, he insisted, but from their merit, which had stood the test of time. The moderns were not necessarily inferior, he admitted, but there had not been enough time to judge whether their works were lasting or not. Boileau thought only posterity capable of deciding the question of superiority. [27]

To ease the bickering of the factions Louis XIV intervened and prodded Perrault and Boileau to declare a truce. Boileau's compromise appeared in a letter to Perrault dated 1700. In it he admitted that there were excellent moderns but insisted they owed their merit to imitation of the ancients. His surrender came in acknowledging, perhaps to please the king, that the age of Louis XIV was superior to the era of Augustus in certain genres, inferior in others, but generally the present surpassed the past.

---

[26] Victor Fournel. *La Littérature indépendante et les écrivains oubliés, essais de critique et d'érudition sur le XVIIe siècle*. (Paris: Didier et Cie, libraire-éditeur, 1862), p. 389.

[27] F. Vial et L. Denise. *Idées et doctrines littéraires au XVIIe siècle*. (Paris: Librairie Ch. Delagrave, 1906), p. 252.

Thus, in the seventeenth century the concept of progress was greatly enlarged to include artistic as well as scientific, intellectual, and material advancement. The yoke of authority and respect for the past, still prevalent to a degree during the Renaissance, disappeared entirely under such fanatical moderns as Desmarets de Saint-Sorlin, Fontenelle, and Perrault. Their extreme optimism will be continued by writers during the eighteenth century, although some cooler heads will seek a compromise in the Quarrel.

The Eighteenth Century: Continuation and Modification of the Quarrel

The truce between Perrault and Boileau did not end the antagonism between the ancients and moderns. After a relatively short interval the literary debate was rekindled. Indeed, during this second phase of the Quarrel the issues were often more heatedly discussed than before.

It was Mme Dacier's translation of the *Iliad* in 1711 which reopened old wounds. In the preface she taunted her contemporaries by suggesting that both Homer and the Greek language were superior to all modern writers and even the mother tongue. She criticized French for lacking the nobility, force, and harmony of Greek and apologized for having rendered Homeric beauties in such an inferior medium. Mme Dacier defended Homer, who had been under attack for over a century, against the widespread accusation of vulgarity by countering that he was no worse than the Bible, his heroes no less refined than the patriarchs. To the accusation that Homer had neglected the depiction of love—the moderns were highly conscious of having a different concept of love than the ancients, which they believed more delicate and refined, more aesthetically pleasing—she replied that the lack of love in the *Iliad* was the reason for its superiority as a work of literature.[28]

Houdar de la Motte, equally fired by patriotism and by

---

[28] Vial et Denise. *XVIIIe siècle*. (1926), pp. 1–5.

modernity, counterattacked with a "Discours sur Homère" in 1714 in which he claimed that the French language was as elegant, harmonious, and precise as Greek, which incidentally he did not know. He insisted that despite Mme Dacier's defense, Homer remained vulgar and unsuitable for refined, cultivated society. To prove his point he set about rewriting Mme Dacier's translation in a language acceptable to the salons. He altered, abbreviated, bowdlerized Homer, omitting all vulgar words, boring speeches and disgusting passions; in short, he "improved" the *Iliad*.[29]

Mme Dacier was not one to cringe from combat and replied to this insolence by a new treatise entitled "Des causes de la corruption du goût"—mainly La Motte's—in 1714. She therein maintained Homer's honor, using as proof of his greatness the esteem he had enjoyed over the centuries. French verse was singularly lacking, she thought; it only reached the level of Greek poetry when it imitated the superior model. She dismissed all innovations as failures. (Vial, *XVIIIe*, pp. 13–15) This last point was in direct reply to La Motte's theory exposed in an earlier treatise, "Discours sur la poésie" of 1707, in which he urged the moderns to innovate in order to surpass the ancients, warning that slavish imitation would at best only make them equals. This theory is the basis of the Romantics' argument a century later, for they had seen the result of the slavish imitation of neoclassicism and knew it brought about atrophy.

Coming to the defense of La Motte was the abbé de Pons, a figure to be remembered, for he will later become the subject of a study by Sainte-Beuve. Pons praised his friend's translation of Mme Dacier's translation as the new improved version of Homer. Pons thought La Motte a hero for having refused to bow to that Greek literary god and called him the "Descartes de la littérature." Pons believed La Motte had brought the same spirit of revolt against authority into the arts that Descartes had brought to science. Pons stressed the advantage of

---

[29] Gilbert Highet. *The Classical Tradition*. (Oxford at the Clarendon Press, 1949), p. 287.

modernizing older works. He believed, and in this respect anticipates the Romantics, that all works of art should be timely. Homer may have been beautiful in his day, Pons argued, but in eighteenth-century France, he seemed dull and tasteless. (Vial, XVIIIe, pp. 16–17)

Coming late in the series of eighteenth-century quarrelers is Turgot. The staunchly pro-modern Turgot proposed that all human endeavors benefit from progress. He, like Pascal, believed that humanity could be represented by a single man, constantly growing, learning and perfecting. The history of humanity, he thought, was the portrait of the civilization process. Man had slowly emerged from "l'état sauvage à la vie aristocratique."[30]

Lecturing at the Sorbonne Turgot distinguished between the roles of the sciences and the arts in the scheme of progress. Each depends upon a favorable milieu for development, he proclaimed, but even in the best environment only science is indefinitely perfectible. The arts have a point of perfection beyond which they cannot progress. In many genres the ancients had reached the outer limit. The moderns would have to content themselves with seeking perfection in areas untouched by the Greeks and Romans. (Vial, XVIIIe, pp. 58–59) Turgot's distinction will be incorporated by Mme de Staël into her theory of progress.

Science, of course, owes its continuous progress to the unending intellectual advance of mankind, according to Turgot. Knowledge constantly augments, although in an irregular fashion. In some centuries, the accomplishments of the past are forgotten, in others lapses are overcome.

Art in particular is hindered by the aesthetic blight which strikes some epochs. Certain artistic lapses can never be overcome, Turgot noted, for art is not dependent upon knowledge as is science and does not enjoy the benefit of intellectual advance. The goal of art is to please, not to instruct, and this cannot be passed along from generation to generation by

---

[30] Georges Sorel. *Les Illusions du progrès.* 5e éd. (Paris: Librairie Marcel Rivière et Cie, 1947), p. 51.

means of a formula. "Si la connaissance de la nature et de la vérité est infinie comme elles, les arts, dont l'objet est de nous plaire, sont bornés comme nous." (Delvaille, p. 397) The technical aspect of art is progressive, however. The moderns' knowledge of perspective has improved their paintings. In literature, contemporaries have the advantage of using local color, imitating nature and more delicately expressing passion, qualities Turgot found to be limited, if not lacking, in the works of the ancients.

Turgot is to be remembered, in addition to his distinction between the arts and sciences, for having coined the term *perfectibility*, later to become the watchword of Mme de Staël. It is Rousseau who will give the word currency, when it is passed from master to disciple to dominate the treatise *De la littérature*.[31]

In addition to the theoreticians and philosophers of the eighteenth century several important literary figures added their comments to the debate on progress. Marivaux in *Le Miroir* in 1755 reasserted that denigration of the moderns stemmed more from jealousy of contemporaries than from preference for classical works. Marivaux also did not believe artistic progress to be continuous but sporadic. He explained that literary genres never die but enjoy varying degrees of health. Only in privileged epochs, when the arts are encouraged, do they flourish and result in masterpieces. Such epochs are highly refined, delicate and polite, in some way similar to eighteenth-century France. Marivaux firmly believed his own times without equal. (Vial, *XVIIIe*, pp. 64–65)

Montesquieu took a more moderate position. He complained about the growing cult of modernity, the love of novelty for its own sake. One reads in the *Lettres persanes* (1721):

Le grand tort qu'ont les journalistes c'est qu'ils ne parlent que des livres nouveaux; comme si la vérité était à jamais nouvelle. Il me semble que, jusqu'à ce qu'un homme ait lu tous les livres anciens, il n'a aucune raison de leur préférer les nouveaux. (Delvaille, p. 294)

---

[31] Arthur O. Lovejoy. *Essays in the History of Ideas.* (Baltimore: The Johns Hopkins Press, 1948), p. 25.

Basically Montesquieu sought a compromise in the Quarrel of the Ancients and Moderns. "La querelle fait voir qu'il y a d'excellents auteurs parmi les anciens et les modernes," he wrote; the ancients, however, held the advantage for they had exhausted the possibilities for plots. Originality was now almost impossible, a complaint to be echoed by some Romantics. "C'est une mine d'or épuisée pour nous." Yet, Montesquieu added to encourage his contemporaries, "si vous suivez toujours les anciens, vous ne serez jamais à côté d'eux." (*Ibid.*)

Voltaire distinguished himself as a judge of the quality of the quarrel, pointing out its excesses, omissions, and its combatants' fondness for generalization. Voltaire took issue with many of the statements of believers in progress, disagreeing particularly with Pascal's theory that humanity could be likened to an individual. Only nations develop in human fashion, he thought. There is no one guiding principle which has directed the development of all of mankind. Voltaire, like Turgot, also insisted on a separation of the arts and sciences when discussing the doctrine of progress. The sciences do progress, but the arts can be produced in an immediately perfected state. The lapse of time has no bearing on their quality. In particular, Voltaire was referring to the abbé Terrasson who had made no distinction between the two. He rebuked the cleric in an article written for the *Gazette littéraire* in 1764.

Le progrès de la philosophie n'a pas, pour comparaison nécessaire le progrès des arts. C'est une erreur de l'abbé Terrasson de croire que les modernes, étant plus grands géomètres que les anciens, ils doivent être plus grands poètes et plus grands orateurs. (Delvaille, p. 408)

More relevant to the perfection of the arts than a general and somewhat vague notion of progress, according to Voltaire, were the specific influences of climate and political institutions, factors often overlooked by the quarrelers.

Voltaire could not endorse a theory of continuous progress because he did not believe the glories of the age of Louis XIV would be reproduced in the foreseeable future. This very reasoning implies a kind of belief in artistic progress, for Voltaire did think the immediate past superior to the far distant one. Voltaire's pride in his own age was based mainly on the accomplishments of French classical playwrights. In "La Toilette de Mme Pompadour" of 1765, pretending to speak to Tullia, Cicero's daughter, he bragged:

> Quand vous venez jouer Phèdre, vous conviendrez peut-être que le rôle de Phèdre dans Racine est prodigieusement supérieur au modèle que vous connaissez en Euripide. J'espère que vous conviendrez que notre Molière l'emporte sur votre Térence. (Vial, *XVIIIe*, p. 77)

Voltaire found other examples of modern superiority in the arts, not all of which were French. He believed that Ariosto and Tasso surpassed Homer and that Renaissance painting was without equal. Greek painting did not compete with it because of the lack of perspective and chiaroscuro. Modern music had no rival in his estimation nor did the architecture of Renaissance Italy.

Although Voltaire often gave the impression of being anti-modern, mainly because of his qualifications of the theory of progress and his jibes at more extreme quarrelers such as the abbé Terrasson, his pro-modern feelings, as expressed above, tended to dominate. By his emphasis on the need of timeliness in art he sided against the past. The ancients were primarily interesting for Greeks and Romans, he thought, but much less so for Frenchmen of the eighteenth century. While showing proper respect for the past, one needed a literature appropriate for one's times. In "Les Lettres écrites en 1719" he argued for timeliness, adding that if ancient playwrights were alive in his day, they would improve upon their works.

> Nous sommes aussi touchés de l'ébauche la plus grossière dans les premières découvertes d'un art, que des beautés les plus achevées lorsque la perfection nous est une fois connue. Ainsi Sophocle et Euripide, tout imparfaits qu'ils sont, ont autant réussi chez les Athéniens que Corneille et Racine parmi nous. Nous devons nous-mêmes, en blâmant les tragédies des Grecs, respecter le génie de leurs auteurs: leurs fautes sont sur le compte de leur siècle, leurs beautés n'appartiennent qu'à eux; et il est à croire que, s'ils étaient nés de nos jours, ils auraient perfectionné l'art qu'ils ont inventé de leur temps. (Vial, *XVIIIe*, p. 78)

Perhaps the most original and certainly the most paradoxical eighteenth-century writer to speak on progress was Rousseau. He believed that mankind degenerated morally as it became increasingly civilized. "Nos âmes se sont corrompues à mesure que nos sciences et nos arts se sont avancés à la perfection," he wrote in the "Discours sur les sciences et les arts" in 1750. Without distinguishing between science and art as others had done, Rousseau thought them both indefinitely perfectible, both of base origin and capable of perverse influence on innocent man. Especially in his *Contrat social* of 1762 Rousseau blamed the arts for man's corruption. In keeping with his belief in a primitive but pure Golden Age, Rousseau maintained that antique art was simpler and more natural, thus morally superior. Increased civilization had caused art to yield to artifice and complexity, resulting in a separation of man from nature. This kind of artistic progress, later heralded by the advocates of decadence such as Baudelaire, was condemned by Rousseau as harmful. Art had become an intellectual game, he believed, not a sincere expression of emotion.[32]

Rousseau's theory that the man of genius is morally and aesthetically superior to his less gifted brothers is more in line with later Romantic thought than his belief in artistic corruption. He had described the genius as the leader of men sent by Providence. Blessed with a superior moral insight and sensitivity to nature, the genius was to direct his more limited brothers from darkness to light, from artifice to nature. (Broome, p. 193) Hugo's theory of the poet as semi-divine prophet as well as Gautier's belief that the artist possessed a sixth sense are later developments of this Platonic theory.

Rousseau's influence on the Romantics' idea of progress will be enormous. Many will agree that increased civilization had brought about moral decay; others will define the role of the poet as savior of mankind. The debate over artificiality will continue, with later Romantics feeling that it is advantageous

---

[32] J. H. Broome. *Rousseau: A Study of His Thought.* (New York: Barnes and Noble, Inc., 1963), p. 187.

to art. While Rousseau's ideas are not always accepted by the Romantics, they are certainly well known and a constant stimulus of discussion.

The last members of the series of proponents of progress to be considered in this historical survey are Condorcet and André Chénier. In many ways both serve not only as an end point but also as a climax to the procession of pro-moderns. Condorcet's enthusiasm and optimism are greater than those of most writers of the eighteenth century, with the exception of the abbé Terrasson, and in the seventeenth century are rivaled only by the partisan attitude of Perrault. His *Esquisse d'un tableau historique des progrès de l'esprit humain* of 1784 is exceptional not only for its wholehearted conviction that progress is a reality but also that it was written during the years of the Revolution when the well ordered world of eighteenth-century France was crumbling. The treatise was finished while the author was held political prisoner. Upon its completion Condorcet committed suicide to avoid the guillotine. The *Esquisse* is thoroughly pre-Revolutionary in character. It can be considered the culminating work of the *Querelle des anciens et des modernes*. Condorcet's immediate heir, Mme de Staël, while reflecting her mentor's philosophic, rationalistic optimism, nonetheless displays the effects of the Revolution in her work *De la littérature*. Condorcet's unbridled optimism is transformed into her cautious faith in the future. His proud account of man's constant progress must then be interrupted by her apologies for unaccountable relapses.

Condorcet patterned his work on that of Turgot, intending to trace the continuous progress of man from his beginnings to the present to which was appended a prognostication of future developments:

Tel est le but de l'ouvrage que j'ai enterpris, et dont le résultat sera de montrer, par le raisonnement et par les faits, qu'il n'a été aucun terme au perfectionnement des facultés humaines; que la perfectibilité de l'homme est réellement indéfinie; que les progrès de cette perfectibilité, désormais indépendante de toute puissance qui voudrait les arrêter, n'ont d'autre terme que la durée du globe où la nature nous a jetés. Sans doute ces progrès pourront suivre une marche plus ou moins rapide, mais jamais elle ne sera rétrograde.[33]

In this march towards perfection Condorcet included the arts, which he claimed were capable of indefinite progress. He explained their advance not only because of the increase of knowledge, the growth of philosophy, and the perfection of artistic techniques—arguments accepted by many other moderns—but also by heredity, a most controversial idea. Condorcet stands almost alone in believing that talent is accumulative, passed from artistic father to son.

The moderns won preeminence over the ancients during the Italian Renaissance, according to the *Esquisse*. During that period epic poetry, painting, and sculpture attained heights of perfection unknown to the Greeks and Romans. The classical age in France, represented by the playwrights Corneille and Racine, extended the primacy to the drama.

> Corneille annonçait que l'art dramatique en France était prêt d'en acquérir une plus grande [perfection] encore, car si l'enthousiasme pour l'antiquité croit peut-être avec justice reconnaître quelque supériorité dans le génie des hommes qui en ont créé les chefs-d'oeuvre, il est bien difficile qu'en comparant leurs ouvrages avec les productions de l'Italie et de la France, la raison n'aperçoive pas les progrès réels, que l'art même a faits entre les mains des modernes. (pp. 219–220)

Condorcet's faith in the ever-augmenting perfection of the arts was bolstered by the productions of the eighteenth century. Music especially showed signs of rapid development and improvement in this period, mainly due to technical discoveries. Painting seemed the exception, however, for it had no great genius who could surpass those of the sixteenth century. Condorcet avoided the word *decadence*, concerning this lapse in pictorial progress, and explained that progress was all the more difficult because of the great advances made in the immediate past. More was needed in the eighteenth century than in the sixteenth to make progress in painting.

---

[33] Condorcet. *Esquisse*. (Paris: Chez Agasse, l'an III de la République), p. 4.

Following Voltaire's lead, Condorcet also acknowledged the role of politics and mores on the fortunes of art. In the eighteenth century they were largely responsible for the retardation of the perfection of painting, he concluded. This explanation by environment is of course the starting point for Mme de Staël's theory of perfectibility, which although she will claim is continuous, she also places at the mercy of sociological events. During the eighteenth century letters were more fortunate than the graphic arts, Condorcet believed. Voltaire carried forward the work of Corneille and Racine. No one improved upon the work of Molière. He stood isolated in his greatness with no rival either prior to his time or following it. "L'art comique doit à Molière d'être parvenu plus promptement à une hauteur qu'aucune nation n'a pu encore atteindre," Condorcet explained. (p. 315)

Condorcet's vision of the future was equally optimistic. He believed that the arts would continue to benefit from man's intellectual advance. Eventually the secrets of artistic production and of talent would be discovered and reduced to a science. Thus, future artists would proceed with greater efficiency to produce masterpieces, avoiding the mistakes of the past and being impervious to the negative influences of external events. (pp. 354–355) In many respects Condorcet announced the doctrines of Romanticism. He believed that future men of talent would benefit from the advance of knowledge and science by becoming better observers of life. Their increased enlightenment would destroy artistic prejudices and extend the sphere of aesthetic activity, lifting definitively the yoke of authority and tradition. Like the Romantics to come, Condorcet argued against imitation—the surest way to end artistic progress. The prejudice that the best has been and that one can only copy the past must be destroyed, he warned. There will always be new beauties, new sentiments whose depiction will enrich future works of art. Art will continue to progress, Condorcet concluded, by moving from simplicity to complexity, an idea to be vigorously championed by such nineteenth-century writers as Balzac and Baudelaire. (pp. 370–371)

Condorcet's optimism is reflected by the most outstanding lyrical genius of the time, André Chénier. Their similar fate and their similar faith in the future is striking. As Condorcet culminates a movement in philosophical history, Chénier ends a series of creators of *poèmes à thèse* which supported the moderns against the ancients. As Condorcet announces Mme de Staël, Chénier announces the Romantic poets by his return to lyricism and his faith in the future progress of art.

Chénier called for new and timely ideas for poetry. Like Du Camp in mid-nineteenth-century France he suggested an inclusion of science in literary topics. He did not propose change in the form of poetry, thinking the classical models sufficient, but he did feel the old moulds should contain new metal. "Sur des pensers nouveaux, faisons des vers antiques."

The manifesto of Chénier's modernism was his poem "Invention" (pub. posthumously 1819). In this work he condemned repetition of the past, man's tendency to look backward and never forward. He fully believed the moderns equal to the ancients, and perhaps superior. He advised contemporaries to do in art what the ancients would do if alive today.

O qu'ainsi parmi nous des esprits inventeurs
De Virgile et d'Homère atteignent les hauteurs,
Sachant dans la mémoire avoir comme eux un temple,
Et sans suivre leur pas imiter leur exemple,
Faire, en s'éloignant d'eux, avec un soin jaloux,
Ce qu'eux-mêmes ils feraient s'ils vivaient parmi nous! . . .
Et qu'en Calliope, élève d'Uranie,
Montant sa lyre d'or sur un plus noble ton,
En langage des Dieux fasse Newton.[34]

Thus in the eighteenth century the discussion of progress, human and aesthetic, continues. An entire spectrum of thought is expressed, ranging from the most negative, that of Mme Dacier, to the most positive, that of Condorcet. Within these end points many shades of opinion are presented. Because those seeking compromise are only partially successful in resolving the difficult issue of progress, the debate does not

---

[34] Vial et Denise. *XIXe siècle.* (1928), p. 110.

end. Even after the shock of the Revolution, when the moderns' faith in human progress appears to have been proved unfounded, writers will continue to determine the extent of progress in man's endeavors, particularly in his art and literature.

Conclusion

In reviewing the history of the *Querelle des anciens et des modernes* one sees that the application of the doctrine of progress to the sphere of literature took the form of a comparison of ancient (Greek and Roman) and modern (seventeenth and eighteenth-century French) authors. In particular, modern French writers were opposed as a group to Homer who had assumed the status of the most complete representative of ancient literary art. It has been demonstrated how the earlier combatants, Saint-Sorlin, Fontenelle, and Perrault, chose to oppose their own era's and own nation's literature to the masterpieces of classical antiquity, while later debaters, Mme Dacier, La Motte, and the abbé de Pons, focused their attention more exclusively on the merits of Homer's *Iliad*. Thus, not only does the French Quarrel consist of two parts but shows an evolution of a restrictive nature in its development. In addition, because of the intensity of the debate and the extravagance of the claims put forth, the Quarrel stands out as a unique chapter in literary history.

Before the formal declaration of war between present and past literatures, Saint-Sorlin's academic discourse, and the eventual subsiding of hostilities, a "quarrel" had always existed. Evidence of it can be found among the ancients themselves. The pitting of the present against the past continued throughout history with growing intensity until and through the Renaissance. Prior to the seventeenth century the tone was less acid. Proponents of progress were less concerned with maligning the past than with flaunting the advantages of the present. Few were bold enough to proclaim the fine arts equal, much less superior, to those produced by their classical ancestors. As one nears the Age of Louis XIV their audacity in-

37

creased. During the early Renaissance Du Bellay comes closest to making the transition. He is no longer satisfied with the promise of equality. He opts for eventual superiority. After the heated debate of the seventeenth century one finds a desire for compromise among the quarrelers of the eighteenth century. A return of sorts to the position of pre-seventeenth-century partisans is indicated. Writers such as Voltaire content themselves with championing the advantages of their own times but are more hesitant than their immediate predecessors to malign the past. Perhaps thinking the quarrelers too hot-headed, the generation of compromisers sought a rational consideration of the issues and were willing to parcel out the laurels of literary achievement impartially to contemporary and ancestor alike. Especially in the case of Voltaire a new note is added. Instead of the hopeful optimism of the Renaissance man, looking forward to the Age of Louis XIV, although unaware of it, the eighteenth-century man tended to look less to the future than to the immediate past. His championing of modernity was more that of the recent past than that of the imminent future. Voltaire frankly did not believe the glories of the past epoch again possible, or at least not for a long time.

Thus, Condorcet distinguishes himself as an exceptional writer among those involved in settling the issues of the Quarrel. He resembles the most fanatical protagonist such as Perrault rather than the more cautious soul of the Renaissance or earlier eighteenth century. His is the last voice of total optimism. Even his closest disciple, Mme de Staël, reflects much less intensely his faith in the future or his assurance that progress is constant, exists in all human endeavors, or that the mere passage of time is the only prerequisite for human advance. All of Condorcet's faith is not lost in the Revolution and indeed the Romantics, however weakly, still reflect his opinion that the arts, especially literature, benefit from the advance of mankind. Still none will champion this doctrine with the same vigor or conviction.

Regardless of the varying quality of the arguments recorded here, their quantity emphasizes the importance of the aesthetic issues of the Quarrel, many of which are of interest even today. The concept of modernity, "le beau moderne" so championed by Baudelaire, owes its origin to this literary debate. The theory of timeliness, an offshoot of the larger question of relative versus absolute beauty, an essential ingredient in the formation of Hugo and Stendhal's literary theories is a product of the discussion. The preference for innovation over imitation, the search for novelty, for absolute freedom in the arts, the cornerstone of the Romantics' doctrine, springs from seeds sown during the Quarrel. The importance of the Quarrel's influence on the development of nineteenth-century French literary aesthetics must not be underestimated.

The moderns of more recent times are heavily indebted to those valiant souls of seventeenth and eighteenth-century France who preferred their contemporaries to the idols of tradition. Even admitting that their vanity exceeded their merits, one must show appreciation for their having infused modern artists with a sense of worthiness and a spirit of competitiveness which otherwise might have been missing. As Gilbert Highet so aptly has pointed out, "the idea of progress may sometimes be a dangerous thing, but it is better for us to be challenged to put forth our best, than to be told the race is hopeless." (p. 288) Montesquieu had recognized this challenge implicitly when he warned his hesitant contemporaries, "si vous suivez toujours les anciens, vous ne serez jamais à côté d'eux."

Men were spurred on by the notion that as latecomers on the cultural scene they could benefit from the general intellectual advance. Whatever their disadvantage in that their rivals had become more numerous, they could profit from the increased richness of a longer artistic tradition and could avoid the mistakes of the past when creating their new and better art. This belief played no small part in strengthening growing optimism as Gillot remarks:

Ce sera désormais [après la Querelle] un lieu commun que les Anciens n'ont point réalisé la souveraine perfection de l'art, qu'il est possible, pourtant, et permis de les corriger; que l'art étant

39

comme la littérature, perfectible, il est possible de faire mieux que les devanciers, en évitant leurs défauts et en profitant de leur expérience. Ici et là, en littérature comme en art, l'idée de progrès, avec tout ce qu'elle comporte de largeur et d'étroitesse, a victorieusement gagné. (Gillot, p. 549)

With the idea of progress by correction of the past came the idea of progress by extension of the past's accomplishments. The doctrine of relativity taught man that the rules were changeable. New models other than those of antiquity were sought out. New genres were created. Art was deemed capable of infinite progress because man's gift for invention was unlimited. Rigault, for one, holds this to be one of the principal merits of the Quarrel.

Proclamer dans la littérature et dans les arts le principe de liberté, et par là, continuer la révolution commencée par Descartes en philosophie; rendre à l'Inspiration ses droits; prévenir la formation d'une orthodoxie littéraire, qu'aurait inventée l'esprit de routine pour la ruine de l'originalité, donner au génie français dont l'humilité diminuait la force, le sentiment de grandeur; étendre et féconder le goût, en abolissant cette vieille idée que les formes de l'art ancien sont les seules formes de l'art et en ouvrant, de toutes parts des issues vers les littératures étrangères et les chefs-d'oeuvre modernes; multiplier ainsi les modèles, enseigner l'intelligence de toutes les portes de beauté, et fonder cette impartialité de goût, est aujourd'hui l'honneur et la supériorité de la critique: voilà des conséquences heureuses de la querelle que le temps a développées. (Rigault, p. 478)

Nor can one overlook the obvious faults of the Quarrel either. Besides the trivial character of many of the arguments, especially those against Homer's crudeness, and the petty hatreds expressed between antagonists, one of the important negative aspects of the debate was that it paved the way for future literary free-for-alls. Highet contends that the gap between literary scholar and the public was widened as the man in the street felt increasingly confident of his literary judgments. Those who considered themselves properly trained to analyze literature resented having their opinions weighed against those of Everyman. The Romantics in particular, being aristocratic in temperament, steeped in the notion of their intellectual, artistic, and sometimes moral superiority, resented the praise or condemnation of the philistine, the untutored. No one better expressed this sort of suffering than Gautier the artist or Saint-Beuve the critic. Had the comparison of literatures not been made a topic of national interest, they would have felt much less threatened by their fellow countrymen.

One should also criticize the Quarrel for its narrowness of scope. The debaters limited themselves to a comparison of French writers of the seventeenth and eighteenth centuries and the classical authors of Greece and Rome. Some exceptions were made on behalf of modern authors of great stature who lay outside the French tradition (Dante and Tasso, Shakespeare and Milton) but none were made among ancient authors outside the Graeco-Roman tradition. The exclusiveness of the quarrelers in thinking that French writers alone were able to oppose the entire tradition seems a product of haughtiness. That they were even partially successful is a tribute to their literary stature. That no thought was given to broadening the scope of the Quarrel to include "barbaric" art may seem strange to the modern viewer, but it must be remembered that the cult of the primitive did not yet exist. Today, of course, a more inclusive view is held and perhaps as a result of the earlier moderns' theories a twentieth-century debater would be more likely to include more varied representatives of art and literature, combining many traditions. Munro suggests that even the time element involved would be lengthened by a contemporary protagonist, for we moderns would be more willing to speak of progress which included slumps lasting as long as a century or even a thousand years. (Munro, p. 189)

That a twentieth-century man would consider reviving the issues of the Quarrel emphasizes the fact that it is never ending. A quarrel existed prior to the seventeenth century and will continue to exist after the twentieth, one may presume. That its issues were very much alive in post-Revolutionary France is attested to by this study. In particular, the epoch of Romanticism witnessed the continued investigation of many of the tenets of the pro-moderns.

41

Chapter Two

Madame De Staël

Madame de Staël serves as an intellectual intermediary between the eighteenth and nineteenth centuries in the continued discussion of progress in France. [1] In the manner of the Moderns of the Enlightenment, she seeks a rationalistic and objective explanation of human advancement, which she labels "human perfectibility." Very much the descendant of Condorcet, she systematically reviews the history of Western civilization, pointing out a growth in knowledge and an increased refinement of the arts. A precursor of Romanticism, Mme de Staël also prophesies the impending literary renaissance and suggests a program of art for social progress.

Mme de Staël's views on literary perfectibility are presented most completely in the analytical treatise *De la littérature* (1800 and 1802). In contrast to her mentor Condorcet, who had allowed no exceptions to his theory of the ever-increasing perfection of man and his arts, Mme de Staël distinguishes between the imaginative and the intellectual arts, excluding

---

[1] An earlier version of this chapter entitled "Mme de Staël, The Continuing Quarrel of the Ancients and Moderns, and the Idea of Progress," appeared in *WSU Research Studies*, March 1982, Vol. 50, No. 1, pp. 33–45.

the former from her theory of progress. Imaginative works, best represented by poetry, were most perfectly produced during the early years of human history, when man was more naïve, less knowledgeable, and consequently more imaginative. The poems of the Greeks in particular have never been surpassed in beauty, according to the author. On the other hand, literary creations such as novels, essays, and dramas, which depend more on the "intelligence" of the writer, i.e. his knowledge of man and the universe, have shown increased perfection in relation to the intellectual advancement of mankind. More recent authors have proven better equipped to portray man with greater insight than their less informed ancestors. As a result of increased knowledge, greater refinement and increased aesthetic sensitivity, i.e. better taste, have come about. Modern authors write not only more profound but also more subtly nuanced works of literature.

Defense and Clarification of Her Theories

Following the publication of *De la littérature* in 1800, Mme de Staël's theories met with considerable hostility from the post-Revolutionary public which, disillusioned by the unfulfilled promises of its leaders and chastened by the remembrance of its terror, was less inclined to view man's development as an uninterrupted march toward utopia.[2] Mme de Staël's eighteenth-century viewpoint was curiously out of step with nineteenth-century reality in the public's opinion. To protect her ideas from ridicule and dismissal, Mme de Staël prepared an extensive preface to the second edition of *De la littérature* in which she sought to dispel misunderstanding about her theory of perfectibility and to convince the doubting reader that progress was still the universal law of mankind.

---

[2] "Ici [dans *De la littérature*] la doctrine du progrès va s'affirmer avec beaucoup plus d'éclat que dans l'essai de Condorcet. Au moment où elle écrivait, les idées des philosophes étaient fort attaquées en France; c'est que la Révolution n'avait guère tenu ses promesses." Georges Sorel, *Les Illusions du progrès*, 5e éd. (Paris: Librairie Marcel Rivière et Cie, 1947), p. 228.

Despite the apparent contradiction of recent events, mankind never ceased to progress, she maintained.

En parcourant les révolutions du monde et la succession des siècles, il est une idée première dont je ne détourne jamais mon attention; c'est la perfectibilité de l'espèce humaine. Je ne pense pas que ce grand oeuvre de la nature morale ait jamais été abandonné; dans les périodes lumineuses, comme dans les siècles de ténèbres, la marche graduelle de l'esprit humain n'a point été interrompue.[3]

As she had written several years earlier in the *Essai sur les fictions* (1795), man's climb toward perfection is unlimited. "Il n'y a sur cette terre que des commencements; aucune limite n'est marquée."[4]

Specifically, the public had misunderstood the meaning of the phrase "la perfectibilité de l'esprit humain," believing Mme de Staël had insisted that man's native intelligence was now greater than before, whereas she had only believed in his increased wisdom. "Je ne prétends pas dire que les modernes ont une puissance d'esprit plus grande que celle des anciens, mais seulement que la masse des idées en tout genre s'augmente avec les siècles." (*Litt.*, p. 10) The necessity of defending a belief in intellectual advance, heretofore a *lieu commun*, reveals the pessimistic mood of the day.

Because she had been taunted for her optimism Mme de Staël wished to set herself apart from other believers in progress who had elaborately described the ever-nearing utopia. Instead of envisioning "un avenir sans vraisemblance," as had Condorcet, for example, Mme de Staël confined herself to the scientifically provable, the progress of civilization "dans toutes les classes et dans tous les pays" up to the present. The author's effort to study as objectively as possible such a subjective topic as perfectibility should be acknowledged, whether or not she succeeded in doing so.

---

[3] Mme de Staël, *De la littérature considérée dans ses rapports avec les institutions sociales*, éd. critique par Paul Van Tieghem (Paris: M. J. Minard, 1959), pp. 42–43.

[4] Mme de Staël, *Essai sur les fictions*, tome II des *Oeuvres complètes* de Mme la Baronne de Staël publiées par son fils (Paris: Chez Treuttel et Würtz, libraires, 1820), p. 176.

Mme de Staël's defensiveness is even more apparent concerning her belief in literary progress. Fearing that her distinction between the imaginative and the intellectual had not been understood, she reiterated in the preface that only in the second group is aesthetic progress possible. Further striving to present herself as an unbiased judge of civilization, Mme de Staël took elaborate care to acknowledge the merits of the past. Above all she wished to protect herself from being accused of lacking respect for the ancients, the label so easily attached to her pro-modern predecessors in the Quarrel. Again this effort toward impartiality should be noted. The tone of the Quarrel had greatly changed since the fanatical pro-modern ergo anti-ancient spirit of a Perrault or a La Motte. Mme de Staël, in the spirit of a Voltaire, chose to prefer the present without denigrating the past. To give credence to her lack of prejudice Mme de Staël praised, one could say to excess, the outstanding accomplishments of the Greeks in poetry.

> L'on m'a dit que je n'avais pas rendu un juste hommage aux anciens. J'ai répété néanmoins de diverses manières que la plupart des inventions poétiques nous venaient des Grecs, que la poésie des Grecs n'avait *été ni surpassée ni même égalée par les modernes.* (*Litt.*, p. 9)

Nevertheless the moderns emerge triumphant in other works of literature because of their increased knowledge of man. The description of love serves as an example.

> Dans les bons ouvrages modernes, l'expression de l'amour avait acquis plus de délicatesse et de profondeur que chez les anciens, parce qu'il est un certain genre de sensibilité qui s'augmente en proportion des idées. (*Ibid.*)

The history of the treatment of love in literature is the history of literary progress, according to the author. Many critics have pointed out that Mme de Staël, far from being the unbiased observer she pretended to be, was attracted mostly by sentimentality in art. Among them René Wellek in his *History of Modern Criticism 1750–1950* traces her view of literature to Diderot, explaining that Mme de Staël believed beauty to be emotional, sensitive, and sad. She was especially fond of works whose tone was pathetic and melancholic. "Sweet sorrow" and "somber reflection" were two qualities of noble art in her opinion.[5] Thus, her Romantic predilections, her fondness for *La Nouvelle Héloïse* and *Die Leiden des jungen Werthers.*

> Si l'on examine avec soin tous les ouvrages de l'antiquité . . . l'on verra que Racine, Voltaire, Pope, Rousseau, Goethe, etc., ont peint l'amour avec une sorte de délicatesse, de culte, de mélancolie et de dévouement qui devait être tout à fait étrangère aux moeurs, aux lois et au caractère des anciens. (*Litt.*, p. 9)

In the preface to *Delphine* published the same year, 1802, her own contribution to the new, improved love literature, Mme de Staël attacked the poor descriptions of love in ancient literature. Her explanation for this failing of antique authors was not based so much on lack of knowledge of man, the premise of *De la littérature*, but rather on the ancients' lack of interest in women as an object of adoration. According to the author, the Greeks and the Romans were too occupied with the affairs of state to be concerned with the complexities of courtship. More obviously women simply did not enjoy a high enough status to inspire a chivalrous attitude among the men.[6]

Whereas the progress of man has been continuous, the perfection of the arts has been seemingly interrupted, Mme de Staël conceded at the close of the preface to *De la littérature*. She

---

[5] Vol. II, *The Romantic Age* (New Haven: Yale University Press, 1955), p. 220. A contemporary critic, Joubert, dismissed her entire theory on the grounds that it was the result of an emotional woman's thought and had no basis in fact. In his *Jugements littéraires* he wrote:

> Il y a dans le monde une femme d'une âme vaste et d'un esprit supérieur. . . . Mme de Staël était née pour exceller dans la morale; mais son imagination a été séduite par quelque chose qui est plus brillante que les vrais biens: l'éclat de la flamme et des feux l'a égarée. Elle a pris les fièvres de l'âme pour ses facultés, l'ivresse pour une puissance, et nos écarts pour un progrès. Les passions sont devenues à ses yeux une espèce de dignité et de gloire. Elle a voulu les peindre comme ce qu'il y a de plus beau, et, prenant leur énormité pour grandeur, elle a fait un roman difforme.

Pensées, maximes et essais, notices et notes par H. Peyre de Bétouzet (Paris: Libraire Hatier, 1932), p. 79.

[6] Mme de Staël, *Oeuvres complètes* (Paris: Firmin Didot, frères, fils et Cie, libraires, 1871), I, 335–336.

takes the stand of Perrault that cultural attainments are like a river, ever flowing forward but sometimes disappearing underground only to emerge at a later date with greater force. Thus, she is able to explain the dark ages following the decline of Rome and the sudden flowering of the Renaissance. From the long view not even art is hindered in its progress, she wrote, although in the shorter view, it seems to suffer relapses and setbacks. (*Litt.*, p. 17) Inevitably art will benefit from the intellectual advance of man.

Proof of Literature's Progress: A Survey of Western Writings

Mme de Staël's survey of Western civilization follows the familiar route from the Greeks through the Romans to the French. Her view becomes pan-European only in the last years covered by her study when she acknowledges the efforts of German and English novelists. Generally speaking, however, her survey is not one of comparative literature, neither among the ancients, for there is no mention of the barbaric or primitive literatures, nor among the moderns. Non-French writers are generally ignored unless they have contributed to the genre of sentimental novels. [7]

By granting preeminence to the Greeks in poetry Mme de Staël was immediately faced with a serious difficulty in demonstrating literary perfectibility. Her solution was simple. She grouped poetry separately as imaginative literature and dismissed it, for unlike La Motte or l'abbé de Pons, she sought no quarrel with Homer, whom she greatly admired. Instead, Mme de Staël cleverly managed to grant the Greeks the honors due them while holding back certain laurels for the moderns. [8]

---

[7] Georges Sorel in his book on Mme de Staël points out that the oversights in her survey are due to her own ignorance. He suggests she preferred the Romans to the Greeks because she knew the former better. She was grossly ignorant of Italian and Spanish literatures, displaying little understanding of Dante and a total ignorance of Cervantes. Sorel, pp. 82–83.

[8] "[La poésie] peut atteindre du premier jet à un certain genre de beautés qui ne seront point surpassées, et tandis que dans les sciences progressives le dernier pas est le plus étonnant de tous, la puissance de l'imagination est d'autant plus vive que l'exercice de puissance est plus nouveau." (*Litt.*, p. 49)

In general, Greek poetry, she commented, magnificent as it is, confines itself to the description of exterior objects, whereas modern poetry moves beyond visual images to a study of human sentiments. (*Litt.*, pp. 48–49) Certainly the shift in focus, the "interiorization" of poetry, was a form of literary progress in her estimation, for it brought about more nuanced studies of love. Mme de Staël's insistence that imagination is more active and artistically productive in early civilizations is a questionable belief. In an effort to be impartial she seems here to have capitulated before having fought. Perhaps because of her eighteenth-century heritage she did not believe imagination to be a quality of the cultivated mind.

Before continuing down the path from ignorance to enlightenment, one should pause to consider a second objection to the theory of progress which Mme de Staël acknowledged but seemed unable to explain away. In apparent contradiction to her belief that man's wisdom and inventiveness have been universally beneficial, she lamented that the invention of printing has lessened the effect of poetry. Again, feeling that poetic beauty was unintellectual, she stated that Greek verse was more beautiful because it was sung, being presented in a flowing, ever-changing manner. Modern poetry, frozen on a printed page, loses this charm. Moreover, modern readers of poetry tend to overlook the simpler beauties of the poem in their insistence on study and analysis. No mention is made of the different and perhaps more profound beauties now accessible to the reader who is able to study a printed text. (*Litt.*, p. 62)

The Romans excelled in history as the Greeks had in poetry, but again in a non-intellectual manner.[9] There are two kinds of history, Mme de Staël explained, philosophical and descriptive, the latter being impassioned accounts written in beautiful language, the forte of Roman historians. (*Litt.*, p. 120) Not even French historians have been able to equal them in this genre in her opinion. (*Litt.*, p. 118) On the other hand,

---

[9] By the author's definition literature includes poetry, eloquence, philosophy, moral studies, and history. (*Litt.*, p. 47)

Roman history, like Greek poetry, avoided analysis and was unconcerned with psychology. In that modern historians, thanks to their intellectual advance, are concerned with character analysis, moral and philosophical observations, they tend to emerge superior to their predecessors. Nevertheless, Mme de Staël recognized an intellectual advance from the Greeks to the Romans which satisfies her requirement that man march continuously toward perfection. The Romans, she maintained, were more philosophical than the Greeks. By philosophical she meant enlightened and rationalistic. (Wellek, II, 221) Because of this intellectual development the Romans also displayed greater sensitivity and refinement in their writings than had the Greeks. The ultimate step in this progression will be, of course, eighteenth-century France where philosophical attitudes, refinement, and good taste reach their apogee in her estimation.

Without having pointed out that progress can only be proved over the long view, Mme de Staël's theory would have disintegrated when forced to incorporate the Middle Ages, which in her day were more often called the Dark Ages. Due to her tenacity, she refused to allow this long lapse of cultural and intellectual advance to deter her from her belief that man moved ever closer to perfection. (*Litt.*, p. 130) It is to her credit that because of her stubbornness she found the medieval period to have some merit when her contemporaries and predecessors dismissed it as "chaos and night."[10] She reasoned that if humanity had not continued its advance during those years, the cultural and intellectual explosion of the Renaissance would have never taken place. Without referring to Perrault's image of the underground river, Mme de Staël suggested much the same metaphor.

> Si l'esprit humain n'avait pas marché pendant les siècles même durant lesquels on a peine à suivre son histoire, aurait-on vu dans la morale, dans la politique, dans les sciences, des hommes qui, à l'époque même de la renaissance des lettres, ont de beaucoup

---

[10] Irving Babbitt, *The Masters of Modern French Criticism* (N.Y.: Houghton Mifflin Company, 1912), p. 11.

dépassé les génies les plus forts parmi les anciens. S'il existe une distance infinie entre les derniers hommes célèbres de l'antiquité et les premiers, qui, parmi les modernes, se sont illustrés dans la carrière des sciences et des idées et des lettres; si Bacon, Machiavelli et Montaigne ont des idées et des connaissances infiniment supérieures à celles de Pline, de Marc-Aurèle, etc., n'est-il pas évident que la raison humaine a fait des progrès pendant l'intervalle qui sépare la vie de ces grands hommes? (*Litt.*, pp. 146–147)

Montaigne epitomizes the gains of this great leap forward. His intellectual point of view is vaster than that of any writer of antiquity. (*Litt.*, p. 120) The result of intellectual progress was readily apparent in the arts. Taste is a matter of education, according to the writer. Thus, a more enlightened, better informed era has higher standards than its more ignorant predecessor. With man's increase in knowledge came a greater understanding of the science of beauty. The Renaissance was a great artistic age because it was a great intellectual age.

Quelle force l'esprit humain n'a-t-il pas montrée tout-à-coup au milieu du quinzième siècle! que de découvertes importantes! quelle marche nouvelle a été adoptée dans peu d'années. Des progrès si rapides, des succès si étonnants peuvent-ils ne se rapporter à rien d'antérieur? et dans les arts mêmes, le mauvais goût n'a-t-il pas été promptement écarté? Les progrès de la pensée ont fait trouver en peu de temps les principes du vrai beau dans tous les genres, et la littérature ne s'est perfectionnée si vite que parce que l'esprit était tellement exercé, qu'une fois rentré dans la route de la raison, il devait y marcher à grands pas. (*Litt.*, pp. 147–148)

Mme de Staël's enthusiasm increases as she approaches her own era. As the Renaissance towered over the Middle Ages and classical antiquity in excellence, so the seventeenth century, the Age of Louis XIV, dominated all that came before it.

So considerably had humanity advanced since antiquity that a comparison between the France of Louis and the Rome of Augustus seemed meaningless. In the opinion of Mme de Staël classical Rome had not produced men equal to Descartes, Bayle, Pascal, Molière, La Bruyère, Bossuet, or here straying into foreign realms, the English philosophers. Because Rome lacked writers who were equally talented moralists and philosophers, its cultural level was ranked much lower. Only by virtue of the augmentation of human knowledge could such an age of intellectual brilliance as the Renaissance have come about. (*Litt.*, p. 118)

The seventeenth century in France is the high water mark in the development of literature. The eighteenth century, although superior to it in philosophy, a more intellectual enterprise than art, has no writers who surpass Racine or Molière. (*Litt.*, p. 271) Racine represents for Mme de Staël the greatest of writers, for he perfected style, refined poetry, and better expressed ideal beauty than any other writer before him. (*Litt.*, p. 274) For all of Racine's progress, he had not reached the ultimate limit of development, however. The eighteenth century with its philosophical outlook would provide new knowledge of the human heart which even Racine had not discovered. (*Litt.*, p. 276)

The progress of mankind culminates for Mme de Staël during the Enlightenment. In her estimation Voltaire epitomizes this progress for he happily married both aspects of man's nature, the intellectual and the imaginative, the philosophical and the literary.

> La littérature du XVIIIe siècle s'enrichit de l'esprit philosophique qui le caractérise. La pureté du style, l'élégance des expressions n'ont pu faire des progrès après Racine et Fénelon; mais la méthode analytique donna plus d'indépendance à l'esprit, a porté la réflexion sur une foule d'objets nouveaux. Les idées philosophiques ont pénétré dans les tragédies, dans les contes, dans tous les écrits même de pur agrément; et Voltaire, unissant la grâce du siècle précédant à la philosophie du sien, sut embellir le charme de l'esprit par toutes les vérités dont on ne croyait pas encore l'application possible. (*Litt.*, p. 281)

Although not equal to Racine in poetry, Voltaire was able to surpass him in drama because of his greater knowledge of mankind. Because of the intellectual advance of the century Voltaire understood better the psychological nature of man. He was thus better able to express his sentiments, in particular the melancholy side of man, and was able to write dramas which more closely approximated life.

Dans ses pièces, les situations sont plus fortes, la passion est peinte avec plus d'abandon, et les moeurs théâtrales sont plus approchées de la vérité. Quand la philosophie fait des progrès, tout marche avec elle; les sentiments se développent avec les idées.[11]

In anticipation of the theme of *De l'Allemagne*, Mme de Staël gives partial credit for Voltaire's superiority to his knowledge of foreign authors. He will later serve as an example in her treatise on Germany as the cosmopolitan author who adapts foreign inspirations to the superior French form. If her contemporaries will follow his example, in the nineteenth century, drawing from Germany as Voltaire had done with England, French literature will be greatly stimulated by new blood, she believed. Voltaire's genius was that "sans limiter les incohérences des tragédies anglaises, sans se permettre même de transporter sur la scène française toutes leurs beautés, il a peint la douleur avec plus d'énergie que les auteurs qui l'ont précédé." (*Litt.*, p. 281)

Along with Voltaire, Montesquieu and Rousseau are singled out for their contributions to literary progress. Montesquieu is noted for his intelligent style, for the clarity and precision of his thought. Rousseau receives praise for his eloquent portrayal of passion. (*Litt.*, p. 284)

The progress of literature is evident in that writers of the eighteenth century stir the emotions of their readers more than had any of their predecessors. (*Litt.*, p. 152) Rousseau, Goethe, and the English Romantic poets represent the superior modern authors of literature of sweet sorrow, according to Mme de Staël. Not until the eighteenth century did the portrayal of love reach full perfection in literature. Then in the *Nouvelle Héloïse, Werther*, and *Tancred* the "sensitive affections" are expressed with greater force and heat than ever before. (*Litt.*, p. 118)

---

[11] *Litt.*, p. 282. "Toutefois si la poésie d'images et de description reste toujours à-peu-près la même, le développement nouveau de la sensibilité et la connaissance plus approfondie des caractères ajoutent à l'éloquence des passions, et donnent à nos chefs-d'oeuvre en littérature un charme qu'on ne peut attribuer seulement à l'imagination poétique, et qui en augmente singulièrement l'effet." (*Litt.*, p. 149)

As literary progress was achieved in the poetic drama of the seventeenth century it is evidenced in the novel of the eighteenth. The mere existence of the novel serves as proof of a kind of progress in literature, i.e. of progress by addition. The novel being a modern genre, its creation has filled a literary lacuna. "Les romans, ces productions variées de l'esprit des modernes, sont un genre presqu'entièrement inconnu aux anciens." (*Litt.*, p. 149) Mme de Staël's pride in the moderns' having achieved this kind of literary progress will be greatly shared by Balzac, who, crediting himself with filling the lacuna, will boast of having done in literature what had never been attempted before. As the nineteenth century progresses, a realization of the uniqueness and importance of the novel will become more widespread. Far-reaching claims for literary progress will be made on its behalf.

In her *Essai sur les fictions* Mme de Staël had pointed out the importance of the novel in the history of literary progress and its potential for further enrichment of the field of letters. Abandoning for the moment her major interest in romantic love, she then argued that if novelists would seek out other subjects for depiction, they could expand immensely the scope of the genre. Love, although "the most violent, universal, and truest of all passions," was the concern mainly of the young, she then explained. Other passions which would interest older readers should become the subject of novels. Immense progress could be made by the inclusion of these passions in literature.

> Une carrière nouvelle s'ouvrirait alors, ce me semble, aux auteurs qui possèdent le talent de peindre, et savent attacher par la connaissance intime de tous les mouvements du coeur humain. L'ambition, l'orgueil, l'avarice, la vanité pourraient être l'objet principal de romans, dont les incidents seraient plus neufs, et les situations aussi variées que celles qui naissent de l'amour. (*Essais*, p. 201)

Mme de Staël's plea will of course be answered in relatively short time by Balzac and Stendhal. One thinks immediately of a Père Grandet or a Julien Sorel. Stendhal is almost prefigured in her appeal for a depictor of ambition.

> Que de beautés ne pourrait-on trouver dans le Lovelace des ambi-

tieux! Quels développements philosophiques, si l'on s'attachait à approfondir, à analyser toutes les passions, comme l'amour a été dans les romans. (*Essai*, p. 209)

The eighteenth century particularly pleased Mme de Staël because its literature had become increasingly didactic. In her opinion, literature profited from the increased knowledge of man by becoming more truthful. Writers like Voltaire and Montesquieu who employed their superior knowledge in their writings to inculcate moral principles, to educate the ignorant, and to liberate the prejudiced, ranked highest in her esteem. Literary progress was a direct product of enlightenment, she concluded. (*Litt.*, pp. 286–287) This opinion will be shared by her later Romantic colleagues—Hugo, Vigny, and Lamartine, in particular—who continue the eighteenth-century tradition of didacticism in literature, which in their words will be known as "art for progress." The longing for realism in literature, more fully expressed later by Stendhal, should also be noted here. Well within the confines of Romanticism, the seeds of Realism will be sown.

The Early Nineteenth Century: Foreshadowing of the Romantic Program

Unfortunately for Mme de Staël her own age did not neatly fit into the scheme of perfectibility. The Revolution appeared as serious a setback as the Middle Ages had been, although a more limited one. Because she believed human perfectibility continuous, she did not feel the recent harm to man's development irreparable, but merely unfortunate and needlessly retardative. Using the same figure of speech as when justifying the apparent lack of progress during the medieval period by the more than compensatory flowering of the Renaissance, Mme de Staël announced with conviction that once the trauma of the Revolution had passed, man's progress would come to light again and be characterized by greater vigor than ever. Without actually stating it, Mme de Staël hinted that a second Renaissance was possible. Later writers will corroborate and more specifically state this opinion. The Romantics particularly were fond of speaking of their times as the second literary rebirth. Mme de Staël's timidity is understandable in that she did not share the Romantics' advantage of hindsight when she prophesied:

> Personne ne conteste que la littérature n'ait beaucoup perdu depuis que la terreur a moissonné dans la France, les hommes, les caractères, les sentiments et les idées. . . . Il est dans la nature même de la révolution d'arrêter, pendant quelques années, les progrès des lumières, et de leur donner ensuite une impulsion nouvelle. (*Litt.*, p. 293)

The literature of the future, of this second Renaissance, will continue in the philosophic and didactic strain of the eighteenth century, according to the author. The writer will work to enlighten his reader, to produce a more harmonious social, political, and moral environment, in short, to hasten the establishment of utopia. The writer, as envisioned by Mme de Staël, will become more and more an orator, for he will seek to stir the emotions of his readers by his philosophical ideas and his melancholic tone. (Wellek, II, 221) With the exception of the last item, Hugo will fill these qualifications. Had Mme de Staël lived in the later 1800's she would have doubtless been impressed by Hugo's ressemblance to her ideal. In addition, Mme de Staël believed that literature would become increasingly intellectual and decreasingly imaginative. She did not foresee the oncoming poetic flowering.

> La poésie d'imagination ne fera plus de progrès en France: l'on mettra dans les vers des idées philosophiques ou des sentiments passionnés; mais l'esprit humain est arrivé, dans notre siècle, à ce degré qui ne permet plus ni illusions, ni l'enthousiasme qui crée des tableaux et des fables propres à frapper les esprits. Le génie français n'a jamais été très remarquable en ce genre; et maintenant on ne peut ajouter aux effets de la poésie qu'en exprimant, dans ce beau langage, les pensées nouvelles dont le temps doit nous enrichir.[12]

Man's progress, intellectual and therefore literary, is in-

---

[12] Cited by Sainte-Beuve in *Chateaubriand et son groupe littéraire sous l'Empire*, nouvelle éd. (Paris: Calmann-Lévy, éditeur, 1889), I, 83.

evitable, Mme de Staël concludes. Its only prerequisite is that it be desired. Thus, retrogression is unthinkable.

> Comment donc forcer l'esprit humain à rétrograder, et lors même qu'on aurait obtenu ce triste succès, comment prévenir les circonstances qui pourraient donner aux facultés morales une impulsion nouvelle? On désire d'abord, et les rois même sont de cet avis, que la littérature et les arts fassent des progrès. (*Litt.*, p. 420)

Mme de Staël announces the Romantic program with her insistence that future literature must find a new way, for imitation would prove fatal to progress. Recasting ancient models, be they Greek, Roman, or from the Age of Louis XIV, regardless of their merit, leads to tiring redundancy and thwarted imagination. (*Litt.*, p. 149) One should distinguish, she points out, between knowledge of and respect for the past and servile imitation of it.[13] The literature of the future will progress by adding to what has come before. Progress does not require destruction of the old nor continuation of it, but addition to it. There can be no limit to such an extension.

> Il est impossible d'être bon littérateur, sans avoir étudié les auteurs anciens, sans connaître parfaitement les ouvrages classiques du siècle de Louis XIV. Mais l'on renoncerait à posséder désormais en France des grands hommes dans la carrière de la littérature, si l'on

---

[13] Mme de Staël is referring of course to the neo-classicists who felt that art had reached its definitive form during the seventeenth century. By wishing to freeze the development of art at this point they were frustrating the creative talent of the nineteenth century and hindering new progress. The author points out that only these authors bold enough to ignore the restrictions of the neo-classicists had shown signs of progress. The rarity of their number reveals the enormous influence of the reactionaries. Her comments forewarn us of the impending conflict of Hugo's *cénacle* and the traditionalists.

> Quelques hommes de génie, ayant à moissonner dans un champ tout nouveau, ont su se rendre illustres, malgré les difficultés qu'ils avaient à vaincre, mais la cessation des progrès de l'art, depuis eux, n'est-elle pas une preuve qu'il y a trop de barrières dans la route qu'ils ont suivie? (*Litt.*, p. 181)

Much the same sentiment is expressed in the preface to *Delphine* of 1802.

> L'esprit dépouillé de l'avenir, il serait condamné sans cesse à regarder en arrière, pour regretter d'abord, rétrograder ensuite, et sûrement il resterait fort au-dessous des écrivains du XVIIe siècle, qui lui sont présentés pour modèles. (*O.C.*, I, 336)

blâmait d'avance tout ce qui peut conduire à un nouveau genre, ouvrir une route nouvelle à l'esprit humain, offrir enfin un avenir à la pensée; elle perdrait bientôt toute émulation, si on lui présentait toujours le siècle de Louis XIV comme un modèle de perfection, au-delà duquel aucun écrivain éloquent ni penseur en pourra jamais s'élever. (*Litt.*, p. 9)

Implicit in this argument is the plea for freedom from rules as well as models. Without total freedom, Mme de Staël, like the Romantics to come, argues, there can be no literary progress.

The new way is announced in 1810 in *De l'Allemagne* when Mme de Staël urges the public to borrow new sources from the recently discovered literature of that neighboring country. Having become increasingly concerned with the stodgy literary climate in neo-classical France, she warned that without new sap the literary plant would wither and die. She had previously pointed out when discussing Racine and Voltaire that foreign inspirations had already enriched French literature. Contemporary authors should follow their examples without fear that the inclusion of foreign sources would necessitate the adoption of barbaric taste. Racine had redressed the Greeks with *bon goût*; Voltaire had eschewed the atrocities of Shakespeare's tragedies. A nineteenth-century author should then be able to take the best from German sources and remold it in an acceptable and superior French form.

Il se pourrait qu'une littérature ne fût pas conforme à notre législation du bon goût, et qu'elle contînt des idées nouvelles dont nous puissions nous enrichir, en les modifiant à notre manière. C'est ainsi que les Grecs ont valu Racine, et Shakespeare plusieurs tragédies de Voltaire. La stérilité dont notre littérature est menacée ferait croire que l'esprit français lui-même a besoin maintenant d'être renouvelé par une sève plus vigoureuse; et comme l'élégance de la société nous préservera toujours de certaines fautes, il nous importe surtout de retrouver la source des grandes beautés.[14]

Mme de Staël had by this time been won over to German literature for she thought it more suited to the northern Euro-

---

[14] Mme de Staël, *De l'Allemagne,* tome X des *Oeuvres complètes,* publiées par son fils, pp. 22–23.

pean temperament than Greek and Roman literatures. Northern literature she called "romantic;" Southern "classical."[15]
The best had already been achieved within the confines of the
latter, she believed. Therefore, the route to progress lay only in
exploiting the virgin territory of non-classical literature. This
progress should be easily brought about for romantic literature
was an indigenous product of French as well as of German
culture; it reflected the national heritage in religion and history.

> La littérature romantique est la seule qui soit susceptible encore
> d'être perfectionnée, parce qu'ayant ses racines dans notre propre
> sol, elle est la seule qui puisse croître et se vivifier de nouveau; elle
> exprime notre religion; elle rappelle notre histoire; son origine est
> ancienne, mais non antique. (*L'Allemagne*, p. 148)

Romantic literature would be free of certain of the im-
pediments of classical literature, in particular mythology. Earlier in the *Essai sur les fictions* Mme de Staël had attacked the
ancients for the use of supernaturalism in their writings.[16]
Because the gods controlled mankind, characters could not be
held responsible for their acts. A hero was not admirable, for
his successes were often the result of divine intervention. A
villain was not detestable, for he was often the victim of fate.
The use of mythological characters had robbed ancient literature of psychological analysis. With the moderns' placement
of responsibility in the hands of man, they had created not

---

[15] Mme de Staël's distinction was not original with her but was based on
A.-W. Schlegel's theory of the two literatures expressed in his *Uber dramatische
Kunst und Litteratur*. A cousin of Mme de Staël's, Mme Necker de Saussure,
had translated this work, based on lectures given in Berlin and Vienna,
entitling her works *Cours de littérature dramatique* (1809 and 1814). Schlegel will
have even greater influence on the French Romantics when in 1817 he pub-
lishes his comparison of Racine's and Euripides' *Phèdres,* granting preeminence to the Greek's. This unprecedented attack on the idol of French literature is but the first step in the reduction of Racine to the status of Romantic *bête
noire.*

[16] "Cette alliance des héros et des dieux, des passions des hommes et des
décrits du destin, nuit même à l'impression des poèmes de Virgile et
d'Homère. . . . Quand les dieux commandent et la colère, et la douleur, et les
victoires d'Achille, l'admiration ne s'arrête ni sur Jupiter, ni sur le héros; l'un
est un être abstrait, l'autre un homme asservi par le destin; la toute-puissance
du caractère échappe à travers le merveilleux qui l'environne." (*Essai,* p. 180)

only more believable but more interesting fictional personalities. While not advocating the replacement of pagan myths by the Christian one, Mme de Staël did detect greater literary possibilities in the use of the *merveilleux chrétien*. Milton had shown the superiority of the Christian approach; his Satan is superior to Homer's Agamemnon, she remarked, for he is not a puppet controlled by a god, but a man, a free agent. (*Essai*, pp. 181–182)

Despite her opposition to pagan literature, Mme de Staël does not embrace Christianity as the panacea for literary ills. In *De l'Allemagne* she points out that romantic literature must be Christian only because that religion is indigenous, but unlike her immediate successor, Chateaubriand, she refuses to grant preeminence to modern literature because it is Christian. Only skirting the arguments in favor of a *merveilleux chrétien* begun by Desmarets de Saint-Sorlin and brought to fullest expression by the author of *Le Génie du Christianisme*, Mme de Staël insists that the moderns' superiority in the artistic realm is due to the progress of knowledge throughout the centuries. In a late preface to *Delphine* contemporaneous with the appearance of Chateaubriand's apologia she explains:

> J'avais essayé de montrer quels étaient les heureux changements que le christianisme avait apportés dans la littérature, mais comme le christianisme date de dix-huit siècles, et nos chefs-d'oeuvre en littérature seulement de deux, je pensais que les progrès de l'esprit humain en général devaient être comptés pour quelque chose dans l'examen des différences entre la littérature des anciens et celle des modernes. (*O.C.*, I, 336)

In conclusion, one may state that Mme de Staël serves as a bridge between two generations. She continues the philosophic outlook of the eighteenth century and summarizes the basic concept of the pre-Revolutionary partisans of progress. She announces the Romantic point of view in calling for liberty in the arts, the rejuvenation of literature by the inclusion of new sources and the cessation of imitation. Thus, she is both an end point and a new beginning for the Quarrel. She is the last author to present a systematic study of literary progress. And she is even one of the last to rewrite Perrault's *Parallèles des anciens et des modernes* (1688–1697). On the other hand, she is very much the Romantic precursor because of her insistence on the development of a literature which is timely. Because of her optimism the Romantic self-confidence will be encouraged. Her prediction of a second Renaissance and its implication of artistic progress become an accepted fact unhesitatingly echoed by the leaders of the new school. The Romantics may differ in their explanation of literary progress, being less sure than she that the augmentation of ideas is responsible for it; nevertheless, their conviction will be equally ardent.

Chapter Three

Chateaubriand

Simultaneously with Mme de Staël, Chateaubriand continues the Quarrel of the Ancients and Moderns in nineteenth-century France. Many striking differences are apparent in their procedure, however. Whereas Mme de Staël attempted to prove both man and art's progress, Chateaubriand limited his defense to the aesthetic question. Within the sphere of the arts, it is Chateaubriand's theory of literary progress alone which is considered here, even though he thought all forms of artistic expression capable of progress.

While both writers worked towards the same end, the demonstration of literary progress since classical times, and while their method was similar, for they both imitated the scheme of Perrault's *Parallèles*,[1] they differed significantly in their ex-

---

[1] "Mme de Staël se trouvait dans une situation analogue à celle de Perrault; elle devrait prouver la supériorité de son temps par des considérations d'ordre littéraire. . . . Chateaubriand va essayer de ramener ses contemporains au catholicisme en faisant des parallèles entre les auteurs païens et les auteurs chrétiens et en démontrant la supériorité de ceux-ci." Georges Sorel. *Les Illusions du progrès.* 5e éd. (Paris: Librairie Marcel Rivière et Cie, 1947), p. 230.

planation of artistic improvement.[2] Chateaubriand credited the influence of Christian morality for all aesthetic progress, discounting the role of increased knowledge or civilization's advance as Mme de Staël in the tradition of the eighteenth century had done. In addition, they disagreed on the extent of literary progress in modern times. Mme de Staël thought the works of eighteenth-century France to be the epitome of perfected literature. Chateaubriand believed literary progress had been temporarily halted with the passing of the Age of Louis XIV, when classicism so aptly blended with the Christian view.

Chateaubriand presents his arguments on behalf of literary progress most completely in his apology, *Le Génie du christianisme* of 1802. They occur previously in outline form in a critique of *De la littérature* and are echoed throughout later works. It is in the review article, which also serves as advance publicity for the forthcoming *Génie*, that Chateaubriand disassociates himself from his contemporary's philosophy of progress.

Critique of *De la littérature:* First Statements on Progress

In 1800, the year of *De la littérature*'s first publication, Chateaubriand, having already formulated the main plan of *Le Génie*, recognized the remarkable similarities and basic differences between his own and Mme de Staël's literary theories. On December 22 of that year he published a review of his contemporary's treatise in the *Mercure de France* in which he emphasized his disagreement with her conclusions, perhaps to protect himself from being labeled her imitator. The article, first entitled "Sur la perfectibilité," was republished on the

---

[2] "Mme de Staël, qui reprenait de son côté, cette vieille 'querelle des anciens et des modernes,' pouvait se reconnaître dans *Le Génie*: 'Il a, s'écrie Benjamin Constant, pillé les idées de l'ouvrage sur la *Littérature*, avec cette différence que, tout ce que l'auteur de ce dernier ouvrage attribue à la perfectibilité, il attribue au christianisme.' " Pierre Moreau. *Chateaubriand, l'Homme et la vie; Le Génie et les libres.* (Paris: Librairie Garnier frères, 1927), p. 96.

occasion of the second printing of *De la littérature* in 1802 as "Lettre au citoyen Fontanes."[3] Chateaubriand characterizes himself and his rival as "deux esprits partant de deux points opposés [qui] sont quelquefois arrivés aux mêmes résultats." (*Corr.*, p. 25) The opposing points of departure are Mme de Staël's estimation of the influence of philosophy, i.e., knowledge, and his recognition of the role of religion on literature's development.[4] They agreed, however, that literature now expresses a deeper understanding of the human heart, for writers' insight and sensitivity had increased since ancient times. (*Corr.*, p. 25)

Modern authors owe their advantage to the moral teaching of Christianity which has brought about a reversal of human values, Chateaubriand explains. Former virtues such as pride are now considered vices, and humility, once scorned as a sign of weakness, is now hailed as a sign of saintliness. Because the Christian outlook is often the opposite of the Greek or Roman one, it offers new interpretations of man's actions. The inclusion of this reversed point of view in art allows for new subjects and new treatment unknown to the ancients. No credit need be given to man's philosophical or intellectual advance for this additional literary potential.

Il résulte de là que nous devons découvrir dans les passions des choses que les anciens n'y voyaient pas, sans qu'on puisse attribuer ses nouvelles vues du coeur humain à une perfection croissante du génie de l'homme. (*Corr.*, p. 26)

In addition, Christianity has served the advance of literature by intensifying the emotional conflict of fictional characters. The new sense of moral responsibility of the individual has increased the significance of his deeds. Thus, restrictions of conscience on man's desires have heightened the struggle

---

[3] Chateaubriand. *Correspondance générale.* Publiée par Louis Thomas. (Paris: Honoré et Edouard Champion, éditeurs, 1912), I, 23.

[4] "Vous n'ignorez pas que ma folie est de voir *Jésus-Christ* partout comme Mme de Staël la perfectibilité. J'ai le malheur de croire, avec Pascal, que la religion chrétienne a seule exprimé le problème de l'homme." (*Corr.*, p. 24)

between flesh and spirit, which lends itself to better dramatic effect.[5]

> S'il existait une religion dont la qualité essentielle fût de poser une barrière aux passions de l'homme, elle augmenterait nécessairement le jeu de ces passions dans le drame et dans l'épopée; elle serait, par sa nature même, beaucoup plus favorable au développement des caractères que toute autre institution religieuse, qui, ne se mêlant point aux affections de l'âme, n'agirait sur nous que par des scènes extérieures. (*Corr.*, p. 27)

Like Mme de Staël, but for different reasons, Chateaubriand had detected an "interiorization" in modern literature. The classics had concerned themselves primarily with external events and explanations. Contemporaries were more interested in inner conflicts and motives, i.e., psychology. As a result, the quality of literature had improved, he believed.[6]

Both Mme de Staël and Chateaubriand found modern literature to be dominated by a new sentiment unknown to the ancients. She called it *douleur*, he will label it in *Le Génie* proper *le vague des passions*.[7] Mme de Staël had reported melancholy to be without antecedent in the past, whereas Chateaubriand saw it instead as the latest form of an ageless sorrow:

> Je ne crois pas, comme Mme de Staël, qu'il y ait un âge particulier de la mélancolie; mais je crois que tous les grands génies ont été mélancoliques. (*Corr.*, p. 26)

Homer, the Bible, and Ossian all manifest this trait. The difference is in degree, not kind. Christianity, with its dual view of this world as a vale of tears and the next as eternal bliss, has

---

[5] "Le Christianisme seul a établi ces terribles combats de la chair et de l'esprit si favorables aux grands effets dramatiques." (*Corr.*, p. 26)

[6] "Tout est machine et ressort, tout est extérieur, tout est fait pour les yeux dans les tableaux du paganisme; tout est sentiment et pensée, tout est intérieur, tout est créé pour l'âme dans les peintures de la religion chrétienne." Chateaubriand. *Le Génie du christianisme.* (Paris: P.-H. Krabbe, éditeur, 1847), II, 4, 16.

[7] "[Le vague des passions] c'est celui qui précède le développement des passions, lorsque nos facultés, jeunes, actives, entières, mais renfermées, ne se sont exercées que sur elles-mêmes, sans but et sans objet. Plus les peuples avancent en civilisation, plus cet état du vague des passions augmente." (*Génie*, II, 3, 9)

produced a new melancholy, unlike that of the Greeks. Its inclusion in modern works of literature has broadened the horizons of art and has offered new opportunities to writers. Chateaubriand never agreed, even after the appearance of *De l'Allemagne* in 1810, that melancholy is a Northern trait. He insisted that it is purely Christian in origin. (*Corr.*, p. 30)

In his review article, the "Lettre au citoyen Fontanes," Chateaubriand is mainly concerned with discussion of literary progress, but he does treat briefly and scornfully Mme de Staël's theory of human perfectibility. Unable to credit Christianity for progress in morality as he had in literature, he dismisses the idea of the perfection of mankind as absurd. Outside the arts there has only been progress in the physical sciences, he notes. The son has not been intellectually or morally superior to the father. (*Corr.*, p. 28)

Le Génie du christianisme:
The Superiority of Christian Art

Chateaubriand's attempt to fuse literary and religious traditions was not an isolated historic phenomenon but had its roots in the seventeenth century. One of the earliest forms of revolt among the moderns of that time was done in the name of Christian art. Desmarets de Saint-Sorlin had fought for the acceptance of a Christian epic, presenting his own "Clovis" and "Marie-Magdeleine" as examples of the improved literature. Other quarrelers such as Vauquelin de la Fresnaye and Charles Perrault repeated his arguments that epic poetry in particular did not have to be pagan and sought an extension of Christian influence in literature in general.[8]

All three agreed, as Chateaubriand was to do two centuries later, that an author's religious convictions bore fruit in his works. A modern Christian writer creates better litterature if he does not have to shed his own religious beliefs and encumber himself with pagan superstitions. These authors felt

---

[8] Mother Maria Consolata, SHCJ. *Christ in the Poetry of Lamartine, Vigny, Hugo, and Musset.* Diss. (Bryn Mawr: 1947), pp. 10–11.

that a superior source of inspiration must produce a superior work of art. Thus, literature, inspired by the holy mysteries of the Bible would necessarily be of greater aesthetic as well as moral value than that which is based on fable, superstition, or unholy actions. Neither the seventeenth-century pro-Christian moderns nor Chateaubriand separated the spheres of morality and art. Each was dependent upon the other for status, they concluded.

The eighteenth century rejected the point of view of the Saint-Sorlins and Fesnayes. It was embarrassed by the religious-literary union and insisted upon dissolving it. The church was not highly esteemed by the deistic *philosophes* and Christ was more often portrayed as human than divine. (Consolata, p. 11) Religious fervor, equated with superstition and fanaticism, seemed out of step with the humanistic and rationalistic age. Those thinking literature had advanced gave no credit to religious inspiration but to man's intelligence and knowledge.

There were two notable exceptions to the non-religious literary point of view in the eighteenth century, the abbés Rollin and Batteux. They will be cited by Chateaubriand as sources for his defense of Christianity. Rollin in his *Traité des études* argued like Perrault that one does not have to be pagan in poetry. Batteux was more forceful. He claimed in his *Cours de littérature* that should a new Homer appear, he would certainly use the Bible to create a Christian *Illiad*.[9]

The nineteenth century Catholic Revival begun by Chateaubriand was an attempt to eradicate the godless attitude of the Enlightenment and return to the Christian-classical traditions of the seventeenth century.[10] Unlike Joseph de Maistre and Lamennais, who worked for an extension of Christian influence in all endeavors, Chateaubriand limited himself to a

---

[9] Chateaubriand. *Les Martyrs. Oeuvres complètes.* (Paris: Ladvocat, librairie, 1826), XVII, 133.

[10] "Il est possible que la somme des talents départie aux auteurs du XVIIIe siècle soit égale à celle qu'avaient reçue les écrivains du XVIIe siècle. Pourquoi donc le second est-il au-dessous du premier? . . . N'en cherchons d'autre cause que notre religion." (*Génie,* III, 4, 5)

championing of the aesthetic worth of the religion, finding faith in beauty. Although Chateaubriand continues the religious tradition of the past, he is also an innovator. Wellek cites this linkage of literary and religious sensitivity as a major contribution to aesthetic criticism.[11] He stresses the importance of Chateaubriand's reinterpretation of seventeenth-century French literature as Christian as well as classical for its originality. (Wellek, p. 233) Chateaubriand's belief that better morality makes better art, zealous as it was, did lead him to discover new paths for literature which had been overlooked by his predecessors, particularly in the treatment of nature. Chateaubriand will claim that the ancients had no descriptive poetry, i.e., of solitude, deserts, and infinite skies where man disappears before God; he will condemn mythology for having reduced nature to a small and petty thing, the habitat of supernatural creatures. Only under Christianity, he will insist, does there appear a feeling for landscapes apart from man. (Wellek, p. 234) Pierre Moreau in his book on Chateaubriand also signals the originality of the author's thinking and its importance for nineteenth-century French literature:

Romantique, le Génie l'est assurément par le souffle de nouveauté qui l'anime. Il appelle, il suscite tout un monde de rêves qui n'ont pas été connus par les Anciens. Il aspire à une poésie neuve, plus pittoresque, où la nature ne serait pas un décor peuplé de vaines déesses. Il déclare que "le genre descriptif" est né du christianisme. . . . A des chrétiens, à des Français, il veut que l'on propose une poésie française et chrétienne. (Moreau, p. 96)

Chateaubriand's claim concerning Christianity's influence in the arts is all encompassing.[12] That which is Chris-

---

[11] René Wellek. *A History of Modern Criticism: 1750–1950.* Vol. II: *The Romantic Age.* (New Haven: Yale University Press, 1955), p. 232.

[12] "De toutes les religions qui ont jamais existé la religion chrétienne est la plus poétique, la plus humaine, la plus favorable à la liberté, aux arts et aux lettres. . . . Le monde moderne lui doit tout, depuis l'agriculture jusqu'aux sciences abstraites, depuis les hospices pour les malheureux jusqu'aux temples bâtis par Michel-Ange et décorés par Raphaël. . . . On devrait dire qu'elle favorise le génie, épure le goût, développe les passions vertueuses,

tian—be it a building, a speech, a piece of music, or a poem—is ipso facto superior to that which is not. While Chateaubriand sets about to prove the beneficent influence of the religion in all the arts, it is his comments on literature which are of pertinent interest here, although the same arguments apply to all aesthetic forms.

One of Chateaubriand's main theses in favor of Christianity is that of timeliness. He felt that modern Christian western European man was so unlike the ancient pagan Greek or Roman that the same artistic forms could not please both.[13] Thus, modern literature must reflect present values and philosophies. Timeliness in this instance is not synonymous with currentness, it should be noted. For Chateaubriand, that which is post-pagan is timely. Later Stendhal will restrict the concept, insisting that only the most recent events and attitudes are timely ones and thus appropriate for artistic creation.

Although the moderns are considered generally superior to the ancients, the latter enjoyed certain qualities which have since been lost, Chateaubriand points out in attempted impartiality. Their taste was surer and their imagination nobler, he remarks. In addition, their works were simpler, more tragic, and truer to life. The moderns have the advantage of being wiser and more delicate than their predecessors. Thus their works are more interesting. Chateaubriand concludes that there has been progress in art because of a movement from the simple to the complex. The ancients concerned themselves with the whole and neglected the details. The moderns show the opposite concern. (*Génie*, II, 2, 2)

To illustrate his theory Chateaubriand draws a parallel between painting and writing. The ancient poet used only the primary colors, he felt, whereas the modern employs an infinite variety of colors and nuances. Thus, more recent writers

---

donne de la vigueur à la pensée, offre des formes nobles à l'écrivain, et des moules parfaits à l'artiste." (*Génie*, I, 1, 1)

[13] "En traitant du génie de cette religion, comment pourrions-nous oublier son influence sur les lettres et sur les arts? influence qui a, pour ainsi dire, changé l'esprit humain, et créé dans l'Europe moderne des peuples tout différents des peuples antiques." (*Génie*, II, 1, 1)

can achieve more subtle effects and greater sensitivity than did their ancestors. (*Ibid*.)

The ancients were also more realistic, i.e. truer to life, Chateaubriand explains, because they had not yet learned to pick and choose. In their works they depicted what they saw without focusing their attention on only relevant aspects of reality. As civilization became more complex, writers learned that they could not continue to be all inclusive in their works. They had to become selective, thus prefer the part to the whole. This process of choosing and hiding, Chateaubriand calls "le beau idéal." Unnatural forms were then created for art, forms more beautiful than nature's. Thus, by the artist's selectivity and emphasis he improved the quality of his creations, and of course Christianity aided in the process.

> Le Christianisme va plus loin que la nature, et par conséquent est plus d'accord avec la belle poésie, qui agrandit les objets et aime un peu l'exagération. (*Génie*, II, 2, 8)

Chateaubriand, like Mme de Staël, traced a continuous progress in artistic development since the time of the Greeks. The Latins who served as a bridge between them and the moderns show signs of this improvement. Retaining the simplicity of the Greeks, the Latins began to be selective and concerned with detail, a tendency not fully developed until modern times. By summing up the old and announcing the new, they had progressed. Virgil is representative of this advance. He is considered superior to Homer by Chateaubriand.

> Les plaintes d'Andromaque, plus étendues, perdent de leur force; celles de la mère d'Euryale, plus resserrées, tombent, avec tous leurs poids, sur le coeur. Cela prouve qu'une grande différence existait déjà entre le temps de Virgile et d'Homère, et qu'au siècle du premier tous les arts, même celui d'aimer, avaient acquis plus de perfection. (*Génie*, II, 2, 6)

For all of Virgil's accomplishments, even greater poetic progress is made by Christian poets. (*Génie*, II, 2, 10) It is Racine whom Chateaubriand considers the Christian writer par excellence. His religious play, *Athalie*, is beyond comparison. Racine best portrays the heightened dramatic intensity of

moral characters. [14] His women are his best creations and Phèdre, the epitome of these. By imposing a Christian conscience
on her, Racine was able to increase her sense of tragedy and to
portray a state of soul unknown to the ancients.

"Moi jalouse! . . .
Jamais mon triste coeur n'a recueilli le fruit."

Cet incomparable morceau offre une gradation de sentiments, une
science de la tristesse, des angoisses et des transports de l'âme que
les anciens n'ont jamais connus. (*Génie*, II, 3, 1)

Outside of French literature, Tasso, like Racine, demon-
strates the superiority of the Christian over the pagan poet.
His characters are moral beings, not soulless humans with
extraordinary strength. Chateaubriand chooses Godefroi as
Mme de Staël had Milton's Satan, not Agamemnon, as the
superior hero.

En faisant abstraction du génie particulier des deux poètes et ne
comparant qu'homme à homme, il nous semble que les personnages de la *Jérusalem* sont supérieurs à ceux de l'*Iliade*. . . . Si par
l'héroïsme on entend un effort contre des passions en faveur de la
vertu, c'est sans doute Godefroi, et non pas Agamemnon, qui est le
véritable héros. Or, nous demandons pourquoi le Tasse, en pei-
gnant les chevaliers, a tracé le modèle du parfait guerrier, tandis
qu'Homère, en représentant les hommes des temps héroïques, n'a
fait que des espèces de monstres? C'est que le Christianisme a
fourni, dès sa naissance, *le beau idéal moral ou le beau idéal des
caractères*, et que le polythéisme n'a pu donner cet avantage au
chantre d'Ilion. (*Génie*, II, 2, 10)

Chateaubriand concludes with the axiom that the more moral
the society, the better it portrays man in art. [15] The progress of
characterization is evident not only in the drama and in epic
poetry, but in the novel as well. Richardson's Clementine and

---

[14] "Une telle religion doit être plus favorable à la peinture des *caractères*
qu'un culte qui n'entre point dans le secret des passions. La plus belle moitié
de la poésie, moitié dramatique, ne recevrait aucun secours du polythéisme; la
morale était séparée de la mythologie." (*Génie*, II, 2, 11)
[15] "La société où la morale parvint le plus tôt à son développement dut
atteindre le plus vite au *beau idéal moral*, ou, ce qui revient, au même, au *beau
idéal des caractères*. Or c'est ce qui distingue éminemment les sociétés formées
dans la religion chrétienne." (*Génie*, II, 2, 11)

Rousseau's Héloïse are without counterparts in antiquity. These heroines reveal a soul-state impossible before Christianity. (*Génie*, II, 3, 1)

The Progress of Descriptive Poetry

Chateaubriand particularly condemned the ancients for their use of mythology, again on moral grounds. The Greek and Roman gods were not superior moral creatures, as are the Christian saints, but merely superhuman ones, still prey to man's foibles and ills. (*Génie*, II, 4, 4) In the same manner as Mme de Staël, he condemned mythology for removing responsibility from fictional characters. A god could always be blamed for the hero's failures or credited for his successes. The hero in ancient literature was reduced to the state of a puppet.

Unlike Mme de Staël, Chateaubriand was more concerned with the ancients' limited view of nature than with their supernatural explanation of man's actions. In contradiction with his earlier remarks that the ancients were more realistic than the moderns because they did not choose and hide, he complained that the ancients were blind to nature, for they only saw mythology. He was amazed at their inability to appreciate landscapes, storms, and sunsets for their own beauty, as he and the other Romantics certainly did, without having to interpret such phenomena symbolically in mythological terms. In his view Christianity had not only freed modern man from the ancients' superstitious fear of being mere playthings of the gods, but it has also opened the artist's eyes to the beauties which surround him. Chateaubriand argues that because of this limited vision the ancients produced no descriptive poetry. By filling this literary lacuna the moderns have made a significant progress.

Le plus grand et le premier vice de la mythologie était d'abord de rapetisser la nature et d'en bannir la vérité. Une preuve incontestable de ce fait, c'est que la poésie que nous appelons *descriptive* a été inconnue de l'antiquité. Les poètes mêmes qui ont chanté la nature, comme Hésiode, Théocrite et Virgile, n'en ont point fait la description dans les sens que nous attachons à ce mot. Il nous ont sans doute laissé d'admirables peintures des travaux, des moeurs

71

et du bonheur de la vie rustique, mais quant à ces tableaux des campagnes, des saisons, des accidents du ciel, qui ont enrichi la muse moderne, on en trouve à peine quelques traits dans leurs écrits. (*Génie*, II, 4, 1)

Chateaubriand, himself a poet of nature, felt only pity for the ancients' blindness. His well known Romantic supersensitivity to the grandeur of the ocean, his ability to commune with its spirit and to find peace made him keenly aware of the classical age's spiritual and aesthetic poverty.

Il faut plaindre les anciens, qui n'avaient trouvé dans l'Océan que le palais de Neptune et la grotte de Protée; il était dur de ne voir que les aventures des tritons et des néréides dans cette immensité des mers, qui semble nous donner une mesure confuse de la grandeur de notre âme; dans cette immensité qui fait naître en nous un vague désir de quitter la vie pour embrasser la nature et nous confondre avec son auteur. (*Ibid.*)

Bernardin de Saint-Pierre had already demonstrated the superiority of the Christian's view of nature in literature. Talent alone was not responsible for his excellence. Without religious faith he would have not responded to worldly beauty as he did.

On dira que ce n'est pas le charme emprunté des livres saints qui donne à Bernardin de Saint-Pierre la supériorité sur Théocrite, mais son talent pour peindre la nature. Eh bien! Nous répondrons qu'il doit encore ce talent, ou du moins le développement de ce talent au christianisme; car cette religion, chassant de petites divinités des bois et des eaux, a seule rendu au poète la liberté de représenter les déserts dans leur majesté primitive. (*Génie*, II, 3, 1)

Uncertainty over Literature's Future Progress

In writing *Le Génie* Chateaubriand had hoped to prepare the way for a renewal of the Christian classical tradition he so much admired in the seventeenth century.[16] To his dismay his

---

[16] Carols Lynes. *Chateaubriand as a Critic of French Literature.* (Baltimore: The Johns Hopkins Studies in Romance Literatures and Languages, XLVI, 1946), p. 80.

followers were those who imitated René and his *mal du siècle*. A tone of bitterness becomes apparent in his writings.

At the time of publication of *Le Génie* Chateaubriand seemed uncertain whether literature was progressing or not. While unwilling to proclaim the arrival of his hoped-for renaissance, he was equally uncertain that literature had entered a period of decadence. In *Le Mercure de France* in 1802 he expressed his wait-and-see attitude:

> Les jugements que l'on porte sur notre littérature moderne nous semblent un peu exagérés. Les uns prennent notre jargon secret et nos phrases ampoulées pour les progrès des lumières et du Génie; selon eux la langue et la raison ont fait un pas depuis Bossuet et Racine; quel pas! Les autres, au contraire, ne trouvent plus rien de passable; et si on veut les en croire, nous n'avons pas un seul bon écrivain. Cependant, n'est-il pas à peu près certain qu'il y a eu des époques en France où les lettres ont été au-dessous de ce qu'elles sont aujourd'hui? (*Martyrs*, p. 133)

Chateaubriand concludes that one cannot accurately judge contemporaries. Only posterity can distinguish between the first and second rate. He quite accurately remarks, and his view will be repeated by other Romantics, that every age is pessimistic concerning the quality of its arts. Man is more inclined to believe in decadence than progress. (*Martyrs*, p. 134)

In viewing the struggle of neo-classicism and emerging Romanticism, Chateaubriand predicted that the former would eventually triumph over the latter. In view of his wish to reinstate the literature of the Age of Louis XIV, this opinion is understandable, whereas considering Chateaubriand's own position as Romantic precursor it seems ironic. Chateaubriand sided with the imitators instead of the innovators because he felt tradition a surer guide than imagination.[17]

---

[17] (*Martyrs*, p. 72) Defending himself against the accusation that he was fanatic in his devotion to everything Christian, Chateaubriand at the same time revealed his hesitation to abandon the tried and the true of tradition for the uncertain success of innovation. Mme de Staël and other moderns also had protested their respect for the ancients while preferring the new. In one sense Chateaubriand is only continuing a defensive tradition. On the other hand, his

The best solution to this conflict of doctrines, he came to believe, would be to wed the classical tradition of the seventeenth century with the experimental attitude of the early nineteenth. As the Latins had preserved the best of Greek literature and announced elements of modern writing, so could contemporary authors bridge the old and the new. Cautiously innovating, writers would further literature's progress, whereas reckless disregard of the past would impede its improvement.

> Enfin ne serait-il pas possible qu'un homme, marchant avec précaution entre deux lignes, et se tenant toute fois beaucoup plus près de l'antique que du moderne, parvînt à marier les deux écoles, et à en faire sortir le génie d'un nouveau siècle?[18]

His advice went unheeded. The innovators, not the imitators, triumphed. Chateaubriand could only stand back in disgust and observe a literary revolution for which he was largely responsible. Instead of tradition and order he saw only barbarity and anarchy.

> Nous irons nous enfonçant de plus en plus dans la barbarie. Tous les genres sont épuisés; les chefs-d'oeuvre de la scène nous en-

---

defense betrays a greater love of the past than that of most moderns. In 1810 in the *Examen des Martyrs* he wrote: "On feint de me regarder comme un homme entêté d'un système, qui le suit partout, qui le voit partout [as indeed he claimed he saw Christ everywhere]; pas un mot de cela. Je ne veux rien changer, rien innover en littérature, j'adore les anciens, je les regarde comme nos maîtres; j'adopte entièrement les principes posés par Aristote, Horace et Boileau; l'*Iliade* me semble être le plus grand ouvrage de l'imagination des hommes, l'*Odysée* me paraît attachante par les moeurs, l'*Enéide* inimitable par le style; mais je dis que le *Paradis perdu* est aussi une oeuvre sublime, que le *Jérusalem* est un poème enchanteur, et la *Henriade* un modèle de narration et d'élégance. Marchant de loin sur les pas des grand maîtres de l'épopée chrétienne, j'essaie de montrer que notre religion a des grâces, des accents, des tableaux qu'on n'a peut-être point encore assez développés; voilà toutes mes prétentions, qu'on me juge." (*Martyrs*, p. 135)

[18] Chateaubriand's suggestion of marrying two literary traditions to create a new and richer one becomes a popular idea among nineteenth-century aestheticians. While Chateaubriand does little more than mention the possibility, Balzac will devise an elaborate theory, claiming the combination of traditions into what he calls "eclectic literature" to be the surest road to literary progress. Gautier also will attribute Romanticism's progress over Classicism in part to the blending of heretofore separate artistic disciplines.

nuieront bientôt; et, comme tous les peuples dégénérés, nous finirons par préférer des pantomimes et des combats de bêtes aux spectacles immortalisés par le génie de Corneille, de Racine et de Voltaire. (*Martyrs*, p. 349)

The inclusion of Voltaire in the list of immortals is significant. Had not the present been so disappointing, Chateaubriand surely would not have thought so highly of that un-Christian writer.

It is in his "Essai sur la littérature anglaise" that one finds Chateaubriand's most violent attack on Romanticism. Here he condemns the attempt to renew language and to discover new forms as retrogression to infancy, not progress. It was the democratization of art by Hugo and his followers which most disturbed him. The new school seemed to be without standards, rules or models. It shunned the superior for the common.

Soutenir qu'il n'y a pas d'art, qu'il n'y a pas d'idéal; qu'il ne faut pas choisir, qu'il faut tout peindre; que le laid est aussi beau que le beau: c'est tout simplement un jeu d'esprit dans ceux-ci, une dépravation du goût dans ceux-là, un sophisme de la phrase dans les uns, de l'impuissance dans les autres.[19]

Whereas Chateaubriand's opinion of the state of literature worsened with the passing years, his view of man became more optimistic. In 1797 in his "Essai sur les Révolutions" he portrayed man as condemned to turn in a tragic circle repeating his errors and atrocities. History he called "une échelle de misères, dont les révolutions forment les différents degrés."[20] Considering the proximity of this work's date to the French Revolution the author's pessimism is readily explained. By 1831, however, at the height of his criticism of Romanticism and just after another political revolution in France, Chateaubriand expresses an almost Staëlian view of man as indefinitely perfectible. In the preface to "Etudes historiques" he expressed this confidence in religious terms:

---

[19] Quoted by Lynes, p. 96.
[20] Quoted by Yves le Febvre. *Le Génie du christianisme.* (Paris: Edgar Malfère, éditeur, 1929), p. 29.

Je cherche à démontrer que l'espèce humaine suit une ligne progressive dans la civilisation, alors même qu'elle semble rétrograder. L'homme tend à une perfection indéfinie; il est loin encore d'être remonté aux sublimes hauteurs dont les traditions religieuses et primitives de tous les peuples nous apprennent qu'il est descendu; mais il ne cesse de gravir la pente escarpée de ce Sinaï inconnu, au sommet duquel il reverra Dieu. La société, en avançant, accomplit certaines transformations générales, et nous sommes arrivés à l'un de ces grands changements de l'espèce humaine. (*O.C.*, IX, 93–94)

Although Chateaubriand's call to faith was largely unheeded, his demonstration of literature's debt to Christianity served a valuable purpose. He awoke others to the beauties of the natural world and made them aware of the important role moral outlook plays in literature. Although others found his position to be extreme and were less inclined than he to equate Christianity with superiority, his fresh point of view did signal the differences in ancient and modern writings and led some to agree that the change had been for the better.

Chapter Four

Stendhal

Stendhal, because of his theories of relative beauty and timeliness, is one of the most ardent supporters of the idea of literary progress in the Romantic era. He believed the newest artistic expression generally to be the best, for it is the most relevant to contemporary men. Regardless of the merits of the masterpieces of the past, they are not equal to the masterpieces of the present, he thought, for they speak to another age whose point of view differed considerably.

It is Stendhal's application of the concept of progress to literature which is of main concern here, although at times he included the other fine arts in his scheme of amelioration. The concept of human—or rather moral progress—is excluded from his general theory. Mankind has progressed only in knavery and vanity, he believed, not in kindness or humility. On the human level, progress has indeed been negative. Stendhal presents his doctrine of progress most fully in the manifesto *Racine et Shakespeare* (1823 and 1825), having first formulated it in his otherwise unoriginal *Histoire de la peinture en Italie* (1817). Many pertinent comments also appear in his journals and letters.

Stendhal, the literary theorist, and Stendhal, the novelist, it will be noted, are much the same man. The same importance is attached to the pursuit of happiness, to the display of passion, to the development of energy. That which gives pleasure, arouses the viewer and speaks of deeds of noble proportions is good, while that which does not arouse, but bores, and that which is ordinary is bad, according to the author. Thus, vital, youthful Romanticism is championed and senile, tired neo-classicism is mocked. Only the new is honored, for only the most recent piques imaginations dulled by too much knowledge of the past. Thus, Stendhal's views of art and the artist are not surprising. Art is that immoral force which "dispose aux séductions de l'amour . . . plonge dans la paresse et dispose à l'exagération."[1] It prefers heart to mind, sentiment to reason. The artist is the Stendhalian hero, "au coeur énergique et agissant [qui] est essentiellement non tolérant. Avec la puissance, il serait un affreux despote."[2] As art exaggerates and arouses love, as the artist gives vent to his energies and emotions, the aesthetic state is improved. In sum, as art becomes more Romantic, it progresses.[3]

Two Main Theories: Relative Beauty and Timeliness

Preeminent among Stendhal's aesthetic doctrines is his belief in relative, not absolute, beauty. In reaction to the classicists' point of view, and especially Winckelmann's, that beauty reached perfection among the Greeks and is almost non-existent in modern times, Stendhal proposed that beauty is not limited to any age or prescribed by any taste, but exists

---

[1] T. M. Mustoxidi. *Histoire de l'esthétique française, 1700–1900.* (Paris: Edouard Champion, 1920), p. 91.

[2] Stendhal. *Histoire de la peinture en Italie.* Etablissement du texte et préface par Henri Martineau. (Paris: Le Divan, 1939), p. 184.

[3] In an article written for publication in England Stendhal explained "les beaux-arts doivent leur existence et leur progrès à la perfection de la sensibilité et à l'excitation forte des passions." *Courrier Anglais, Lettres à Strich, Paris Monthly Review,* January, 1822. Etablissement du texte et préface par Henri Martineau. (Paris: Le Divan, 1935), p. 271.

everywhere and always. The theory of ideal and absolute beauty is erroneous, he thought; it proposes one perfect masterpiece, ceaselessly imitated—a rather monotonous view of art.

Les âmes tendres et exaltées, qui ont eu la paresse de ne pas chercher l'*idéologie* dans les philosophes, et la vanité de croire l'avoir apprise dans Platon, sont sujettes à une autre erreur: elles disent qu'il y a un *beau idéal absolu*; que, par exemple, s'il eut été donné à Raphaël et au Titien de se perfectionner à chaque instant davantage, ils seraient arrivés un beau jour à produire *identiquement* les mêmes tableaux.[4]

On the contrary, there are as many concepts of beauty as there are men to conceive them. (*R et S*, p. 108) Thus, there can be no iron-clad rules, such as established under classicism. Freedom to experiment is necessary to the development of art. Innovation must always be preferred to imitation, an obviously Romantic point of view.

Man's concept of beauty is not unchanging but instead is dependent upon many circumstances. Like Mme de Staël, Stendhal attached importance to the influence of climatic, social, and political conditions. He also turned to eighteenth-century theorists such as l'abbé Dubos and Montesquieu to develop a concept of humours to explain variances in taste and in expressions of beauty.[5]

Depending upon the individual's physical makeup, he was either sanguine or bilious, phlegmatic, or melancholic, the ageless theory maintains. Stendhal accepted this view and proposed that the artist takes these differences of temperament into account. A writer most certainly must understand the theory of humours in order to create realistic fictional characters, he believed.

Werther ne sera pas indifféremment sanguin ou mélancolique; Lovelace, flegmatique ou bilieux. Le bon curé Primerose, l'aimable

---

[4] Stendhal. *Racine et Shakespeare, études sur le romantisme.* (Paris: Michel Lévy frères, libraires-éditeurs, 1854), p. 106.

[5] Pierre Moreau. *Le Romantisme.* Vol. VIII of *Histoire de la littérature française.* Publiée sous la direction de J. Calvet. (Paris: J. de Gigord, éditeur, 1932), p. 423.

Cassio, n'auront pas le tempérament bilieux, mais le juif Shylock, mais le sombre Iago, mais lady Macbeth, mais Richard III. (*Hist.*, p. 240)

Not only the creator, but also the admirer, must submit to the laws of temperament. A sanguine man cannot have the same preferences as the melancholic, thus the existence of many kinds of beauty, necessary to please all tastes. (*Hist.*, p. 244)

In *Les Promenades dans Rome* of 1829 Stendhal illustrated his belief by means of a fable. He told of a nightingale and a mole who found each other's tastes unacceptable. The mole could not understand the bird's love of light nor the nightingale the rodent's love of darkness. Transposed to the sphere of art, moles—changed into nineteenth-century classicists—cannot understand the preferences of nightingales, nineteenth-century Romantics, nor vice versa. It would be wrong for one to try to convince the other, Stendhal decides after *Racine et Shakespeare*, for one can only speak of art with those who feel the same way.[6] How foolish this quarrel will seem to posterity, he had even remarked in anticipation as early as 1817 in the *Histoire*:

Quelle excellente source de comique pour la postérité! les La Harpe et les gens du goût français, régentant du haut de leur chaire, et prononçant hardiment des arrêts dédaigneux sur leurs goûts divers, tandis qu'en effet ils ignorent les premiers principes de la science de l'homme [the science of humours]. De là l'inanité des disputes sur Racine et Shakespeare, sur Rubens et Raphaël. On peut tout au plus s'enquérir, en faisant un travail de savant, de plus ou moins grand nombre d'hommes qui suivent la bannière de l'auteur de *Macbeth*, ou de l'auteur d'*Iphigénie*. Si le savant a le génie de Montesquieu, il pourra dire: "Le climat tempéré et la monarchie font naître des admirateurs pour Racine. L'orageuse liberté et les climats extrêmes produisent des enthousiastes à Shakespeare. (*Hist.*, p. 182)

There must be both a Racine and a Shakespeare, Stendhal concludes. Majorities of opinion have no effect. If one man exists who prefers darkness to light, he should be granted the

---

6 Stendhal. *Promenades dans Rome*. (Paris: Calmann-Lévy, 1923), II, 33.

enjoyment of his preference which is determined only by his sensations. Stendhal's theory of relativity appears in his other works, both critical and imaginary. Mustoxidi points out that the famous love-theory of crystallization is but another affirmation of aesthetic tolerance. Beauty is in the eye of the beholder, be it verbal or corporal. "Ce que j'appelle cristallisation," wrote Stendhal in *De l'amour* in 1822, "c'est l'opération de l'esprit, qui tire de tout ce qui se présente la découverte que l'objet a de nouvelles perfections."[7] Beauty, Stendhal goes on to say, is pleasure which varies in kind with each individual. There is no absolute beauty, as there is no absolute or universal pleasure.

La beauté que vous découvrez étant donc une nouvelle aptitude à vous donner du plaisir, et les plaisirs variant comme les individus, la cristallisation formée donc dans la tête de chaque homme doit porter les couleurs des plaisirs de cet homme.[8]

As a corollary to the axiom that beauty is relative, Stendhal develops the doctrine of timeliness, that art must be current and relevant or it becomes boring, an interesting relic of the past perhaps, but still a museum piece, an oddity in modern times, out of kilter with the new. In *Racine et Shakespeare* Stendhal states most succinctly his belief in timeliness in his definition of Romanticism and Classicism. Typically, aesthetics are related to hedonism.

Le *romantisme* est l'art de présenter aux peuples les oeuvres littéraires qui, dans l'état actuel de leurs habitudes et de leurs croyances, sont susceptibles de leur donner le plus de plaisir possible.

Le *classicisme*, au contraire, leur présente la littérature qui donnait le

---

[7] Mustoxidi, p. 90. Martineau in his edition of the *Oeuvres complètes de Stendhal* makes a similar observation of the author's repeated belief in relativity. "En admettant ainsi l'évolution de l'idée du beau et en plaçant la physiologie à la base de toutes ses études, Beyle tient déjà le fil conducteur de toute son oeuvre, car la même idéologie qu'il applique ici à la peinture, le guidera quand il parlera de la musique ou qu'il dissertera de l'amour ou bien même quand avec *Racine et Shakespeare*, il développera ses idées romantiques dans le domaine des lettres pures." (*Histoire*, préface de l'éditeur, p. xxi).
[8] Stendhal. *De l'amour*. (Paris: Le Divan, 1927), I, 63.

plus de plaisir possible à leurs arrière-grands-pères. (*R et S*, pp. 32–33)

Romanticism, because it is better suited to the taste of the day, is to be preferred. No mention is made of an improved aesthetic quality. Romanticism and classicism removed from time are perhaps equal. Romanticism's superiority is revealed only when it is situated in the present environment, i.e., of the early 1800's, whose cultural needs it fulfills.[9]

By his theory of timeliness Stendhal argues for truth or realism in art. Progress, one could say, occurs as art more faithfully reproduces man. A post-Revolutionary Frenchman, being so far removed in taste from his pre-Revolutionary ancestor, demands an artistic representation of man which includes facts and opinions brought to light by intervening historical events. To pretend that the world had remained the same from 1720 to 1820 and that thus fictional characters should have the same beliefs and attitudes is to produce art in a vacuum, detached from reality. By so doing art becomes untruthful, thus inferior. Only by being abreast of the times can art accurately depict its subject—man—and thus maintain its quality.[10]

Stendhal's insistence that man changes continually is more than documented by a glance at the turbulence of the late eighteenth and early nineteenth centuries in France. The old aristocratic order had been overthrown by the Revolution; Napoleon had built an empire and lost it. With such severe historical lessons, the Frenchman of 1830 could not be ex-

---

[9] Literature is like clothes, Stendhal observes later in the manifesto, tailored to fit the man. The comparison comes dangerously close to labeling both utilitarian, for here Stendhal emphasizes the variance in man's taste (like his body's proportions) and never speaks of the difference in quality in the many kinds of clothes and/or literature. "Car voici la théorie romantique: il faut que chaque peuple ait une littérature particulière et modelée sur son caractère particulier, comme chacun de nous porte un habit modelé pour sa taille particulière." (*R et S*, p. 247).

[10] As Harry Levin in his *Gates of Horn: A Study of Five French Realists* points out, Stendhal favors Romanticism only because it is the most recent form of literature. "Had *le réalisme* been more current, it would better have suited his argument." (New York: Oxford University Press, 1963), p. 110.

pected to see life as had his grandfather. Stendhal emphasizes these factors in his call for an updating of literature:

> De mémoire d'historien, jamais peuple n'a éprouvé, dans ses moeurs et dans ses plaisirs, de changement plus rapide et plus totale que celui de 1780 à 1823; et l'on veut nous donner toujours la même littérature. (*R et S*, p. 38)

Neo-classicists refused to admit that their audiences were no longer the courtiers of Versailles. Forgetting that Molière was *romantic*, i.e., timely, in his own era, they copy him two centuries later naïvely believing him to portray contemporary man. Their imitation, their lack of adjustment, makes them *classical*, i.e., antiquated and thus inferior.

> Molière était romantique en 1670, car la cour était peuplée d'Orontes, et les châteaux de provinces d'Alcestes fort mécontents. A le bien prendre, *Tous Les Grands Ecrivains Ont Eté Romantiques De Leur Temps*. C'est un siècle après leur mort, les gens qui les copient au lieu d'ouvrir les yeux et d'imiter la nature, qui sont classiques. (*R et S*, p. 172)

Nothing could be less similar than a nineteenth-century bourgeois and a seventeenth-century nobleman, Stendhal went on to argue; Corneille, Racine, and Molière wrote for "marquis couverts d'habits brodés et de grandes perruques noires, coûtant mille écus." (*R et S*, p. 1) A nineteenth-century author should write "pour nous, jeunes gens raisonneurs, sérieux et un peu envieux, de l'an de grâce 1823." (*R et S*, p. 2)

The Positive and Negative Effects of Progress

Stendhal at times referred to the change in society as one of perfection, employing the term, however, in the opposite sense of Mme de Staël's definition. Only negative qualities, such as vanity, had been perfected, he believed. Man had learned to flatter with increasing skill over the years. In such a negative manner civilization had progressed since the Age of Louis XIV.

> Il me semble que [*Les Amants magnifiques* de Molière] est une preuve que la société s'est bien perfectionnée depuis Molière. C'est-à-dire que l'homme qui occupe aujourd'hui une position semblable . . . à

83

celle d'un homme sous Louis XIV, sait bien mieux ne pas blesser la vanité et la flatter que cet homme de Louis XIV. [11]

Stendhal thus concludes that there is more "bon ton" in the nineteenth century than in the seventeenth—"bon ton" meaning skillful use of flattery. Consequently, society has progressed, [12] for vanity is the product of perfected civilization. (*Pensées*, p. 297)

A more honest statement concerning man's "a-perfectibility" is to be found in a letter to Sainte-Beuve dated December 31, 1834. Here Stendhal mocks the concept of progress as a meaningless, but favored, cliché of unthinking people. Mankind ages, it does not progress, Stendhal preferred to say:

> Je saisis l'occasion d'écrire à un homme que je voudrais voir, c'est ce qui ne m'arrive presque jamais. Je ne parle jamais de notre chère littérature sans être Ovide: *Barbarus hic ego sum quia non intelligor illis*. Je reçois la *Revue des Deux Mondes*, et *Rétrospective* et l'*Edinburgh Review*. Ah! Monsieur, quels styles! et par compensation quelle absence d'idées! M. Loeuve-Weimars me console, et cette fois M. Magnin, quoi qu'il dise: Le siècle *progresse*! Quel joli mot qui rime avec graisse! Mais enfin il y a des idées. Si vous voyez M. Magnin . . . rappelez-moi à son souvenir. Mais demandez-lui pourquoi il invente *progresse* et fait usage de *hiératique* et autres mots grecs que Dieu confonde! Il faut laisser ces pauvres ressources à ces hommes qui n'ont pas une idée. (*Corr.*, 1834)

The arts, like civilization in general, progress but again with certain negative effects. Increased civilization has its price, for example, the loss of the poetic in day-to-day life.

---

[11] Stendhal. *Pensées, Filosofia Nova*. Etablissement du texte et préface par Henri Martineau. (Paris: Le Divan, 1931), p. 292.

[12] In obvious mockery of Mme de Staël he states: "Il faut donc qu'en 1670 le bon ton fût bien plus rare qu'en 1804 (134 ans après). Etudier bien cette idée de *perfectibilité* qui me mènera si je la trouve fondée à un état de l'âme bien doux, l'*optimisme* (on sait quel optimisme j'entends)" (*Pensées*, p. 293). The idea recurs in a letter to his sister Pauline in 1804. Speaking of *Les Amants magnifiques*, he remarks: "Regarde combien les moeurs se sont perfectionnées depuis Louis XIV; ce qui n'était qu'à la cour est actuellement dans deux mille maisons de Paris. Tout se perfectionne." *Correspondance, 1800–1842*. Publiée par Ad. Paupe et P.-A. Cheramy. (Paris: Charles Bosse, 1908), 7 juillet 1804.

Here Stendhal is echoing Mme de Staël who believed modern man to be less imaginative than his forebears. He also suggests Hugo and his theory that poetry flourishes only in humanity's childhood. Without the elaborate explanations of either of the other two writers, Stendhal simply states, however, that poetic qualities have disappeared in the modern world of harsh realities. (*Pensées*, p. 21)

Stendhal does not survey the history of Western writings in order to prove literature's continuous progress. Generally he dismissed pre-Romantic works as inferior and based his claim for perfection of the art of writing on quite recent examples. Unlike Mme de Staël, who thought the eighteenth century the epitome of literary production, for she valued reason over sentiment, philosophy over imagination, Stendhal generally condemned the age as one of little literary merit. He reasoned it was an artificially structured age, unnatural, and most importantly dispassionate. Without passion, without spontaneously and naturally expressed emotions, writers of the eighteenth century were unpoetic. They were rimers of maxims, to be sure, but never lyricists. He hoped that nineteenth-century writers would reverse this trend and restore poetry, imagination, and emotion to a more honored position.

Il faut donc avoir en horreur les *maximes*, le défaut le plus desséchant de la poésie du XVIIIe siècle; il faut reconnaître les vices du siècle et se jeter dans les défauts opposés. (*Ibid.*)

Stendhal was basically optimistic over literature's future in his own century. He believed that contemporaries, now free of classical rules, could profit from their knowledge of the past and avoid its mistakes. With the proper ambition and diligent application of energy the writer could achieve literary progress. To support his optimism Stendhal cited evidence of such an accomplishment among his own generation. His choices may be of questionable taste, but he was convinced they were obvious proof of literature's perfection.

Like Mme de Staël he noted an improved representation of melancholy in modern times. Without specifically attributing this advance to Voltaire as she had done, Stendhal instead thought it the product of society's progress. "Il me semble que depuis Racine la tendresse proprement dite s'est perfectionnée et que nous pouvons mettre en scène une mélancolie plus touchante que la sienne."[13] Heroism also was better portrayed in the nineteenth century than before. As proof he cites *Le Philinte de Molière ou la suite du Misanthrope* (1790) by Fabre d'Eglantine in which the principal character is stronger morally, in Stendhal's opinion, than Molière's Alceste. (*Journal*, p. 604) Generally heroism is now better portrayed because it is no longer limited to noble characters. Again referring to the importance of timeliness Stendhal remarks that a playwright can no longer expect empathy from an audience for whom "des rois et des reines pleins de vanité, qui sont presque les personnages les moins aimables possibles pour nous." After the Revolution one would better depict the heroism of a bourgeois or a peasant, "des êtres qui, abstraction faite de leur passion, seraient encore les plus aimables du monde à nos yeux." (*Ibid.*) The sincerity of this statement is more than proved by the creation of Julien Sorel.

Harking back to earlier moderns' claim that contemporary man has more knowledge at his disposal than did his ancestor, Stendhal credits recent writers' improved depiction of humanity to "notre science." Looking into the future Stendhal expressed wonder at the literary possibilities which would be available one thousand years hence. Presumably the progress would be enormous. (*Pensées*, p. 12)

Stendhal believed that for nineteenth-century literature to be timely it must be emotional.[14] Like Hugo he thought his age disposed toward the dramatic (the emotional), not the epic

---

[13] Stendhal. *Journal, 1801–1814*. (Oeuvre posthume) (Paris: G. Charpentier et Cie, éditeurs, 1888), p. 604.

[14] In the *Histoire de la peinture en Italie* Stendhal had characterized the nineteenth century as one of passion: "Les jouissances que l'homme demande aux arts vont revenir sous nos yeux presque à ce qu'elles étaient sous nos belliqueux ancêtres. . . . Il est difficile de ne pas voir ce que cherche le XIXe siècle: une soif croissante d'émotions fortes est son vrai caractère. . . . C'est la passion elle-même que nous voulons. C'est donc par une peinture exacte et enflammée du coeur humain que le XIXe siècle se distinguera de tout ce qui l'a précédé" (*Histoire*, p. 87)

(the intellectual). Racinian tragedy, he explained, gave only epic pleasure to its spectators by its expression of noble sentiments in beautiful verse. It was unmoving, however. Stendhal excused Racine for this "fault," saying that he did not know tragedy could be written any other way. Thanks to the present-day emancipation from the classical rules and the awareness of contemporaries that more than intellectual beauty is needed, the "fault" can be corrected. Romantic tragedy can now be a bit spicier, it can create "des pièces qui les [font] pleurer et frémir, ou en d'autres termes, qui leur donnent des plaisirs *dramatiques.*" (*R et S*, p. 7) Stendhal even goes so far as to say that if Racine were living in the nineteenth century, he would become dramatic and in so doing produce superior plays. "S'il vivait de nos jours, et qu'il osât suivre les règles nouvelles [those encouraging the depiction of strong emotion], il ferait cent fois mieux qu'*Iphigénie.*" Instead of limiting himself to inspiring only admiration, he would cause his spectators to cry copiously. (*R et S*, p. 18) "Les beaux-arts . . . doivent leur existence et leur progrès à la perfection de la sensibilité et à l'excitation forte des passions," he concludes.[15]

Painting had already undergone the necessary readjustment from the epic to the dramatic, Stendhal believed. Once imitators, such as Lagrénée, Fragonard, and Vanloo, dominated the scene. The public tired of their epic paleness and artificiality. David, who recognized the need for emotionalism, came to the fore as the leading artist of his time.

Enfin, et c'est ce qui lui vaudra l'immortalité, il s'aperçut que le genre niais de l'ancienne école française ne convenait plus au goût sévère d'un peuple chez qui commençait à se développer la soif des actions énergiques.[16]

Sculpture, Stendhal believed, was at the same turning point in

---

[15] Cf. note 3.
[16] (*R et S*, p. 2). The reduction of boring passages is characterized as progress in the sphere of music as well. Recitatifs have been replaced by ensemble works "qui, par leur vivacité et leur tenue musicale, tiennent l'ennui à distance . . . (donc) la musique . . . a fait un progrès considérable." (*Courrier*, p. 288)

the 1820's. Imitators of antiquity were being replaced by inno-vators, sculptors more aware of their era's aesthetic needs. Stendhal echoes Montesquieu's famous warning.

L'art statuaire est à la veille d'une révolution: faut-il copier servile-ment l'antique, comme la plupart des sculpteurs français? On sait le triste sort réservé aux copistes. "Si vous suivez toujours les anciens, vous ne serez jamais à côté d'eux," disait Montesquieu.[17]

A reproduction can never surpass its model and rarely equals it. Thus equality with the past inevitably implies inferiority, Stendhal concluded. "L'homme qui . . . ne fera que des ou-vrages égaux à ceux de Corneille, Molière et Racine sera donc dans le fait moins grand qu'eux." (*Pensées*, p. 153)

Despite Stendhal's call for dramatic literature, as op-posed to epic, he did not believe the theatre's potential to be very great in the nineteenth century. Instead, the means of literary progress seemed to be connected with the novel. After *Racine et Shakespeare* Stendhal became increasingly convinced that comedy was not a suitable genre for the era. He explained in an article entitled "La Comédie est impossible en 1836" that manners were changing too rapidly to be satirized.[18] Like other Romantics who thought of themselves as members of the elite because they were artists, Stendhal was disturbed by the amalgamating process of democracy, the domination of the common man. The old class distinctions which were once an excellent source of comedy were now gone. Society had become uniform.[19] The theatres were now filled with vulgar crowds too unsophisticated to appreciate fine comedy. The true artist must seek a special audience. The novelist must create for the "happy few," those capable of appreciating the

---

[17] Stendhal. *Mélanges d'art et de littérature.* (Paris: Michel Lévy frères, libraires-éditeurs, 1867), p. 254.

[18] This opinion is in direct opposition to one expressed in 1805. Then Stendhal believed the comedy to be the genre of the future. "L'empire de la comédie est bien plus considérable chez nous que parmi les anciens, donc si le monde continue à se civiliser cet empire augmentera sans cesse." (*Pensées*, p. 48)

[19] René Wellek. *A History of Modern Criticism: 1750–1950.* (New Haven: Yale University Press, 1955), II, 250.

joke. (Levin, pp. 107–108) Where better than in the novel could the writer display his superior knowledge of the human heart? What better place for accurate descriptions of passion? (Wellek, II, 250) In *Racine et Shakespeare* Stendhal had advised dramatists to become novelists in order to be superior "Eh bien! au moyen de quelques descriptions ajoutées, transformez vos comédies en romans et imprimez à Paris." (*R et S*, p. 133)

In typical fashion Stendhal championed the novel because he believed it less boring than the drama. Its potential as a pleasure giver was greater than any other genre's. In terms appropriate to a businessman with an eye on expanding markets, he pointed out the unavailability of theatres in the countryside and the need to escape boredom felt by vacationing Parisians. With novels they were equipped with portable theatres with which to amuse themselves on long rainy evenings. Boredom was the chief factor in the overthrow of the theatre and in the establishment of the primacy of the novel, Stendhal remarked.

> Ainsi, l'*ennui* a déjà brisé toutes les règles pour le roman; l'*ennui*! ce dieu que j'implore, ce dieu puissant qui règne dans la salle des *Français*, le seul pouvoir au monde qui puisse faire jeter les La Harpe au feu. (*Ibid.*)

The novel had first been mocked because it was not a classical genre. Instead the critics should have acclaimed the addition of a new genre to literature as a sign of progress. The age of the theatre has ended. Stendhal, foreshadowing Mallarmé, believed literature is to be contained in a book:

> Quels tragiques, suivants d'Aristote, ont produit, depuis un siècle, quelque oeuvre à comparer à *Tom Jones*, à *Werther*, aux *Tableaux de famille*, à la *Nouvelle Héloïse* ou aux *Puritains*? Comparez cela aux tragédies françaises contemporaines; vous en trouverez la triste liste de Grimm. (*R et S*, p. 56)

As Levin so aptly sums up "[Stendhal's] opinions proceed from a historical relativism toward a theory of literary progress, in which *le romantisme* figures as simply the most recent phase. Its recentness is what appeals to Stendhal. Throughout he sustains the unromantic assumption that the novel has eclipsed all the other genres." (p. 110)

Timeliness Not Fad

In the interest of fairness it must be pointed out that Stendhal distinguished between timeliness and fad. Although his preferences seemed most often based on the recentness of the product as Levin has noted, Stendhal also sought lasting qualities in art. In his *Pensées* he made the distinction:

> Le mauvais goût, c'est de confondre la mode qui ne vit que de changements, avec le beau durable, fruit de tel gouvernement, dirigeant tel climat. Un édifice à la mode, dans dix ans, sera à une mode surannée. (*Pensées*, p. 83)

He illustrated the difference humorously by referring to a painting of Jeanne d'Arc by Vinchon, no longer fashionable because the subject seemed unrefined and uncoquettish, much too interested in the beauty of her own shoulders and too obviously corseted. Because of changing feminine fashion the painting was now unsuitable. Had the artist been less timely in detail, i.e., less accurate in his depiction of fashion, he would have produced a work of more lasting quality.

> L'essence de la mode est de changer sans cesse . . . tandis que le *beau idéal* ne varie que tous les dix siècles avec les grands intérêts des peuples. (*Mélanges*, p. 228)

To exemplify the slower changes in beauty Stendhal divides the history of art into the pre- and post-gunpowder ages. Beauty for the ancients had a useful character, he believed. It expressed physical force.

> La belle statue de Méléagre avait donc par sa force mille choses intéressantes à dire. S'il paraissait beau, c'est qu'il était agréable; s'il paraissait agréable, c'est qu'il était utile. (*Hist.*, p. 278)

In modern times, by contrast, physical force has been replaced by intellectual force.

> A mes yeux la beauté a été dans tous les âges du monde la prédiction d'un caractère utile. Le poudre à canon a changé la manière

90

d'être utile; la force physique a perdu tous ses droits ou respect. (*Promenades*, II, 280)

Stendhal's preoccupation with time distinguishes him from other writers. He developed a Janus-like perspective, contemplative of the past and watchful of the future. He wished to attain immortality and feared that by an erroneous choice of fashionable instead of durable beauty his works would suffer the same fate as Vinchon's. All works have a limited lifetime, he believed. Molière and Racine were already outdated. Voltaire could not survive beyond the twenty-first century. To find the right combination of timeliness and time-lessness became his obsession. He once lamented: "Je croirai être loin de mon siècle et je serai encore tout près, tant ce que nous voyons chaque jour a d'influence sur nous." (*Pensées*, p. 21) To avoid classification as superannuated he advised himself: "Il faut me sortir entièrement de mon siècle, et me supposer sous les yeux des grands hommes du siècle de Louis XIV. Travailler toujours pour le XXe siècle." (*Pensées*, p. 16) Relenting in his attack on the outmoded classicists he admitted he would like to be considered their contemporary. "Je veux que dans trois cents ans l'on me croie contemporain de Corneille et de Racine." (*Journal*, p. 87) Apologetically he praised the targets of his Romantic zeal. France would probably not see the equal of Voltaire, Racine, or Molière for eight or ten centuries. In an effort at compromise he admitted that the first-rate of any century would last and be preferred to the second-rate, regardless how timely they were.

Il se peut qu'un homme de génie, en faisant des ouvrages qui plaisent infiniment aux hommes d'une des époques de la civilisation, donne encore plus de plaisir aux hommes d'une époque absolument différente que les artistes médiocres de cette seconde époque. (*R et S*, notes p. 42)

Stendhal seems then to retreat a bit from his insistence on timeliness. Actually he remained as obdurate as ever. The second-rate are those who copy another's view of reality. The first-rate are those who view life for themselves. Stendhal never abandons his opinion that all great writers were roman-

91

tics in their day, timely and relevant to their age. To fulfill these requirements in the nineteenth century the first-rate author must be a novelist, for only in that genre could originality flourish. By more truthfully, realistically if you will, portraying man, the novelist would achieve progress in literature.

Chapter Five

Victor Hugo

Victor Hugo in many ways is only a repeater and popularizer of the Romantic theories which came before him. He extracts the essence of Mme de Staël's, Chateaubriand's, and Stendhal's manifestoes, reclothes it in his own oratorial prose, and presents to a forewarned public "The Romantic Document," proclaiming the supremacy of his school's works over its rival's and suggesting its superiority to all that came before. But Victor Hugo is also an innovator. Unlike previous debaters he personalizes the Quarrel of the Ancients and the Moderns, starring himself in the role of creator of the new superior art form and its chief defender against servile and decadent oppressors. As the years pass by, Hugo more and more assumes the role of idealistic champion. He extends his benevolence beyond the sphere of letters to include the people in his fatherly embrace. He links art with social and political progress, imagining himself a second Moses leading the people to the Promised Land. Towards the end of his life Hugo becomes a bit more cautious, however, and qualifies his belief in the progress of art. Without abandoning his vision of himself as the unique seer and translator of God to man, he forsakes the rhetoric of the Quarrel and explains art's movement as an open-ended series of masterpieces, equal links in an infinite chain, of which he is only one of many units. In typical Hugolian fashion, however, he remarks that perhaps some links are more important than others.

Hugo's Debt to the Past

While Hugo recapitulates what comes before, like all first-rate geniuses, he does more than merely summarize; he digests and reforms tradition to prepare the way for the new. His debt to the immediate past is nevertheless enormous, for his future theories depend heavily on the ideas of foreign as well as French literary theoreticians.

Like other French Romantics, Hugo was familiar with the efforts of foreigners to overthrow classical gods and to allow the emerging Romantic movement the necessary freedom from rules needed to express itself completely. Inspired by such men as Schlegel and Manzoni, both of whom had attacked classical tragedy for its outmoded laws of composition, Hugo sought a new formula for drama, appropriate for the nineteenth century.[1]

It was his fellow countrymen, however, to whom Hugo was most indebted. Mme de Staël heads his list of creditors. Souriau, in his critical edition of *La Préface de Cromwell*, acknowledges Hugo as the popularizer of the ideas of *De l'Allemagne*. He also states that Hugo remoulded them considerably enough that the original author probably would not have recognized them.[2] According to Souriau, Hugo's early admi-

---

[1] August-Wilhelm Schlegel (1767–1845) had given impetus to the newly emerging Romantic Movement with his condemnation of classical tragedy, especially Racine's *Phèdre*, in his *Cours de littérature dramatique*, one of Mme de Staël's prime sources for *De l'Allemagne*. Alessandro Manzoni (1785–1873), Italian Romantic, best known for his novel *I Promessi Sposi*, exerted influence on French thinkers with his attack on the dramatic unities in the *Lettre à M. Chauvet sur les deux unités classiques* which served as a preface to Fauriel's translation of his *Tragédies* in 1823, the year of the publication of *Racine et Shakespeare*.

[2] Maurice Souriau, éd. *La Préface de Cromwell*. (Paris: Boivin et Cie, éditeurs, 1928), p. 35.

ration for Germany was due to Mme de Staël as was his comparison of pagan antiquity and Christian modernity. (Souriau, p. 34) More important, however, Hugo's views on human perfectibility and literary progress are derived from *De la littérature* as well as Hugo's insistence on the rapport between the origin of a genre and its social milieu. The *Préface* and *De la littérature* are strikingly similar in their form as discourses on the universal history of literatures in the manner of eighteenth-century *querelleurs*. As was said about Chateaubriand and Mme de Staël, the same applies to Hugo and the authoress, they both had the same point of departure but arrived at different conclusions. (Souriau, p. 36)

Hugo acknowledges his indebtedness to Mme de Staël earlier than the time of *Cromwell*. In the preface to *Odes et Ballades* of 1824 he credits her with adding the term *romantic* to the French lexicon. He also considers literature as a product "du ciel, des moeurs et de l'histoire du peuple dont elle est l'expression," an idea previously expressed by Stendhal as well.[3]

As a royalist, monarchist, and Christian, Hugo is of course reflective of Chateaubriand, his schoolboy idol. The mystico-literary theories of the *Préface* are derived from *Le Génie du christianisme*, in particular the belief that Christianity gave modernity a new genre, *le drame*, and a new sentiment, *la mélancolie*. (Souriau, p. 41) Unlike his mentor, however, Hugo did not agree that a new religion requires a new literature and agreed more with Mme de Staël that the un-Christian writers of the eighteenth century, Voltaire in particular, were equally admirable. Hugo found Christianity beautiful but was reluctant to accept its tenets as true. More honest than Chateaubriand, he admitted to being an admirer of religious aesthetics, not religious dogmas. Hugo and Chateaubriand also differed in their preferences of genres, the author of *Le Génie* favoring the epic although never writing one in the traditional sense, and the future author of *La Légende des Siècles* preferring the

---

[3] Victor Hugo. *Oeuvres complètes poétiques*. Réunies et présentées par Francis Bouvet. (Paris: Jean-Jacques Pauvert, éditeur, 1963), p. 4.

drama. Hugo did agree that modern literature differed from the antique by its insistence on "le beau idéal, l'art de choisir et de cacher" but even so varied from Chateaubriand's more ordinary view that Beauty was the artist's goal and proposed instead the Characteristic. "Si le poète doit *choisir* dans les choses (et il le doit), ce n'est pas le beau, mais le caractéristique . . . [parce que] tout ce qui est dans la nature est dans l'art."[4]

Stendhal's *Racine et Shakespeare* must be counted along with *De la littérature* and *Le Génie* as a prime source of the *Préface de Cromwell*. The idea "à peuple nouveau, art nouveau," echoed in the preface to *Hernani* is obviously from Beyle.[5] Stendhal also had opposed the continued influence of classical rules, e.g., the unities of time and place and the exclusion of all but "noble" language in classical tragedy. Stendhal's desire was to move the public more dramatically, that is emotionally, not epically or intellectually, a sentiment certainly repeated in the preface to *Marion Delorme* of 1831.

Des siècles passés au siècle présent, le pas est immense. Le théâtre maintenant peut ébranler les multitudes et les remuer dans leurs dernières profondeurs. Autrefois, le peuple, c'était une épaisse muraille sur laquelle l'art ne peignait qu'une fresque.[6]

Hugo Continues the Quarrel in His Own Way

Hugo's originality is expressed by his divergence from a narrow literary point of view to a wider concept of the Quarrel. He more than his predecessors linked Romanticism with the social and political currents of the day.

Hugo insisted upon the parallel revolutions in politics and literature. In an article entitled "Guerre aux démolisseurs," he remarked:

Car, il faut bien, nous le répétons, que les oreilles de toute grandeur

---

[4] Quoted by Souriau, p. 42.
[5] Victor Hugo. *Littérature et philosophie mêlées, 1819–1834.* (Paris: J. Hetzel et Cie, 1882), p 313.
[6] Victor Hugo. *Oeuvres dramatiques complètes.* Réunies et présentées par Francis Bouvet. (Paris: Jean-Jacques Pauvert, éditeur, 1963), p. 290.

s'habituent à l'entendre dire et redire, en même temps qu'une glorieuse révolution politique s'est accomplie dans la société, une glorieuse révolution intellectuelle s'est accomplie dans l'art. (*Litt. et phil.*, p. 377)

The Romantic Era which was dawning was certain to be a glorious one, he proclaimed. Napoleon's greatness in military matters was to be seconded by a poet's triumphs in the arts. A century which produced a Charlemagne would also bring forth a Shakespeare. (*Litt. et phil.*, p. 15) (Hugo was never bothered by the historical incongruity of this slogan.) Most likely casting himself in the starring role, Hugo devised an elaborate theory, which one could call the "binomial of greatness," which maintained that each important epoch had two outstanding representatives, a doer and a thinker. The nineteenth century was to follow suit. With a little more care for historical accuracy, Hugo dropped Charlemagne from his list and began the binomial series with Luther and Shakespeare, then added Richelieu and Corneille, Cromwell and Milton, leading up to Napoleon and "*l'inconnu.*" Until the equation was completed the parallel artistic revolution would not be ended, he thought. To unify the spirit of the century the unknown poet would have to be found. With a flair for showmanship, Hugo rhetorically called him forth:

Laissons-le donc venir, le poète! et répétons ce cri sans nous lasser! laissons-le sortir des rangs de cette jeunesse, où son front plonge encore dans l'ombre, ce prédestiné qui doit, en se combinant un jour avec Napoléon selon la mystérieuse algèbre de la providence, donner complète à l'avenir la formule générale du dix-neuvième siècle. (*Litt. et phil.*, p. 379)

Hugo's faith in the efficacy of these parallel revolutions was enormous. Artistically the nineteenth century was expected to blaze in a glory unknown to the past. Until the arrival of the poet-leader, the glory was to be stifled somewhat. Hugo worked hard to turn attention from the past where many felt France's literary glory lay to the future where he predicted it would appear. Paradise was not lost, he seemed to say; it had just not yet arrived. In the "Journal d'un jeune Jacobite de 1819" he optimistically prophesied:

Nous sommes à l'aurore d'une grande ère littéraire, et cette flétrissante opinion voudrait que notre époque, si éclatante de son propre éclat ne fût que le pâle reflet des deux époques précédentes! La littérature funeste du siècle passé a, pour ainsi parler, exhalé cette opinion antipoétique dans notre siècle comme un miasme chargé de principe de mort. (*Litt. et phil.*, p. 158)

With the ardor of the most extreme modern, Hugo would tolerate no worship of the past. With ever increasing insistency he maintained that his era was the best yet known and that its literature would be without parallel. Art's progress had been and would continue to be enormous during his lifetime. Much later in 1839 the older Jacobite wrote to the staff of the journal *Les Ecoles* to bolster their flagging faith. The letter with its extravagant claims is worthy of Napoleon inciting his troops to build an empire.

Courage, Messieurs, courage! vous êtes de la génération qui a l'avenir. En philosophie, en littérature, en religion, vous ferez de grandes choses. . . . Quoiqu'on en dise, l'époque où nous vivons est une belle époque. L'art et la pensée n'ont en aucun temps monté plus haut. Il y a partout de grands commencements de tous.[7]

As late as 1866, while in self-imposed exile on Guernesey, Hugo was to maintain his faith, proclaiming progress in all things, even the arts, to one he felt was responsible for poetry's advance, Paul Verlaine:

Une des joies de ma solitude, c'est, monsieur, de voir se lever en France, dans ce grand dix-neuvième siècle, une jeune aube de vraie poésie. Toutes les promesses de progrès sont tenues, et l'art est plus rayonnant que jamais. (*Corr.*, II, 547)

Of course, Hugo, like the other early Romantics, met with considerable opposition in his effort to break loose from the past and to sail freely into the future. Respect for the seventeenth-century greats was enormous and even their mediocre nineteenth-century imitators were generally esteemed.

---

[7] Victor Hugo. *Correspondance*. (Paris: Albin Michel, 1952), I, 562.

The struggle of the new versus the old, the familiar *Querelle*, was very real in the early nineteenth century.

Hugo's argument against imitation is a close approximation of Stendhal's. Copying the ancients, he remarked, produces only cold and false works. (*Litt. et phil.*, p. 289) Imitation is the scourge of art, whether models are new or old. Not above imitating Stendhal, however, Hugo wrote in the preface to *Odes et Ballades* of 1826:

> Celui qui imite un poète *romantique* devient nécessairement un *classique* puisqu'il imite. Que vous soyez l'école de Racine ou le reflet de Shakespeare, vous n'êtes toujours qu'un écho et qu'un reflet.

An imitator can never capture the soul of his model's work. The creator's genius cannot be duplicated. Only an original work will have that spark of imagination which characterizes the first-rate.

Hugo argues against imitation as did Stendhal on the grounds that older works regardless of their quality are anachronistic in today's world. Timeliness is an essential quality, the two agreed.

> Il faut . . . déclarer qu'il n'existe aujourd'hui qu'une littérature comme il n'existe qu'une société; que les littératures antérieures tout en laissant des monuments immortels, ont dû disparaître et ont disparu avec les générations dont elles ont exprimé les habitudes sociales et les émotions politiques. Le génie de notre époque peut être aussi beau que celui des époques les plus illustres, il ne peut être le même; et il ne dépend pas plus des écrivains contemporains de ressusciter une littérature passée, qu'il ne dépend du jardinier de faire reverdir les feuilles de l'automne sur les rameaux du printemps. (*Litt. et phil.*, pp. 270–271)

In place of imitation Hugo preferred innovation. The new was to be tried at all costs. "Faisons autrement. Si nous réussissons, tant mieux; si nous échouons, qu'importe," he once cavalierly remarked. Freedom became his watchword: freedom from rules and models, those vestiges of another era's idea of good taste. Literature's existence, not just its progress, depended upon absolute liberty. Again linking politics with art, he proclaimed: "Espérons qu'un jour le dix-neuvième siècle, politique et littéraire, pourra être résumé d'un mot: la liberté dans l'ordre, la liberté dans l'art." (*Odes et Ballades*, 1828)

Only total liberty was acceptable to Hugo; he wished no limits on the artist's imagination, no hindrances to his will to innovate. Especially in the preface to *Les Orientales* of 1829 does one find the Hugolian formula for literary progress. His insistence on the catholic nature of art prefigures his later doctrine of aesthetic opposites, e.g., the juxtaposition of the grotesque and the sublime in art. In 1829 Hugo maintained:

> Il n'y a, en poésie, ni de bons ni de mauvais sujets, mais de bons et de mauvais poètes. D'ailleurs, tout est sujet; tout relève de l'art; tout a droit de cité en poésie.

By insisting there could be no limitation to art as an argument for innovation, Hugo simultaneously was purporting that art continually progressed. No matter how high a summit the masterpieces of the past may have attained, they had never reached an end point. Art by its very nature is infinite. Without fully developing this idea Hugo nevertheless suggests it when defending his own innovations in poetic form, speaking of himself in the third person:

> Il a toujours répondu que ces caprices étaient ses caprices, qu'il ne savait pas en quoi étaient faites les *limites de l'art*; que de géographie précise du monde intellectuel, il n'en connaissait point; qu'il n'avait point encore vu de cartes routières de l'art, avec les frontières du possible et de l'impossible tracées en rouge et en bleu. (*Les Orientales*, 1829)

Total freedom to Hugo seemed utter anarchy to his opponents. Their fears seem justified when one considers the belligerent way in which he condemned artistic restrictions. Doubtless the neo-classicists, the *ultras* as he called them, felt a certain terror on reading the rousing war cries of this ardent revolutionary. Despite this literary Danton's zeal, he did keep in mind that art, too, must submit to certain discipline. He carefully delineated between the eternal laws—those limitations imposed by subject matter and nature—and the variable laws—rules and models imposed by well intentioned but misguided men. [8] The difficulty of separating the eternal from the temporal plagued many a Romantic and will lead to interesting discussions by Gautier and Baudelaire. Stendhal with his differentiation between the timely and the timeless had already attempted to elucidate this complex problem.

One of the most obvious variables in literature is language. Hugo was intensely dedicated to the destruction of all restrictions in the matter of form. Because of his valor other Romantics, especially the novelist Balzac, will have an easier time when they attempt to tailor language to fit the character they are describing. The French had been extremely conservative on the question of the evolution of language since the efforts of Vaugelas (1585–1650) and his fellow academicians to fix for eternity good usage. Although others were perhaps equally aware that classical seventeenth-century French was anachronistic in post-Revolutionary times, it was Hugo who distinguished himself as its most ardent opponent.

It is in the *Préface de Cromwell* that the author first presents an organized attack on this sacred cow of the past. There he argues that a fixed language is a dead one. Because "l'esprit humain est toujours en marche," that is to say progressing, language must follow in its step, by adapting itself to new conditions and meeting the new demands of the times. In Stendhalian terms Hugo explains that each era has its own favorite ideas and a language appropriate for expressing them. The nineteenth century being no different needs a new and vital idiom to convey its point of view. Inevitably certain beauties of the older tongue will be sacrificed in the process but for every loss there is a gain. (*Cromwell*, pp. 40–41)

Many years later Hugo takes up the same theme in "Réponse à un acte d'accusation" written in 1854 but predated to appear contemporaneous with the earlier struggle to free French verse. Hugo pictures himself in this poem as a liberator. Replying to a M. Duval who had called him the

---

[8] Victor Hugo. *Oeuvres complètes, Cromwell.* (Paris: Vve Alexandre Houssiau, libraire-éditeur, 1869), I, 147.

Robespierre of literature, Hugo takes up the images obviously delighted by the comparison:

Je me borne à ceci: je suis ce monstre énorme,
Je suis le démagogue horrible et débordé,
Et le dévasteur du vieil ABCD.
Je fis souffler un vent révolutionnaire.
Je mis un bonnet rouge au vieux dictionnaire.

Hugo in mock epic form divides words into aristocrats and laborers who repeat the struggle of the Revolution for "lìberté, fraternité, égalité." He, of course, sides with the people against their noble oppressors:

Oui, je suis ce Danton! je suis ce Robespierre!
J'ai contre le mot noble à la longue rapière
Insurgé le vocable ignoble son valet. . . .
J'ai pris et démoli la bastille des rimes.

Continuing Stendhal's plea for new words to clothe new ideas, Hugo upgrades the sentiment by suggesting that without perfect freedom of expression there can be no freedom of thought.

Et j'ignorais pas que la main courroucée,
Qui délivre le mot, délivre la pensée.
L'unité des efforts de l'homme est l'attribut.
Tout est la même flèche et frappe au même but.

The artist is thus recast not only as a thinker, but as a politician and social reformer. He must participate in and aid man's progress in all spheres.

Grâce à toi, progrès saint, la Révolution
Vibre aujourd'hui dans l'air, dans la voix, dans le livre . . .

Art to Serve Progress: The Poet to Serve Humanity

Victor Hugo, along with Mme de Staël, was a fervent believer in human progress. Unlike his predecessor, however, he interpreted the theory of perfectibility in a wider sense, for he thought man progressed morally as well as intellectually. He envisioned the poet as an active participant in the human advance and a leader of it, not simply a beneficiary of increased knowledge as Mme de Staël had done. Hugo's image of the poet was Saint-Simonian in character. He was to be a missionary, a carrier of the message of truth and love. He was to be a prophet, a seer and a guide of his people in the same manner as the Old Testament patriarchs had been "des voyants qui, à la lueur de leurs illuminations, aperçoivent la route que le peuple hébreu doit suivre." ("Fonction du poète," *Les Rayons et les Ombres*) The nineteenth-century poet, Victor Hugo himself more particularly, was to be the messenger of progress.

Le poète en des jours impies
Vient préparer des jours meilleurs.
Il est l'homme des utopies,
Les pieds ici, les yeux ailleurs.
C'est lui qui sur toutes les têtes,
En tout temps, pareil aux prophètes,
Dans sa main, où tout peut tenir,
Doit, qu'on l'insulte ou qu'on le loue,
Comme un torche qu'il secoue,
Faire flamboyer l'avenir!

To carry out this duty, Platonic as well as Biblical in inspiration, the poet could no longer content himself with a small select public such as Stendhal's "happy few" but should embrace all manner of men.[9] Art must become democratic, Hugo argues, although in typical Romantic fashion, he elevates himself above the masses to a state of semi-divine leadership, becoming the modern Prometheus bringing light to a darkened world. He hopes that the public will recognize the value of such a leader and follow him.

Peuples! écoutez le poète!
Ecoutez le rêveur sacré!
Dans votre nuit, sans lui complète,
Lui seul a le front éclairé.
Des temps futurs perçant les ombres,

---

[9] "Au siècle où nous vivons, l'horizon de l'art est bien élargi. Autrefois le poète disait: le public; aujourd'hui le poète dit: le peuple." *Préface d'Angélo* (1835).

Lui seul distingue en leurs flancs sombres
Le germe qui n'est pas éclos. . . .
Car la poésie est l'étoile
Qui mène à Dieu rois et pasteurs.[10]

Hugo worked equally hard to convince his fellow poets of their mission to lead as he did to persuade the people to follow. Especially while in exile on Guernesey he became absorbed with the idea of the poet's shaping man's destiny. In *William Shakespeare* he pleaded with the reluctant second generation Romantics:

Ah! esprits soyez utiles! servez à quelque chose. Ne faites pas les dégoûtés quand il s'agit d'être efficaces et bons. L'art pour l'art peut être beau mais l'art pour le progrès est plus beau encore. Rêver la rêverie est bien, rêver l'utopie est mieux [car] le poète est chargé de ce soin immense, la mise en marche du genre humain.[11]

Two colleagues were particularly opposed to the new collaboration of art and progress, for they equated the latter with science and technology, antipodes of art.[12] Neither Théophile Gautier, chief of the Art for Art's Sake Movement, nor his friend Charles Baudelaire, fellow hater of the utilitarian bourgeois climate of his century, was eager to assume the prophet's responsibility. Hugo therefore had to use greater persuasion and skillfully combined his request with flattery in a letter to the author of *Les Fleurs du mal* in 1859:

Je n'ai jamais dit: l'art pour l'art; j'ai toujours dit: l'art pour le progrès. Au fond c'est la même chose, et votre esprit est trop pénétrant pour ne pas le sentir. En avant! c'est le mot du progrès; c'est aussi le cri de l'art. Tout le verbe de la poésie est là. *Ite.* . . . Le poète ne peut aller seul, il faut que l'homme aussi se déplace. Les pas de l'humanité sont donc les pas mêmes de l'art.—Donc, gloire au Progrès. (*Corr.*, II, 314)

---

[10] The similarity between Hugo's image and Vigny's is striking. In *Chatterton* the young poet explains his mission: "[Le poète] lit dans les astres la route que nous montre le doigt du Seigneur."

[11] Victor Hugo. *William Shakespeare*. (Paris: J. Hetzel et Cie, 1882), p. 253.

[12] "L'histoire entière constate la collaboration de l'art au progrès," Hugo wrote in the chapter "Le Beau serviteur du vrai." *Shakespeare*, p. 261.

Despite Hugo's diplomacy, his mission was unsuccessful. Baudelaire never joined the ranks of the partisans of progress. Hugo viewed human progress as inevitable in much the same manner as had Mme de Staël. "Le progrès n'est autre chose qu'un phénomène de gravitation," Hugo wrote in *Pendant l'exil* of 1860. Man progresses as naturally as rocks fall and rivers flow into the sea. The world is hurled by God towards light. In *Les Misérables* Hugo is equally convinced of man's direction, although admitting there are interruptions in his march.

> Le Progrès est le mode de l'homme. La vie générale du genre humain s'appelle le Progrès; le pas collectif du genre humain s'appelle le Progrès. Le Progrès marche; il fait le grand voyage humain et terrestre vers le céleste et le divin; il a ses haltes, où il rallie le troupeau attardé; il a ses stations, où il médite . . . il a ses nuits où il dort. . . . Dieu est peut-être mort, disait un jour à celui qui écrit ces lignes Gérard de Nerval, confondant le Progrès avec Dieu.[13]

The question of man's ups and downs could not be avoided at a particularly grave historical moment such as France's humiliating defeat in the Franco-Prussian war. In *L'Année terrible* of 1872 Hugo, although saddened by the present, remains optimistic about the future. Like Goethe who had described man's progress as an eternal spiral, Hugo then explains:

> Le genre humain gravit un escalier qui tourne
> Et plonge dans la nuit pour rentrer dans le jour;
> On perd le bien de vue et le mal tour à tour; . . .
> Les sages du passé disent:—l'homme recule;
> Il sort de la lumière, il entre au crépuscule,
> L'homme est parti de tout pour naufrager dans rien.
> Ils disent: Bien et Mal. Nous disons: Mal et Bien.
> ("Loi de la formation du progrès")

Hugo's belief in moral progress had been longstanding. It was most clearly attested however in *La Légende des siècles* (1859), a series of poems providing an epic account of humanity's long climb from darkness to light. This mammoth work was to demonstrate in verse what Mme de Staël had done in

---

[13] Victor Hugo. *Les Misérables*. (Paris: J. Hetzel, 1862), 5e partie, I, 20.

prose, the perfectibility of the human race.[14] The poem continues the progressive tradition of earlier centuries. It is a universal history in the manner of the eighteenth century. It resumes the arguments of the utopians of the nineteenth. The work is unique in form, however, for while most moderns wrote their treatises in philosophical prose, Hugo wrote his in philosophical verse.

Optimism prevades the *Légende*. In the preface Hugo announces that he has set about to record man's continuous progress throughout history. (*Légende*, I, 12) With rich imagery, he refers to mythology, likening progress to the thread which guides man through the labyrinth of life towards utopia. (*Légende*, I, 15) Waxing religious in a manner suggestive of Lamartine, he also describes man's ascent as "une espèce d'hymne religieux." (*Légende*, I, 18)

Of particular interest in the larger work is the poem "Plein Ciel," one of two entries which depict twentieth-century human progress. Here Hugo's optimism exceeds its former bounds. Unfettered as he had been in describing man's past progress, for all too often history proved it severely limited, Hugo enjoyed the great freedom afforded by prophesy, which could not be immediately disproved, to announce a great step forward in the future.

In "Plein Ciel" Hugo ventures into scientific realms to acquire the proper imagery for his prophesy. Impressed by the invention of the gas balloon, he chose the airship to symbolize man's ascent or progress to heights undreamed of in the past. The airship image represents a high point in Hugo's faith in mankind. Goethe's spiral, which Hugo himself had later borrowed as a symbol, is much more cautious an image. Man's ascent, according to Goethe, is not perpendicular, but circular. To advance man must turn back upon himself. Thus much

---

[14] "Exprimer l'humanité dans une espèce d'oeuvre cyclique; la peindre successivement et simultanément sous tous aspects, histoire, fable, philosophie, religion, science, lesquels se résument en un seul et immense mouvement vers la lumière . . . voilà de quelle pensée, de quelle amibition, si l'on veut, est sortie *La Légende des siècles.*" *Préface, La Légende.* (Paris: Nelson, s.d.), I, 12.

effort is required to rise but a small distance. How much bolder the vision of man soaring unimpeded heavenward, like a rocket towards the infinite. The vertical image of progress reappears, as has been noted, in 1860 when Hugo compares progress to gravity. In *Pendant l'exil* he describes both as unalterable natural laws affecting human behaviour. Of interest here is the variation of the stock image. Gravity is vertical, but downward. How much more forceful the reverse image, flight.

Somewhat contradictory on the subject of gravity, Hugo in "Plein Ciel" equated man's freedom from gravity with the beginnings of a new era of unparalleled progress. Man's freedom from earth represents the culmination of his advancement. From relatively immobile primitive man, who was capable of moving horizontally only, as through a labyrinth, to completely mobile modern man, who can now move vertically as well, being capable of traveling on earth, sea, and in the air, there has been a huge step forward. Released from gravity, i.e., physical limitation, man is likewise released from moral fetters.

La pesanteur, liée au pied du genre humain,
Se brisa; cette chaîne était toutes les chaînes!
Tout s'envola dans l'homme, et les fureurs, les haines,
Les chimères, la force évanouie enfin,
L'ignorance et l'erreur, la misère et la faim,
Le droit divin des rois, les faux dieux juifs ou guèbres,
Le mensonge, le dol, les brumes, les ténèbres,
Tombèrent dans la poudre avec l'antique sort,
Comme le vêtement du bagne dont on sort.
(*Légende*, III, 325–326)

The voyage upward becomes sacred in character. It is the pilgrimage of imperfect man toward perfect God. Man's destination, Utopia, represents the fusion of created and Creator.

Hors de la pesanteur, c'est l'avenir fondé;
C'est le destin de l'homme à la fin évadé,
    Qui lève l'ancre et sort de l'ombre!
Ce navire là-haut conclut le grand hymen.
Il mêle presque à Dieu l'âme du genre humain.

Il voit l'insondable, il y touche;
Il est le vaste élan du progrès vers le ciel.
(*Légende*, III, 331)

Hugo never questioned his assumption that increased technical knowledge would result in improved morality. In 1862, three years after the publication of *La Légende*, he further glorified man's conquest of the skies in *Les Misérables* likening the inventor to a god.

Jadis les premières races humaines voyaient avec terreur passer devant leurs yeux l'hydre qui soufflait sur les eaux, le dragon qui vomissait du feu, le griffon qui était le monstre de l'air et qui volait avec des ailes d'un aigle et les griffes d'un tigre; bêtes effrayantes qui étaient au-dessus de l'homme. L'homme cependant a tendu ses pièges sacrés de l'intelligence, et il a fini par y prendre les monstres. Nous avons domptés l'hydre, et elle s'appelle le steamer; nous avons dompté le dragon, et il s'appelle la locomotive; nous sommes sur le point de dompter le griffon, nous le tenons déjà, et il s'appelle le ballon. Le jour où cette oeuvre prométhéenne sera terminée, et où l'homme aura définitivement attelé à sa volonté la triple Chimère antique, il sera maître de l'eau, du feu et de l'air, et il sera pour le reste de la création animée ce que les anciens dieux étaient déjà pour lui.(*Misérables*, 5e Partie, I, 5)

Twentieth-century critics, for example Bellesort, have pointed out Hugo should not have so readily abandoned caution but should have remained more sceptical about the future. Science is amoral, the critics maintain, interested in knowledge alone, not in its application to man's benefit. Hugo's naïveté, the natural result of his idealism, leads Bellesort to question his true understanding of the human race.

On lui reproche tout bonnement d'avoir méconnu la nature humaine au point de supposer que les inventions de la science pourraient la transfigurer et que tous les peuples deviendraient frères, toutes les âmes droites et pures, quand on saurait diriger les ballons. [15]

Hugo prided himself on his humanitarian efforts which could serve as an example to others of the sincerity of his belief

---

[15] André Bellesort. *Victor Hugo: Essai sur son oeuvre.* (Paris: Perrin et Cie, 1930), p. 184.

that the poet must lead his brothers. Toward the end of his life Hugo expresses self-satisfaction in a letter to Alfred Barbour in 1879. In characteristic egotism, the author ranks himself with the greatest of humanitarians.

Quoi que soit le jugement qu'on porte sur moi, je suis tranquille. Ma tentative littéraire, ma tentative politique, ma tentative sociale, sont trois efforts vers le bien. Je n'ai jamais eu de colère que contre le mal.

Humaniores litterae. Nous sommes avec tous ceux qui ont eu le désir de voir décroître la souffrance humaine. Si diverses que soient les surfaces, le fond, le progrès est toujours le même. Ce qu'a voulu Socrate est voulu par Molière, ce qu'a voulu Jésus est voulu par Voltaire. (*Corr.*, III, 69)

Artistic Progress Denied?

Despite Hugo's life-long commitment to the belief in man's perfectibility, the poet was less staunch a supporter of the idea of progress in the arts. In his earliest enthusiasm there seemed no hesitation to extend the influence of the benevolent law into the realm of aesthetics, whereas in later years Hugo adamantly proclaimed art inherently unprogressive. Looking beyond these pronouncements one suspects, however, that Victor Hugo never totally abandoned the idea of artistic progress, for perhaps it would have been personally too costly. Two main texts treat the question of progress in the arts. The first, representative of youth and fiery Romanticism, comes closest to proclaiming literary perfectibility. It is, of course, the famous manifesto, the *Préface de Cromwell* of 1827. The second text, *William Shakespeare* of 1864, indicative of a more contemplative period, for it was written on Guernesey, manifestly debunks the notion of art progressing while insinuating that in special circumstances and limited ways it does.

The preface, being a work of propaganda contrived to win public favor for a much maligned new literary school, is not known for its complete objectivity. To prove his point, Hugo took short cuts in logic and made fullest use of his nimble pen to give his side every advantage. In spite of these faults there is much of value in the manifesto, notably the introduction of the theory of the grotesque in literature.

Being convinced even at this early date that man had continually progressed, Hugo based his literary theories on that proposition. Borrowing a metaphor from Pascal, he divided humanity's lifetime into three ages—childhood, adulthood, and old age—reckoning as had his seventeenth-century source that humanity could be compared to an individual. Man, the collective being, produced literatures appropriate for his age group. Childhood, the "primitive age," was lyrical and most adept with the ode. According to the author Genesis is the finest example. Adulthood, or the "antique" age was epic in nature and chose that genre to express itself. Homer and Virgil are its best representatives. Old age, or more kindly maturity, since there is no hint of senility in Hugo's scheme, is the "modern" age which is dramatic in character. Shakespeare is its leading writer.

Hugo's thesis that as man progresses his art is forced to adapt to a changing environment is, of course, repetitive of Mme de Staël and Stendhal. Hugo's choice of genres befitting each age was entirely his own idea, for which he received much criticism. Biré has pointed out that Hugo would have been more accurate had he reversed the position of the ode and epic. Genesis, according to this critic, is epic in nature, as Chateaubriand himself had noted when comparing Homer and the Bible. It is not until David and the prophets that lyricism appears in the Old Testament. It was equally erroneous to label the Greeks exclusively epic, Biré continues, for they were equally lyrical and dramatic. Their poets were legion. Homer himself was lyrical along with Pindar, Sapho, and Anacreon. Their tragedians, Aeschylus, Sophocles, and Euripides, are still revered and imitated.[16]

Abandoning these inconsistencies and turning our attention to the third epoch, modernity, we find Hugo echoing Chateaubriand, but again in his own fashion. Like his boy-

---

[16] Edmond Biré. *Victor Hugo avant 1830*. Nouvelle éd. (Paris: Librairie Académique Didier, 1902), pp. 427–428.

hood idol, Hugo credited Christianity with definitively dividing the old world from the new. He agreed that it provided a new genre, the drama, and a new sentiment, melancholy.[17] The new religion's insistence on man's duality also served as a springboard for Hugo's theory of the grotesque. Paganism, Hugo contends, was one-sided in its art. It rejected all that did not conform to its rigid ideal of beauty. The ideal type was magnificent, he concedes, but fake and conventional. Christianity awoke man from the pagan dream and confronted him with reality. Poetry turned from fiction to truth. This step toward realism, Hugo like Stendhal argued, was a sign of progress.

> Le Christianisme amène la poésie à la vérité. Comme lui, la muse moderne verra les choses d'un coup d'oeil plus haut et plus large. (*Cromwell*, p. 141)

With the veil torn from the poet's eyes, he discovered that all nature was not beautiful, that a duality existed in all things. Complementary to the beautiful and the good was the ugly (the deformed and the grotesque) and the evil. Incorporating the negative with the positive in his poems, the poet opened new horizons to art.[18] By providing contrast for the positive, he highlighted the ideal, an invention Hugo proclaims is "la plus riche source que la nature puisse ouvrir à l'art." (*Cromwell*, p. 142) Modern literature with its newly found advantage then surpassed its primitive and antique predecessors, for "le contact du difforme a donné au sublime moderne quelque chose de plus pur, de plus grand, de plus sublime enfin que le beau antique et cela doit être." Quantitatively as well as qualitatively, the new aesthetic provided for greater depiction. "Le beau n'a qu'un type; le laid en a mille." (*Ibid.*)

Hugo's historical accuracy is again questionable. He

---

[17] "Avec le christianisme et par lui s'introduisait dans l'esprit des peuples un sentiment nouveau, inconnu des anciens et singulièrement développé chez les modernes, un sentiment qui est plus que la gravité et moins que la tristesse: la mélancolie" (*Cromwell*, pp. 140–141).

[18] "[C'était] un grand pas, un pas décisif, un pas qui, pareil à la secousse d'un tremblement de terre, [changerait] toute la face du monde intellectuel." (*Cromwell*, p. 141)

111

maintained that antiquity was unaware of the grotesque and consequently was lacking comedy. (*Cromwell*, p. 141) The ancients' concept of grotesqueness was at best embryonic. Their deformed characters lacked force because they had the compensation of being divine. In modernity the grotesque has come to full flower. Its impact is immense. Because of its cultivation works such as Dante's *Inferno*, Milton's *Paradise Lost*, and Shakespeare's *Macbeth* were made possible.

Biré again takes Hugo to task for his sweeping claims. Antique literature was steeped with grotesque figures. He cites Thersites in the *Iliad*, Ulysses' companions turned to swine, Cacus in the *Aeneid*, and Horace's sorcerer Candide. An entire genre of the grotesque existed, Biré maintains, satyric drama whose main characters were Pans or satyrs with either the feet or heads of goats. Aeschylus produced five of these plays, Sophocles seven, and Euripides another five. (Biré, p. 429) Equally untenable was Hugo's statement that comedy was lacking among the ancients. He had simply overlooked Plautus and Aristophanes for convenience's sake. (Biré, p. 430)

More sympathetic to Hugo is Maurice Souriau. In his critical edition of *La Préface de Cromwell* he ranks the theory of the grotesque Hugo's most important aesthetic contribution, although he too takes the author to task for having slighted Aristophanes, "celui qui a poussé le grotesque jusqu'au lyrisme, et qui renferme toutes les antithèses, étant à la fois, comme le remarque Musset, 'Tendre et terrible, pur et obscène, honnête et corrompu, noble et trivial.' "[19]

However shaky the factual foundation of his theory, Hugo believed that only modern literature as represented by the drama is complete and true. The earlier genres were mere preparatory stages, fragmented and biased, he thought. With Shakespeare literature makes great progress. It arrives "à la sommité poétique." (*Cromwell*, p. 143) The moderns having the advantage of hindsight are able to incorporate the best of

---

[19] Musset. *Lettres de Dupuis et Cotonnet.* Ière Lettre.

the past into a superior literary form. Hugo's belief in progress is unquestionable when he writes:

> C'est . . . pour cette dernière raison que le drame, unissant les qualités les plus opposées, peut être tout à la fois, plein de profondeur et plein de relief, philosophique et pittoresque . . . [Car] le drame est la poésie complète. L'ode et l'épopée ne le contiennent qu'en germe; il les contient l'une et l'autre en développement; ils les résument et les enserrent toutes deux. C'est donc au drame que tout venait aboutir dans la poésie moderne. (*Cromwell*, pp. 143–144)

The second important document by Hugo on the subject of literary progress is *William Shakespeare*, published in 1864 on the three-hundredth anniversary of his birth. François-Victor Hugo, the poet's second oldest son, had just completed a translation of Shakespeare's plays to which his father's essay was to serve as a biographical and critical commentary. Instead the older Hugo used Shakespeare as a springboard for the discussion of his own theories on the nature of art, the character of genius, in sum his philosophy of literature. Within a few pages one discovers that the real subject of the work is not the English poet-playwright but his French counterpart, Hugo himself.

Whereas Hugo had strongly intimated that literature progressed in the *Préface de Cromwell*, he abandons this position in *William Shakespeare*, at least superficially. With the passing of years the poet had become slightly more conservative in his claims about the artistic revolution while he had become more positive and assertive in his belief about the human one. He was convinced that man marched nearer to utopia with each passing year, whereas art sometimes seemed only to exist in a void, moving neither forward nor backward.

Hugo was always aware of the technological innovations of his time and was preeminent among the poets in recognizing the importance of science in his century. In his *Shakespeare* he makes use of a comparison between art and science to establish his belief that only the latter enjoyed progress, not the former. Science is self-annihilating, thus temporal. The best, the most recent, replaces what came before, he explained. Art, on the other hand, is eternal. Newer masterpieces, regardless of their merit, do not take the place of the old. Science is relative; art, definitive. For these reasons there can be no perfectibility in art.

> Le chef-d'oeuvre d'aujourd'hui sera le chef-d'oeuvre de demain . . . Les poètes ne s'entre-escaladent pas. L'un n'est pas le marchepied de l'autre. . . . On se succède, on ne se remplace point. Le beau ne chasse pas le beau. (*Sh.*, p. 84)

The change in art, Hugo calls undulations of beauty, they are neither forward nor backward movements.[20] Man's expression of beauty may differ from age to age and from genius to genius, but this difference cannot be measured qualitatively. The masterpiece, a perfect work by definition, cannot be further perfected (*Sh.*, p. 85).

Art has a potential for growth at least, if it does not have a potential for progress. There is no limit to the number of masterpieces or creative geniuses. The embrace of art is extended in every succeeding age. Hugo had first presented this idea in the 1830's in his *Littérature et philosophie mêlées*. He elaborates upon it in 1860 in a letter to Champfleury:

> Eschyle reste Eschyle, même après Shakespeare, Homère reste Homère, même après Dante, Phidias reste Phidias, même après Michel-Ange; seulement la venue des Shakespeare, des Dante, et des Michel-Ange est indéfinie; les constellations d'hier ne barrent pas la route aux constellations de demain; et cela pour une bonne raison, c'est que l'infini ne s'encombre pas. Donc en avant! Il y a place pour tous. On ne peut dépasser les génies, mais on peut les égaler. Dieu, qui fait le cerveau humain, ne s'épuise pas, et le remplit d'étoiles. (*Corr.*, II, 330)

In the work on Shakespeare Hugo further develops his theory of the expanding number of geniuses, these "hommes-océans," the human reservoirs of the knowledge of each age.[21]

---

[20] "Ces mots, si souvent employés, même par les lettrés, *décadence, renaissance*, prouvent à quel point l'essence de l'art est ignorée" (*Sh.*, p. 95).

[21] "L'auteur pense que tout poète véritable . . . doit contenir la somme des idées de son temps" (*Préface des Rayons et des Ombres* [1840]). In that each genius was to be the sum of all knowledge in his time, Hugo might have argued that since men advanced intellectually, the latest genius would possess more knowledge than his predecessor and thus represent a kind of progress.

Three or four of these semi-divine creatures are allotted to each century, according to the author, each the equal of the other (*Sh.*, p. 36). Hugo's sense of equality was not absolute, however. Among the mighty equals he was able to distinguish a hierarchy, at least in terms of literary talent, if not in overall genius.

> Peut-être à l'extrême rigueur . . . pourrait-on désigner comme les plus haut cimes parmi ces cimes Homère, Eschyle, Job, Isaïe, Dante et Shakespeare.
>
> Il est entendu que nous ne parlons ici qu'au point de vue de l'art, et dans l'art, au point de vue de littérature.
>
> Donc, dans la région supérieure de la poésie et de la pensée, il y a Homère [et] Shakespeare.
>
> Ces suprêmes génies ne sont point une série fermée. L'auteur de Tout y ajoute un nom quand les besoins du progrès l'exigent. (*Sh.*, pp. 67 and 75)

It is most interesting to note that despite all previous defiance exhibited toward the idea of artistic progress, Hugo here reverses himself almost totally. He introduces the relative into the realm of the absolute and distinguishes among geniuses.[22] By detecting "scientific" characteristics in the domain of art, he allowed for the possibility of progress in the realm of aesthetics.

Further inequalities among the absolutes are exposed. Certain geniuses are "suns," others "planets," and others "moons." Three distinct grades of genius are thus mentioned. Another source of inequality is the varying distances at which the planets gravitate around their sun and the moons around

---

Hugo never expounds this idea, however. Although he believed in the progress of knowledge, he was more fascinated by the concept of the progress of morality.

[22] In this instance Hugo completely contradicts himself within the space of thirty pages. He had earlier insisted that the word *genius*, like *masterpiece* and *art*, was incomparable. "Comme l'eau qui, chauffée à cent degrés, n'est plus capable d'augmentation calorique et ne peut s'élever plus haut, la pensée humaine atteint dans certains hommes sa complète intensité. Eschyle, Job, Phidias, Isaïe, Saint Paul, Juvénal, Dante, Michel-Ange, Rabelais, Cervantes, Shakespeare, Rembrandt, Beethoven, quelques autres encore, marquent les cents degrés de génie." (*Sh.*, p. 36)

their planet. The realm of the absolute is again proved most relative.[23]

Preeminence is given to the genius who epitomizes an era. Reverting to the ideas of the *Préface de Cromwell*, especially to the theory of the ages of man, Hugo once again describes human history in terms of cycles which are each represented by a sun genius. Also, as in his binomial theory, Hugo here contends that all revolutions are intimately bound together and that a man of thought as well as a man of action epitomizes the spirit of each age.

> Les génies recommençants, c'est le nom qui leur convient, surgissent à toutes les crises décisives de l'humanité; ils résument les phases et complètent les révolutions. Homère marque en civilisation la fin de l'Asie et le commencement de l'Europe; Shakespeare marque la fin du moyen âge. . . . Comme Homère, Shakespeare est un homme cyclique. Ces deux génies . . . forment les deux portes de la barbarie, la porte antique et la porte gothique. . . . La troisième crise est la révolution française; c'est la troisième porte énorme de la barbarie, la porte monarchique, qui se ferme en ce moment. (*Sh.*, p. 66)

Without doubt Hugo chose himself to close that door.[24] By increasing the number of geniuses with the passing of time, and possibly by adding to the number of suns as well as planets and moons, a kind of artistic progress is accomplished. Again it must be pointed out that art never replaces itself.

---

[23] "Homère, comme le soleil, a des planètes (Virgile, Lucain, Tasse, Arioste, Milton, Camoëns, Klopstock et Voltaire) qui gravitent sur Homère, et, renvoyant à leurs propres lunes sa lumière diversement réfléchie, se meuvent à des distances inégales dans son orbite démesurée." (*Sh.*, p. 39)

[24] As Edmond Biré points out in his *Victor Hugo après 1852* (Paris: Librairie Académique Didier, 1894), pp. 173–174, the poet carefully wrought his artistic hierarchy in order to place himself at its apex. "L'Humanité a produit quatorze grands génies. Puis, ramassant toutes ses forces, elle en a enfanté un quinzième, qui incarne en lui tous les autres, qui est plus grand, à lui seul, qu'Homère, Job, Eschyle, Isaïe, Ezéchiel, Lucrèce, Juvénal, Saint Jean, Saint Paul, Tacite, Dante, Rabelais, Cervantes et Shakespeare réunis. Ce génie, Victor Hugo, est la plus haute cime de l'esprit humain. Il est le Soleil, à qui les *Quatorze* font cortège, comme autant de satellites, astres errants, dont les principaux, Homère et Shakespeare, sont pareils, à cette planète que nous habitons, qui nous paraît si grande et qui est quatorze cent mille fois plus petite que le soleil autour duquel elle circule!"

Shakespeare does not efface Homer. However, by extending the horizons of artistic endeavor, each new genius, each successive masterpiece contributes to the perfection and progress of art. As Hugo had contended much earlier, there are no frontiers to art. Progress by extension and by innovation is the subject of the famous letter of Hugo to Charles Baudelaire quoted in part earlier. While denying once again that art is perfectible, Hugo credits Baudelaire with having contributed to literature's progress.

> En avant! c'est le mot du progrès; c'est aussi le cri de l'art. Tout le verbe de la poésie est là. *Ite.*
>
> Que faites-vous quand vous écrivez ces vers saisissants: *Les Sept Vieillards* et les *Petites Vieilles* . . . vous marchez. Vous dotez le ciel de l'art d'on ne sait quel rayon macabre. Vous créez un frisson nouveau. (*Corr.*, II, 314)

Hugo goes so far as to say that for art to maintain its standards, for contemporaries to equal the greats of the past, they must surpass them. Either art progresses or it dies, and as it moves forward art must carry with it humanity.

> Personne ne dépassera Eschyle [ni] Phidias; mais on peut égaler; et pour les égaler; il faut déplacer les horizons de l'art, monter plus haut, aller plus loin, marcher. Le poète ne peut aller seul, il faut que l'homme aussi se déplace. Les pas de l'humanité sont donc les pas mêmes de l'art. — Donc gloire au Progrès.

The nineteenth century had witnessed notable progress, both human and aesthetic, Hugo felt. Through expanded education the number of the literate had increased bringing a wider and better public to the writer as well as allowing more men to create than before. As the process continued the future ranks of geniuses were to swell until one day the summits of thought now almost deserted would be covered with avid souls. (*Sh.*, pp. 80–81) Such optimism was founded on the unique nature of the nineteenth century which Hugo hoped would be perpetuated, for in his own age, man had linked progress to art.

> Stimuler, presser, gronder, réveiller, suggérer, inspirer, c'est cette

fonction, remplie de toutes parts par les écrivains, qui imprime à la littérature de ce siècle un si haut caractère de puissance et d'originalité. Rester fidèle à toutes les lois de l'art en les combinant avec la loi du progrès, tel est le problème, victorieusement résolu, par tant de nobles et fiers esprits. (*Sh., p.* 308)

Two genres particularly fulfilled this double function of art and progress, the novel and poetry. The novel, by virtue of its newness, represented an extension of art's boundaries. Its mere existence represented progress in literature, as Hugo remarked in a letter to Champfleury:

Le roman est presque une conquête de l'art moderne . . . Il est une des puissances du progrès et une des forces du génie humain en ce XIXe siècle. (*Corr.*, II, 33)

In addition, the recent perfection of the genre, i.e., its increased evidence of social concern, further attested to literature's progress. Hugo, of course, felt partially responsible for this advance, for in *Les Misérables* he had not only aided in the formation of the genre but had used his novel as an instrument for social progress.

Hugo, like the other Romantics treated here, was impressed by modernity's invention of an important genre and foresaw in its development immense possibilities for literature's advancement. Mme de Staël had urged that the unchartered territory revealed by the novel be immediately probed and that totally modern masterpieces be created to give contemporaries the advantage over the ancients. It is Balzac, however, who most forcefully expresses this idea, when in his boast of being secretary to his epoch, he points out that by having filled such an important literary lacuna, he had achieved great progress in art. Hugo's relative quiet on the subject is surprising, for his accomplisments were notable. An explanation may be that in believing the modern age to be dramatic, he expected theatre, not novels, to reign supreme in the nineteenth century. Only we, with the advantage of hindsight, can recognize this mistake, and wish that Hugo had been more conscious of the truly innovative character of *Notre Dame de Paris, Le Dernier Jour d'un condamné,* and *Les Misérables.*

Hugo was not as hesitant concerning poetry, however, for having led the forces for its restoration, he firmly believed that its flowering in the nineteenth century was a sign of progress. The lyrical rebirth, due greatly to poetry's freedom from classical restrictions, supported his optimism. Poetry's alliance with social idealism under the early Romantics further encouraged Hugo who had preached "l'art pour le progrès." His self-confidence and pride were further bolstered by his belief that in having written a poetic history of mankind, *La Légende des siècles*, a work never before undertaken, in having created a new poetic genre, the dramatic epic, he had been greatly responsible for progress in art. In the preface to *La Légende* he wrote:

> Ce livre a été écrit, l'esprit de l'auteur étant pour ainsi dire sur l'une des frontières les moins explorées et les plus vertigineuses de la pensée, au point de la jonction de l'élément épique et de l'élément dramatique . . . le confluent d'Homère et d'Eschyle; lieu sombre où le Romancero rencontre Job, où Dante se heurte à Shakespeare qui écume.

Thus we find Hugo, like Balzac, boastful of having corrected the omissions of past authors, of having filled a significant literary lacuna. Suggestive of later Romantics, Hugo also purports that progress is often the result of combining two heretofore separated traditions in art into a new and stronger discipline. Whereas Hugo merely flirts with the idea, Gautier and Balzac will attach great importance to it, for in the fusion of divergent aesthetic areas do they see the promise of unparalleled progress.

In conclusion, one may state that Hugo's thesis is that art progresses with humanity. By extending aesthetic horizons, by swelling the ranks of the cultured elite, and by improving the lot of mankind, poets more forward toward an artistic, intellectual, and moral utopia. No poet more than Hugo thought literary progress possible despite his repeated comments otherwise. An ego such as Hugo's could not accept the idea that his own contributions had not improved the quality of literature. Considering Hugo's output, one must admit that his pride was well founded, even if flaunted in the typically immodest Romantic fashion.

Chapter Six

Vigny

Alfred de Vigny, philosopher-poet of the Romantics, despite a profoundly melancholy nature, was an ardent believer in the doctrine of progress.[1] Throughout his life he maintained that mankind marched continuously toward a better tomorrow. He envisioned that pilgrimage led by the Poet, to whom he gave the double role of savior and martyr of society. Art also traveled the route of progress, he believed. Literature and the other fine arts shared in the general amelioration of civilization.

Vigny's philosophy of progress contains elements already found in the writings of the four authors previously discussed. Despite his repetition of their ideas, his expression is original and reflective of his personality. He combines Hugo's belief that the poet should guide the masses with Mme de Staël's and Chateaubriand's portrait of the artist, the gifted

---

[1] Portions of this chapter, entitled "Alfred de Vigny on Progress: An Optimistic Pessimist," were presented before the Pacific Northwest Council on Foreign Languages, Victoria, B.C., in April 1970, and subsequently appeared in its *Proceedings*, 1970, Vol. XXI, pp. 27–33.

one, as society's pariah.[2] Agreeing with Stendhal that timeliness is essential to the health of art, he warns that the theory of timeliness is a two-edged sword. It benefits the present at the expense of the past and it favors the future to the detriment of the present.

Vigny's originality also comes from his peculiar point of view. Borrowing a future expression from Baudelaire, one could well describe him as an "homo duplex," a dual personality, a synthesis of opposing forces. Basically aristocratic, Vigny disdained the common, yet he embraced all of mankind in a paternalistic pity. Pessimistic over the present state of human affairs, he remained ultimately optimistic that good would triumph over evil. Thinking the poet deserving of the highest position in society, Vigny portrayed him as an outcast, condemned to suffer and to die at the hands of those he was chosen to save.

Vigny's thoughts on progress are more concerned with the moral and social condition of man and the role of the poet in the creation of utopia than with the question of artistic improvement. Unwilling to campaign for the domination of one school of art over all others, Vigny remained relatively aloof from the propaganda battles of the Hugos and the Stendhals. Yet Vigny believed Romanticism's innovations to have produced progress in art. His call for a truer, more natural, and nationalistic poetic expression reflects the opinion of other Romantics that timely works, derived from indigenous sources, were superior to the less relevant and somewhat artificial creations of the preceding century.

The Perfecting of Imperfect Society

Vigny himself explains his conflicting attitude toward man in a note appended to the unfinished novel *Daphné*. There he confesses that he has chosen to pose as a severe father to

[2] Marc Citoleux. *Alfred de Vigny, Persistances classiques et affinités étrangères.* (Paris: Librairie Ancienne Edouard Champion, 1924), p. 470.

humanity, more ready to criticize than to flatter, hoping that his prodding will result in the improvement of the child.

En ayant l'air de désespérer des progrès d'un enfant, on les lui fait faire. Il faut lui dire: "Je suis sûr que vous êtes incapable de jamais vous élever jusqu'à cette hauteur;" il fait effort et s'y élève. Il faut piquer d'*honneur* les enfants et les sociétés. C'est ce que je veux faire par mes consultations.[3]

Vigny had previously employed this method in *Stello ou les Consultations du Docteur Noir* and in *Chatterton*. Unsatisfied with his child's progress, he decided to continue with *Daphné*. As Marc Citoleux remarks in his study of the poet, for Vigny to believe society perfectible, he had to believe it imperfect. (Citoleux, p. 213)

Vigny's pessimism does not however resemble Rousseau's, whose thesis, that civilization corrupted man, the poet planned to refute in *Daphné*.[4] Civilization is man's greatest accomplishment, he had already asserted in "La Sauvage," where he depicted an American Indian woman abandoning the barbarity of the primitive life for the material security and moral superiority of the Anglo-Saxon settler's world. In a Hugoesque manner he described the savage leaving the darkened forest and entering the brightly illumined home of the white man, viewing progress as did his colleague as man's voyage from darkness to light. Vigny's pessimism was due rather to his impatience with human failings, his irritation at man's frail idealism and his slowness to progress. Humanity advanced in spite of itself, the poet was wont to believe. Arnold Whitridge characterizes Vigny's pessimism as essentially heroic and compares it to Rousseau's more cowardly complaining.[5] To maintain the faith without encouragement

---

[3] Vigny. *Daphné, Deuxième Consultation du Dr. Noir*. Ed. déf. par Fernand Gregh. (Paris: Librairie Ch. Delagrave, 1913), p. 196.

[4] "Quoique j'aime J.-J. Rousseau, ma conscience m'a forcé de prendre le thème contraire au sien." Quoted by Citoleux, p. 212.

[5] "No doubt there is an element of courage in philosophic pessimism that was deeply sympathetic to Vigny. To certain temperaments pessimism is the postulate of heroism, the necessary stimulus of conservation and progress. It is only the cowardly thinkers like Rousseau who impute all the ills of the

required a profound idealism found only among the noblest of men.

Man's rate of progress was disappointing, for although he advanced continuously, his movement was often impeded. To the casual observer it would often seem that man did not advance at all. One should not lose faith, however, for ultimate success is guaranteed by God. Man's progress may be circular, Vigny had written in "La Sauvage," but it is ever-expanding. Vigny's choice of a circle to symbolize progress, a variation of Goethe's spiral, well suited his ambivalent attitude. The circle, like the spiral, suggests both pessimism and optimism, in contrast to Hugo's unqualified faith in human progress as revealed by his image, the airship. Unlike Hugo's unimpeded flight upward, Vigny's progress follows a circuitous and earth-bound path. The circle is a pessimistic symbol, for one traveling in its perimeter is condemned to return to his point of departure. Thus the observer of man's progress would appear justified in his belief that although much effort has been expended, man's resulting progress was non-existent. Vigny, like Goethe, qualifies his pessimism, however. Man's progress is a spiral, the German poet had remarked, but an ever-expanding one. Vigny likewise called his circle of progress "l'anneau grandissant."[6] Man may return to his starting point, but with each expansion of the circle, the distance traveled as well as the space enclosed is greater.

In "La Bouteille à la mer" the poet again illustrates his presently pessimistic but eventually optimistic view of progress. The bottle, symbolizing man's advance, cast overboard by the drowning captain carries important knowledge. Its chance of reaching shore seems minimal, for the waves toss it

---

world to accident, which prevents Nature from producing spontaneously the complete triumph of reason, justice and goodness, who persist in optimism." *Alfred de Vigny*. (London: Oxford University Press, 1933), p. 174.

[6] "La Sauvage," *Les Destinées*. Ed. critique par Verdun L. Saulnier. (Genève: Librairie Droz, 1963), p. 96. Cf. Georges Poulet, *Les Métamorphoses du cercle* (Paris: Plon, 1961), for a complete discussion of Vigny's use of the circle in his poetic imagery. Goethe's image of the ascending spiral can be found in *Die Metamorphose der Pflanzen, Sämmtliche Werke*, Bd. 2, S. 248, and in the Walpurgis Nacht scene, *Faust II*, vs. 8379–8383 and v. 12094.

about helplessly, causing it to surge forward and to recoil from its goal. Ultimately, however, the bottle completes its course, led by God to its destination. Despite the ebb and flow of progress man's advance has never ceased. Vigny explains that a just God could do no less, for

> . . . Dieu peut bien permettre à des eaux insensées
> De perdre des vaisseaux mais non pas des pensées;

Progress is founded upon justice, Vigny had also stated in "La Sauvage."

> C'est la Loi qui sur vous s'avance en vous pressant
> Mais son cercle est divin, car au centre est le Juste.

Vigny encourages all men to have the same faith as the dying captain in ultimate, if distant, success.

> Jetons l'oeuvre à la mer, la mer des multitudes:
> —Dieu le prendra du doigt pour la conduire au port.[7]

Progress is costly and painful. Knowing the price humanity must pay saddened the poet, for, as he wrote in his *Journal*, "Il est certain que la création est une oeuvre manquée ou à demie accomplie, et marchant vers sa perfection à grand'peine."[8] Progress will be a battle of good over evil, of the spiritual over the material. In the fight many will perish, but victory will eventually be won. (*Daphné*, p. 40) It must be remembered, however, that only the individual succumbs, not the race. (*Journal* 1847) Man must stoically accept his unimportance in view of the total labor.

Vigny was fond of phrasing his thoughts on progress in military terms. He envisioned mankind as an army, progress as a march or a battle. Speaking to the Academy in 1846, the poet incited its members to join the fight despite the hardships and promised ultimate success:

---

[7] "La Bouteille à la mer," *Les Destinées*, p. 189. Compare Chatterton's explanation of his semi-divine role in achieving progress where he says "[Je lis] dans les astres la route que nous montre le doigt du Seigneur."

[8] Vigny. *Journal d'un poète*. Ed. déf., recueillie et publiée par Louis Ratisbonne. (Paris: Librairie Ch. Delagrave, 1911), entry from 1835.

L'espèce humaine est en marche pour des destinées de jour en jour meilleures et plus sereines, . . . la chute de chaque homme n'arrête pas un moment la marche de la grande armée. L'un tombe, un autre se lève à sa place, et, une fois arrivé sur l'un de ses points élevés d'où l'on parle avec plus d'autorité, notre devoir est de penser, dès ce jour même, à ceux qui viendront après nous; pareils à ces glorieux soldats, qui d'une main plantent leur drapeau sur la brèche, et tendent l'autre main à celui qui, après eux, marche au premier rang.[9]

With a modesty that was rare among the Romantics Vigny de-emphasized the importance of any individual's contribution to human progress. "Quels que soient les monuments qu'ils laissent, les hommes éminents d'une génération ne sont rien que les éclaireurs de la génération qui les suit." (*Ibid.*)

The Role of the Poet in Man's Advance

While believing that humanity moved steadily toward perfection, Vigny distinguished among the rates of progress of its members. An entry in the *Journal* for 1829 warns with military abruptness those who resist the movement of the times. "Malheur aux traînards! Rester en arrière, c'est mourir." Those participating in progress comprise three groups. Using the image of the clock, a variation of the circle, Vigny equates progress with the passage of time indicated by its three hands, the three strata of society. Slowest of advance are the masses, who without commotion, as imperceptibly as the hour-hand, inch forward. With greater speed the enlightened element of society, the thinker, progresses, in a manner comparable to the advance of the minute-hand. The poet outdistances all others, for his special gifts allow him to race ahead of his times like a speeding second-hand.[10] The poet moves ahead of humanity because he is superior, a rare being, semi-

---

[9] Vigny. "Discours de réception à l'Académie française," le 29 janvier, 1846 (*Journal*, p. 320).
[10] Vigny. "Lettre à Lord *** sur la soirée du 24 oct. 1829 et sur un système dramatique, servant comme préface d'*Othello, Le More de Venise,*" *Théâtre.* Ed. déf. par Fernand Baldensperger. (Paris: Louis Conard, libraire-éditeur, 1926), I, 346.

divine.[11] Like the noble lion, he marches alone, shunning cowardly associations. (*Journal* 1847) His nobility, his divinity has its price, nevertheless. The great are often lonely, sometimes abandoned, sometimes persecuted. The dying Christ received no answer from his cross; Moses shared no communion with his people. The poet, Stello or Chatterton, experienced sharp rejection from society because he differed from the common man.

Vigny thought of the poet as a prophet, a leglislator, and a philosopher. Like Moses or Christ, the poet shared a messianic mission. His task was to lead man to God.[12] With the disappearance of the old nobility of birth, a new nobility of intelligence was to rule the world. Force was to be replaced by thought, Vigny believed. The poet, the aristocrat of the spirit, was to bring about progress.[13]

The serious and tragic irony of the poet's capability and desire to lead mankind in progress and society's rejection and persecution of him became a philosophical leitmotif in Vigny's works. The poet, the rarest of God's creations, went unappreciated by materially oriented and utilitarian man. To *Chatterton*, perhaps Vigny's most poignant defense of the poet and sharpest condemnation of society, he affixed a preface which reiterated his astonishment and sorrow over the poet's dilemma in modern times.

> On croirait, à vous [the masses] voir en faire si bon marché, que c'est une chose commune qu'un Poète. —Songez donc que lorsqu'une nation en a deux en dix siècles, elle se trouve heureuse et s'en orgueillit. Il y a tel peuple qui n'en a pas un, et n'en aura jamais. (*Chatterton*, p. 812)

Modern society alone could not be blamed for the misunderstanding and scorn it showed the poet. In *Stello* Vigny had

---

[11] "Un artiste ne doit et ne peut aimer que lui-même. Il est la manifestation d'une supériorité; il est une faculté." (*Journal*, 1830)

[12] Vigny. *Chatterton. Oeuvres complètes.* Texte présenté et commenté par F. Baldensperger. Ed. de la Pléiade. (Paris: Gallimard, 1948). Cf. note 7.

[13] Fernand Baldensperger. *Alfred de Vigny.* (Paris: La Nouvelle Revue Critique, 1929), pp. 150–151.

noted that since the time of the Greeks, the poet has been an outcast, rejected because he was thought useless even by the philosophers. Plato, for instance, bans Homer from his republic because he felt he served no purpose. Coming to that poet's and all poets' aid, Vigny would have had Homer answer that the poet is society's most useful member, for he performs a task few could fulfill. He teaches love and pity, he lights the way to progress for a lost and wandering humanity. In addition, the poet's gifts are the rarest of all mankind's, for imagination appears less frequently than judgment among men. Philosophy abounds while poetry is strictly rationed. Imagination is also a greater power than reason, Vigny believed, for it embraces both judgment and memory. Imagination is the connecting link between man and God, by which the poet expresses through art the divine will. Art is rarer than science, Vigny adds, for unlike the latter it cannot be learned, it cannot be transmitted intact from father to son. The creator of art then is an elected one, chosen for a holy duty.

Plato had correctly argued that the poet builds no institutions, gives no laws nor preaches any doctrines which specifically aid one nation or one age. Instead the poet serves all humanity by his creations.

> Je ne suis d'aucune ville, mais de l'univers [the poet replies], vos doctrines, vos lois, vos institutions, ont été bonnes pour un âge et un peuple, et sont mortes avec eux, tandis que les oeuvres de l'Art céleste restent debout pour toujours à mesure qu'elles s'élèvent, et toutes portent les malheureux mortels à la loi impérissable de l'*Amour* et de la *Pitié*.[14]

In speaking for the poet Vigny was, of course, expressing his own beliefs. His desire was to serve humanity. He broadened the demands of *noblesse oblige* to embrace the entire human race. Vigny attested to his humanitarianism ceaselessly in his works. Saddened by man's fate at the hands of a cruel nature or society, he dedicated himself to the defense of the persecuted. In his *Journal* of 1835 he remarked:

---

[14] Vigny. *Les Consultations du Docteur Noir, Première Consultation: Stello.* Ed. déf. (Paris: Ch. Delagrave, s.d.), pp. 274–275.

J'aime l'humanité. J'ai pitié d'elle. La nature est pour moi une décoration dont la durée est insolente, et sur laquelle est jetée cette passagère et sublime marionnette appellée l'homme.

In 1844 he maintained that the purpose of his "Poèmes philosophiques," especially "La Maison du berger," was to express his paternalistic sentiments—love, pity, and benevolence—toward man.

"J'aime la majesté des souffrances humaines." Ce vers est le sens de tous mes poèmes philosophiques. L'esprit de l'humanité, l'amour entier de l'humanité et de l'amélioration de ses destinées.

Stello had justified his calling to poetry because of these same sentiments.[15]

Despite the nobility of the poet's desires or the usefulness of his talent, he is always rejected. Vigny compares the poet to a swan bitten by a snake. Although the bird, the poet-prophet, carries the reptile, humanity, towards the ideal, "l'azur du ciel . . . la lumière," his burdened flight representing man's difficult progress, the snake struggles to kill his benefactor. (*Journal* 1847) With noble self-effacement Vigny accepts the eternal martyrdom of the poet in the belief that even this great sacrifice is worthwhile if man is benefited. Through Stello he explains that the individual counts less than humanity. Having described a pilgrim crushed by a crowd of blind men he had been leading, Docteur Noir remarks:

Voyez ces aveugles, . . . ils ont bien l'instinct vague de leur chemin, mais ils écrasent sans pitié l'homme qui remonte leur courant.

Eh! qu'importe, dit Stello, si le bien est accompli, que l'on soit ou non foulé aux pieds. (*Daphné*, p. 10)

Again in the *Journal* Vigny states that some must be lost to save the others:

---

[15] "Je crois fermement à une vocation ineffable qui m'est donnée, et j'y crois à cause de la pitié sans bornes que m'inspirent les hommes, mes compagnons de misère, et à cause du désir que je me sens de leur tendre la main et de les élever sans cesse par des paroles de commisérations et d'amour" (*Stello*, p. 31).

La pensée est semblable au compas qui perce le point sur lequel il tourne, quoique sa seconde branche décrive un cercle éloigné.

L'homme succombe sous son travail et est percé par le compas; mais la ligne que l'autre branche a décrite reste gravée à jamais pour le bien des races futures. (*Journal* 1847)

The compass too describes the "divine circle whose center is Justice." From God radiates progress in all directions.

The Progress of Art

Vigny's pessimism is practically nonexistent in his attitude toward the arts. He, like the other Romantics, was excited by the abundance of creativity his century had produced. Unlike his colleagues, however, he did not feel that Romanticism was the culmination of art's progress, but merely another rung on the infinite ladder of intellectual and aesthetic advance, "l'échelle continue des idées." ("Discours," p. 319)

The nineteenth century had proved to be a second Renaissance, he remarked in the preface to *Othello*. Whereas the eighteenth century was noted for its philosophical accomplishments, the nineteenth would be remembered for its art. (*Journal* 1828) The rebirth began during the Bourbon Restoration when literature as well as the other fine arts experienced a resurgence of energy and productivity, rare in the history of man. Poetry, the novel, and the theatre, under Romanticism, showed progress by venturing into realms previously untried in France. Architecture and sculpture, the academic disciplines, also participated in the artistic flowering and produced new forms. Painting was bathed in a new light. Music expressed new harmonies, larger and more powerful than the old. ("Discours," p. 318)

Vigny shared the Romantic belief that the road to progress lay through innovation and that nothing proved more fatal to the arts than enforced imitation of a "perfect" earlier style. Speaking to the Academy in 1846 he hailed the Romantics as this "autre génération littéraire novatrice" which unlike the former, the classicists, sought its inspiration from native sources instead of continuing the tradition of imitating the far

129

distant and far past Greeks and Romans. Vigny shared Mme de Staël's contention that literary progress was more readily attainable in "romantic" rather than "classical" works, innovation being easier with better known but less worked over indigenous sources. Vigny was particularly proud of his generation's poetry which reflected the nation's character, its religion, and history. Because of its "romantic" qualities he believed it to be more natural and true, thus better, than the artificial works of the neo-classicists. The acceptance of French sources for art and literature, sought by artists since the Middle Ages, was an important triumph of the Romantic era. Because works "de plus en plus rapprochés de la nature, de la vérité dans l'art et du génie réel de notre nation" were now possible to be produced, literature had made considerable progress. ("Discours," p. 316) It must be remembered, however, that Vigny did not equate greater truth in art with greater realism. By truth he meant naturalness as opposed to foreignness or artificiality. In his "Réflexions sur la Vérité dans l'Art" of 1827, Vigny, like Chateaubriand, had remarked that reality must be modified by art. "L'*Art* ne doit jamais être considéré que dans ses rapports avec sa *Beauté idéale*. Il faut le dire, ce qu'il y a de Vrai n'est que secondaire."[16]

Vigny, during his days of association with the *Cénacle*, had been particularly disdainful of classicism because of its condemnation of innovation. The attitude of these "ancients" was harmful to creativity, he believed, for it venerated routine. Not realizing that art thrived on movement and change, these curators of the past sought to fix forever the acceptable expression of beauty. Vigny's scorn was harsh toward those whom he called the lazy and infirm minds, "ces malades . . . qui aiment à entendre aujourd'hui ce qu'ils entendaient hier; mêmes expressions, mêmes sons," instead of the new, and perhaps better, ideas, expressions, and sounds being produced by the Romantics. (*Othello*, p. 332)

Had the classicists been more successful in their attempt

---

[16] Vigny. "Réflexions sur la Vérité dans l'art," préface de *Cinq Mars*. Ed. déf. (Paris: Librairie Delagrave, 1918), p. 18.

to preserve the standards of the past, which by Vigny's reasoning would have been impossible, for the progress of art cannot be halted, they then would have merited respect. Instead even the most reactionary had found themselves induced to innovate despite their resistance. Those who believed that "tout ce qui est nouveau . . . [est] ridicule, tout ce qui est inusité, barbare" had been forced to incorporate some of the new in their antique art. (*Ibid.*) As a result, their traditional works were ridiculously anachronistic, neither antique nor modern, and consequently inferior. Vigny particularly ridiculed the neo-classical playwrights who attempted to portray modern subjects in antique form resulting in "des Chinois, des Turcs, et des sauvages de l'Amérique [qui] parlent à chaque vers de l'hyménée et de ses flambeaux." (*Othello*, p. 338) The Romantics risked making the same mistake because of their idolatry of Shakespeare. It must be remembered, he noted, that Shakespeare reached his summit according to his times and that Romantic literature must strive for perfection while expressing its own era. (*Othello*, p. 344)[17]

---

[17] Yet the Romantic debate on literary progress, particularly theatrical, relies greatly on Shakespeare's dramatic system. Long before either Stendhal, Hugo, or Vigny had produced their manifestoes, François Guizot had argued the need for the French to understand the English playwright if there was to be any significant progress in the French theatre of the nineteenth century. In 1820 Guizot had revised Le Tourneur's translation of Shakespeare's work and in a preface entitled "Sur la vie et les oeuvres de Shakespeare" (reprinted in 1822, 1823, and 1852) contrasted Voltaire with the Bard, calling the latter's plays "indigenous and modern," the former's "borrowed and ancient."

The importance of timely works for modern viewers became, of course, a basic tenet of Stendhal's *Racine et Shakespeare* (1823 and 1825). In *Le Globe* as well a campaign was also waged during the 1820's against neo-classical drama based on the theory that through the incorporation of new ideas into the theatre, progress would surely result, as had already occurred in the realms of philosophy and science. In 1827 Hugo's *Préface de Cromwell* equated the Romantic theatre with realism and modernity, Shakespeare being the prime example of literary progress. Thus, as Robert T. Denommé explains in "French Theatre Reform and Vigny's Translation of *Othello* in 1829" (in *Symbolism and Modern Literature. Studies in Honor of Wallace Fowlie*. Marcel Tetel, ed. Durham, N.C.: Duke University Press, 1978), pp. 81–102, "by the time [Vigny] had joined the Romanticists' campaign for a new theatre, he had embraced the Doctrinaire idea of literary progress," (p. 92) and was thus an heir to Guizot. Vigny had even thought of founding a journal, *La Réforme de la Littérature et des*

Combining the theories of Mme de Staël and Stendhal, Vigny called for intellectual timeliness in art. Inspiration and human nature lay outside the scope of man's advance, he believed, and thus remained changeless in the art of all periods. Man's ideas did evolve, however, and it was the writer's duty to express man's new and greater wisdom in his creative works. Art then progressed as a benefit of man's intellectual advance. "Ce qui est philosophie divine ou humaine doit correspondre au besoin de la société où vit le poète; or, les sociétés avancent." (*Othello*, p. 345)

Because Vigny believed intellectual and therefore artistic progress to be unending, he realized the danger that today's moderns were destined to become tomorrow's ancients. As intellectual progress is "l'échelle continue des idées," literature's successive schools and movements are but the artistic expression of this advance. Each represents a progress over the work of its predecessor, but those yet to come will doubtless manifest an improvement over what exists today. Art is destined to ascend the ladder of ideas. Resistance to its progress would be futile. ("Discours," p. 342)

In addition to the image of the ladder which expressed man's continued intellectual and artistic ascent towards perfection, Vigny was fond of employing the image of the harvest to emphasize his belief that no artistic expression can be definitive. Each era's art sprang from seed, flourished for a moment, then was cut down. It fertilized the ground for the next crop of masterpieces which, deriving their strength from past accomplishments, would be stronger and richer than before. As the individual should be willing to be sacrificed for the ultimate good of humanity, individual schools of art must accept their temporary position in the long route of aesthetic advance. By giving way to the new, each succeeding artistic expression

---

Arts, along with Victor Hugo and Emile Deschamps, to champion the ideas of progress and reform (p. 95). It was in fact the manifestoes of Guizot, Stendhal, and Hugo added together which "coalesced the Romanticists in their drive to modernize the theatre with Shakespeare as a symbol," according to Denommé, and led to Vigny's translation/adaptation, *Othello ou Le More de Venise* of 1829. (p. 81)

contributes to an ever-augmenting heritage which aids future artists to come closer than before to perfection. With unblemished faith in the future and rare modesty for the present Vigny predicted in 1846:

Notre époque est une époque de renaissance et de réhabilitation tout à la fois; je ne dirai jamais cependant que la loi nouvelle doive être impérissable, elle passera avec nous, peut-être avant nous, et sera remplacée par une meilleure: il doit suffir à un nom d'homme de marquer un degré de progrès. Plus la civilisation avance, et plus l'on doit se résigner à voir les idées que l'on sème, comme un grain fécond, s'élèver, mûrir, jaunir et tomber promptement, pour faire place à une moisson nouvelle, plus forte et plus abondante, sous les yeux du premier cultivateur. (*Ibid.*)

While Vigny's statements on artistic progress are few, they are revealing. Equally convinced that art, like man, progressed, he displayed none of the irritation or pessimism he exhibited towards the human condition in his view on the present and future of the arts. Artistic progress was to be the result of the continuous intellectual advance of mankind, he believed, thus inevitable and eternal. Romanticism, the most recent, but not the last, example of this progress, had surpassed its predecessors by its innovative use of national sources to create a truer, more natural art. Its replacement, profiting from Romanticism's progress, would in turn surpass it in creating works of greater perfection, the result of further innovations. Vigny's attitude is typically Romantic. Recognizing that man's increased knowledge when incorporated into his art gave a truer view of life, he, like Stendhal, announced the arrival of Realism. Yet, like Chateaubriand, he wished to see reality transformed by art.

With Vigny one also discovers a change in tone in the nineteenth-century Quarrel. The issues are less heatedly debated and are less personal. The blind fanaticism of the earliest Romantics turns to more temperate consideration of the issues by later authors who, benefiting from the triumphs of their predecessors, were less obliged to destroy the old before building the new. Vigny, unlike Hugo or Stendhal, did not feel the necessity of leading the battle against the past. Instead his thoughts were concerned with the preparation of the future.

Chapter Seven

Lamartine

Lamartine, somewhat later than Hugo and Vigny, became a poet of progress. He, after an initial hesitation, came to share their basic belief that mankind moved indefinitely toward perfection, led by the poet whose talents especially enabled him to guide humanity from darkness to light. Lamartine also believed that as man progressed so did poetry. He, too, voiced the Romantic opinion that nineteenth-century France enjoyed a second cultural Renaissance, begun by poetry but shared by the other literary arts as well.

Lamartine continues the progressive tradition, human and literary, often rephrasing arguments advanced before. Like Mme de Staël, he acknowledged intellectual progress and a decline in the importance of imagination, a typical eighteenth-century belief. Like Chateaubriand, he credited Christianity with having set modern man apart from his pagan ancestors and with having brought a new source of beauty to the arts. In agreement with Stendhal, Lamartine espoused the doctrine of historical relativism, preferring timely works to outmoded masterpieces.

Lamartine is also the last member of a group. He forms with Hugo and Vigny a trio of socialistic and philosophic artists who keenly felt the poet's responsibility in achieving human progress. Beginning with Alfred de Musset, attitudes will change and the old clichés of poetry's double role as beauty and propaganda will be abandoned by those who think art separate from politics and sociology. Already with Vigny a more tolerant tone had been evident in the literary quarrel of neo-classicists and Romantics. Like Vigny, Lamartine remains relatively uninvolved in the bickerings of nineteenth-century ancients and moderns. With the same large view of literary history he acknowledges the fact that Romanticism was but one of the many phases through which literature would pass. While it evidenced improvements over neo-classicism, future schools would in turn produce new expressions of beauty, in some ways surpassing those of the present moment. Lamartine should also be singled out for his personal approach to the philosophy of progress. Less historical than Hugo and less philosophical than Vigny, Lamartine, more like Chateaubriand, interpreted progress in religious terms, believing man's ultimate destiny to be his reunion with God.

On Human Progress

Lamartine had not always believed in human perfectibility. As a young man of noble birth he had witnessed the destruction of an old and favored order and saw it replaced by a new regime of force. Having personally suffered from the French Revolution he looked askance at other nations' political upheavals. In 1820 revolution struck Italy. In dismay the young man wrote to a more optimistic friend, the Count of Saint-Aulaire, that he believed man eternally condemned to repeat the mistakes of the past.

> Vous espérez donc qu'un monde nouveau va sortir de ce mouvement déréglé comme des nuages agités du premier chaos. . . . Vous croyez que les hommes et l'humanité s'améliorent. . . . Je crois, moi, que chaque génération apporte dans ce monde les mêmes passions et la même inexpérience.[1]

---

[1] Quoted by Pierre Moreau. *Le Romantisme*. (Paris: J. de Gigord, éditeur, 1932), p. 174.

During the next decade Lamartine became increasingly optimistic. Perhaps his change in attitude can be traced to his literary and social success, to his self-satisfaction. In any case he embraced the doctrine of human progress with fervor, to relinquish it only at the very end of his life when personal misfortunes again plagued him. Then with the cynicism of a dying man whose dreams of utopia had not been fulfilled, Lamartine denounced progress as an illusion.[2] Within these negative boundaries, however, one finds repeated affirmation of his faith in man and a better future.

Lamartine interpreted man's progress as the fulfillment of a religious destiny. Progress, like the mystery of creation and life, could only be partially understood by man.[3] But like the mysteries of birth and death, progress was a universal phenomenon, in which individuals collectively and eternally participated.[4] Through successive phases man attained a fuller knowledge of truth and virtue, a greater understanding of the divine. Ultimately God himself would be revealed and the creator and created united.[5]

In the shorter view Lamartine spoke of progress in predominantly human terms, placing the responsibility of hu-

---

[2] One finds the darkest note of pessimism in Lamartine's *Cours familier de littérature* (1862), a rambling work written for profit. There the self-pitying poet complained "quand on s'est lancé hardiment avec une sainte pensée dans le coeur, au milieu d'un peuple en révolution, pour l'apaiser et le diriger vers des destinées plus hautes . . . quand on a participé à cette illusion des grandes âmes, qu'on l'a vue s'éteindre, on a trop vécu" (Moreau, p. 491).

[3] "L'homme n'a rien de plus inconnu autour de lui que l'homme même. Les phénomènes de sa pensée, les lois de sa civilisation, les phases de ses progrès ou de ses décadences, sont les mystères qu'il a le moins pénétrés." "Des Destinées de la poésie," seconde préface des *Premières Méditations poétiques*. (Paris: Hachette et Cie, éditeur, 1895), p. xxv.

[4] In the "avertissement de Jocelyn" of 1836 Lamartine explained that all religions and philosophies had taught men "qu'il n'était qu'une partie imperceptible d'une immense et solidaire unité, que l'oeuvre de son perfectionnement était une oeuvre collective et éternelle." *Jocelyn, épisode, Journal trouvé chez un curé de village*. (Paris: Hachette et Cie, éditeur, 1895), p. iv. Cf. A. J. George. *Lamartine and Romantic Unanimism*. (New York: Columbia University Press, 1940).

[5] Avertissement de la *Chute d'un ange, épisode*. (Paris: Hachette et Cie, éditeur, 1887), pp. viii–ix.

manity's improvement on man. Governments in particular were called upon to implement the human advance, for they were to serve as an instrument of ideas, a propagator of reason. ("Chute," p. xiv) In this respect Lamartine aligns himself with the eighteenth-century *philosophes* and their nineteenth-century disciple Mme de Staël, for he recognized the intimate rapport between governments and the moral, social, intellectual, and artistic climates of a nation. Sharing Mme de Staël's dislike of the Napoleonic tyranny, he welcomed the Bourbon Restoration and believed it responsible for the subsequent rebirth of the arts.

All of history marks the slow progress of thought, Lamartine told the Academy in 1829, but more recent history has shown a quickening of the pace. Like Vigny, Lamartine thought man's progress particularly noticeable in the first three decades of the nineteenth century. Despite the great strides forward man could not yet afford to indulge in contented complacency, however. More remained to be done, especially in the area of social improvements. Man's thirst for moral and social perfection should never be quenched. The search for truth was unending. With faith that the quest would continue Lamartine prophesied that the nineteenth century would be an outstanding chapter in the history of man's advance. "Tout annonce . . . un grand siècle, une des époques caractéristiques de l'humanité."[6]

The Poet and Progress

Continuing a tradition already established by Hugo and Vigny, Lamartine looked upon himself as a prophet and leader of men, in his own words "un conseiller du peuple." The poet, a paradoxical creature more human than the average man and at the same time somewhat divine,[7] was to serve as an inter-

---

[6] "Discours de réception à l'Académie française," *Recueillements poétiques*. (Paris: Hachette et Cie, éditeur, 1888), p. 367.

[7] In the "Destinées de la poésie" he described poets as "hommes plus hommes que le vulgaire, *mens divinior.*" "Destinées," p. xxxvi.

mediary between man and God. In "Des Destinées de la poésie" of 1834 Lamartine explained the poet's responsibility. He was to reveal to man the divine side of human nature.

> [Le peuple] est plus poète par l'âme que nous, car il est plus près de la nature: mais il a besoin d'un interprète entre cette nature et lui; c'est à nous de lui en servir, et de lui expliquer, par ses sentiments rendus dans sa langue ce que Dieu a mis de bonté, de noblesse, de générosité, de patriotisme et de piété enthousiaste dans son coeur. ("Dest.," p. lxi)

During the early years of his career Lamartine had been unaware of his humanitarian responsibilities as a poet and had concerned himself in his verses with highly personal themes and emotions. The "sincere Lamartine" as he came to be known epitomized the Romantic ego which glorified in its own contemplation. Later upon accepting the quasi-messianic mission of poetry in the struggle for progress, Lamartine reproached himself for having been egotistical and decided to subordinate self to the entirety of humanity.

The old pose of Romantic dreamer had to be abandoned for that of man of action. Isolation from the world was a luxury the poet could not afford. As Hugo before him and Balzac afterward, Lamartine envisioned himself as a literary Napoleon, a combination of thought and action, of theory and practice. (Moreau, p. 257) In the "avertissement de Jocelyn" Lamartine emphatically proclaimed that during such times of progress the poet must cooperate with his brothers in "le grand combat de la patrie ou de la civilisation . . . dans le terrible enfantement des idées ou des choses." ("Jocelyn," p. vi) It is especially in the "Recueillements poétiques" of 1837, however, that Lamartine publicly accepts the social mission of poetry and chastises himself for previous egotism. In a poem addressed to Félix Guillemardet, Lamartine relates his change of heart.

> Puis mon coeur, insensible à ses propres misères,
> S'est élargi plus tard aux douleurs de mes frères;
> Tous leurs maux ont coulé dans le lac de mes pleurs;
> Et, comme un grand linceul que la pitié déroule,
> L'âme d'un seul, ouverte aux plaintes de la foule,
>   A gémi toutes les douleurs.

138

The reference to the "lake of tears" is striking, for no poem had been more representative of the "egotistical" Lamartine than "Le Lac." The old sorrow of a lost loved one is now forgotten for the larger, more important sorrows of suffering humanity. One finds a point of comparison with the attitude of Vigny, for like that poet, Lamartine was ready to pity humanity and was equally concerned with its ultimate destiny.

Further reference is made in the collection to Lamartine's new sense of unity with mankind and of his duty to work with others in improving the human lot. Most significant in the collection is the poem "Utopie," Lamartine's poetic expression of Vigny's sentiments found in the drama *Chatterton*. Like his colleague, Lamartine compares the poet to the pilot of a ship, as Chatterton had said, the one "qui lit dans les astres la route que montre le doigt du Seigneur." Lamartine describes the poet as the astronomer, who perched upon the mast, scans the horizon, and then plots the course of humanity. Once this task is accomplished, the poet-astronomer descends from his elevated position to mingle among the crowd below, working shoulder to shoulder to reach the common goal.

L'astronome chargé d'orienter la voile
Monte au sommet des mâts où palpite la toile,
Et, promenant ses yeux de la vague à l'étoile,
    Se dit: "nous serons là demain!"

Il descend sur le pont où l'équipage roule,
Met la main au cordage et lutte avec la houle.
Il faut se séparer, pour penser, de la foule,
    Et s'y confondre pour agir!

The Progress of Poetry

Again one must think of Hugo when considering Lamartine's conception of the history of poetry. Like his predecessor, the author of "Des Destinées" believed the life of humanity to be divided into periods of infancy, childhood, youth, virility, and old age, each having a poetic expression appropriate to its temperament. Although Lamartine borrowed heavily from the ideas of the *Préface de Cromwell*, he varied from them considerably as will be apparent in the following discussion. Lamartine's point in delineating the ages of poetry was to insist that no one historical period monopolized the creation of verse. Instead each age devises a new expression appropriate to the times.[8] This argument was most clearly advanced by Stendhal and will have support as late as Baudelaire, whose concept of "le beau moderne" is but another variation of the common theme. The idea of progress does not immediately enter into the argument, for relativism allows no superiority, only equality. Nevertheless, the Romantics were not impartial relativists and did believe their own epoch to have produced not only different but superior poetry. Some, like Vigny and Lamartine, awaited even better artistic creations in the future.

In reviewing Lamartine's historical sketch, one finds it more detailed and less generalized than Hugo's. Nor does he abandon verse for drama. The author denotes seven stages of poetry up to the present time. During the cradle years of civilization, verse was simple and naïve, befitting the character of infant humanity. During childhood, it was narrative and miraculous; for youth, loving and pastoral; for virility, warlike and epic. From these vaguer groups of time Lamartine turns to more specific historical eras and describes a mystical, lyric, and prophetic poetry which flourished during the time of the theocracies of Egypt and the Holy Land. He groups together the civilizations of Rome, Renaissance Florence, and the Age of Louis XIV because of their sophistication and decadence and describes their poetry as grave, philosophic, and corrupting.

---

[8] Preferring timely works as did Stendhal, Lamartine rejected even the notion of translating earlier masterpieces into the modern idiom, for the spirit of a work cannot be detached from its historical milieu. In his speech to the Academy Lamartine attacked the perpetrators of the classics for giving living men dead literature. He explained:

> D'ailleurs, dans la poésie d'un autre âge, il y a toujours une partie déjà morte, un sens des temps, des moeurs, des lieux, des cultes, des opinions, que nous n'entendrons plus, et qui ne peut plus nous toucher! Otez à une poésie sa date, sa foi, son originalité, enfin, qu'en restera-t-il? ce qui reste d'une statue des dieux dont la divinité s'est retirée, un morceau de marbre plus ou moins bien taillé! ("Discours," pp. 359–360)

Between this last epoch and the early nineteenth century was a transitional age, a time of convulsion and ruin, the era of revolution. Poetry appropriately reflected the tenor of the times and was "wild and screaming." The present Lamartine characterizes as an age of rebirth and reconstruction whose verse is melancholic, uncertain, and timid.

Projecting his view into the future, for Lamartine unlike Hugo did not believe his own age nor the present literary movement to be the highest point attainable on the curve of progress, the author predicts that in mankind's old age, poetry will become sad, complaining, and discouraged, a mixture of presentiment and nostalgic dreaming. Most remarkable is Lamartine's prophesy that poetry will have no end but will continue after the demise of the present world, when mankind is resurrected or transformed into a new being. Neither mankind nor poetry is mortal, he believed. ("Dest.," pp. xxxv-xxxvi)

To document the idea that poetry had not only evolved but also progressed, one has only to turn to Lamartine's pronouncements concerning the nineteenth century. Recognizing his political bias one understands his denunciation of the early years, the Napoleonic sterility, and his approbation of the era of the Bourbon Restoration. In literature the earlier epoch was dominated by classical imitation, the latter by Romantic innovation. A new soul entered poetry with the reestablishment of liberty in politics, he believed. Under the new regime talent flourished and a second renaissance occurred. ("Dest.," p. xxxiii) The present intellectual and artistic age was without parallel in the opinion of Lamartine. It was "le plus hardi mouvement intellectuel qu'aucun de nos siècles eût encore vu." ("Dest.," p. xxxiv)

Poetry's new vigor was due not only to the favorable political change, Lamartine wrote, but also to the Catholic Revival begun by Chateaubriand. Once Christianity had won a place in literature, the old hypocrisy caused by Christian writers producing pagan verses was ended. With one philosophy in religion and art, the nineteenth century could create with unhampered sincerity and freedom. ("Discours," p. 360)

As a result nineteenth-century France had its Christian Homer, its modern equivalents of Plato, Pliny, and Quintillian. There was no reason to feel inferior to any previous age. ("Discours," p. 366) Poetically the present was unparalleled.

Je me demande s'il y eut jamais dans les époques littéraires un moment aussi remarquable en talents éclos et en promesses qui éclorent à leur tour? . . . Non, il n'eut jamais autant de poètes et plus de poésie qu'il y en a en France et en Europe, au moment où j'écris ces lignes, au moment où quelques esprits superficiels ou préoccupés s'écrient que la poésie a accompli ses destinées et prophétisent la décadence de l'humanité. ("Dest.," p. lx)

Lamartine's optimism extended far into the future. The old age of mankind which he had prophesied was yet quite far off. In the meanwhile poetry had new and great destinies to fulfill. ("Dest.," p. lviii) Adapting to the future needs of man, verse was to become "la raison chantée," that is to say, philosophic, religious, social, and political. It was to be the conscience of humanity, the popularizer of truth, love, and reason. Poetry was to become the guardian angel of mankind. ("Dest.," p. lxii) In the progress of man, poetry and the poet were to play important roles.

Dans cette oeuvre, la poésie a sa place quoique Platon voulût l'en bannir. C'est elle qui plane sur la société et qui la juge, et qui, montrant à l'homme la vulgarité de son oeuvre, l'appelle sans cesse en avant, en lui montrant du doigt des utopies, des républiques imaginaires, des cités de Dieu, et lui souffle au coeur le courage de les atteindre. ("Dest.," p. lx)

Taking his own advice to heart Lamartine attempted to produce poetry of "sung reason." He began an epic account of humanity's progress which he entitled "Visions." Of the projected work the author completed but two episodes, "Jocelyn" in 1836 and "La Chute d'un ange" in 1838. Lamartine felt he had truly innovated in creating this work, for two decades prior to Hugo's "La Légende des siècles" he was attempting the first epic which was not narrowly national but universal, whose subject was the destiny of all mankind. ("Jocelyn," p. v)

In conclusion, one may state that no other poet of the Romantic era rivaled Lamartine in his idealistic optimism and faith in mankind and poetry. A partisan of progress like Hugo and Vigny, Lamartine surpassed them both in the purity of his vision and the innocence of his faith. Without Hugo's bombast or Vigny's underlying cynicism, Lamartine looked contentedly at the present and expectantly to the future. Perhaps his religious beliefs are what compel us to distinguish him from his predecessors. In any case, he alone truly believed in the ultimate union of man and God and the transfiguration of human poetry into divine hymn.

Chapter Eight

Musset

Although Alfred de Musset completes the quartet of Romantic poets under investigation here, he cannot be grouped with the other three as a proponent of progress, human or aesthetic. Fiercely independent in attitude, Musset discounted the theory of human perfectibility, rejected the idea of the poet's duty to any other but himself and renounced the concepts of artistic progress and decadence as meaningless clichés.

Many factors contributed to the poet's negative attitude. His basic discontent with himself and his century caused him to appear misanthropic and led him to yearn for a distant golden age and a more satisfying experience. His irritation with and jealousy of Hugo entrenched his separateness from the *Cénacle*. He refused to side with one school against another and argued he was capable of appreciating the contributions of all great artists, be they ancients or moderns. Instead of continuing the Quarrel in the nineteenth century as many of his fellow writers had done, Musset, with a tolerance not unlike that so esteemed in the eighteenth century, preferred to see peace between the warring traditionalists and innovators, with each contributing what he would to the creation of art.

144

Nostalgia and Negativism

Musset's very Romanticism sets him apart from his contemporaries. Individualism was his prized characteristic, discontent his most frequent attitude. Adoring the *moi* which gave him uniqueness, Musset lamented his isolation and suffering, his intense *mal du siècle*. Noble in an unaristocratic age, Alfred de Musset dreamed of a princely existence which reality had denied him. Of moderate means, he wished for a great fortune. Born for another life, he was condemned to lead one far from his choosing. "La nature m'avait fait riche et le hasard m'avait fait pauvre," he once characterized his predicament.[1] Opportunity had passed him by. Life in nineteenth-century France was humdrum. His only escape was in dandyism and dreams.

Like Stendhal, a fellow malcontent, Musset looked longingly to past heroic ages. Most recently Napoleon had offered opportunity for young men to find glory. Previously Renaissance Italy and ancient Greece were propitious historical eras, when action was venerated and art admired. In contrast France of the Restoration appeared weak and mediocre. Indeed it seemed to Musset he was born too late in a century too old. Musset's scorn for his epoch is scathing. "En vérité, ce siècle est un mauvais moment," he wrote in a "Sonnet au lecteur." It is a time when "tout s'en va, les plaisirs et les moeurs d'un autre âge; les rois, les dieux [sont] vaincus."[2] Instead of proclaiming his times the greatest in all history as more optimistic contemporaries had done, Musset complained that "notre siècle est l'antipode des grands siècles."[3]

Of all past heroic ages, it was ancient Greece to which the poet looked most longingly, that incomparable land, mother of the arts, which had produced Homer and Aristotle. Like another amateur of Hellenism, Du Bellay, who nevertheless preferred his native France to Greece or Rome, Musset rhap-

---

[1] Pierre Moreau. *Le Romantisme.* (Paris: J. de Gigord, éditeur, 1932), p. 381.

[2] Musset. *Poésies.* (Paris: Alphonse Lemerre, éditeur, 1904), I, 332.

[3] Musset. "Un Mot sur l'art moderne," *Mélanges de littérature et de critique.* (Paris: Alphonse Lemerre, éditeur, 1909), p. 854.

145

sodized the grandeurs of the past, borrowing that predecessor's style.

> Grèce, ô mère des arts, terre d'idolâtrie,
> De mes voeux insensés éternelle patrie,
> J'étais né pour ces temps où les fleurs de ton front
> Couronnaient dans les mers l'azur de l'Hellespont.
> Je suis un citoyen de tes siècles antiques.
>   ("Les Voeux stériles")

Antique paganism particularly appealed to Musset. Ignoring the Catholic Revival of his century and the belief that Christian art is superior, the poet maintained his preference for colorful, exotic, and imaginative mythology, whose morals were freer and gods more poetic. In "Rolla" Musset lists the lost assets of that wondrous age, all of which he now deeply regrets. Blaming Christianity for depoetizing the world, he violently rejects its founder:

> Je ne crois pas, ô Christ! à ta parole sainte:
> Je suis venu trop tard dans un monde trop vieux.
> D'un siècle sans espoir naît un siècle sans crainte;
> Les comètes du nôtre ont dépeuplé les cieux.
> Maintenant le hasard promène au sein des ombres.
> De leurs illusions les mondes réveillés,
> L'esprit des temps passés, errant sur leurs décombres,
> Jette au gouffre éternel tes anges mutilés.

Being so thoroughly negative about the nature of his era, Musset in no way agreed with those proclaiming human perfectibility and progress. If anything humanity continuously regressed deeper into imbecility, Musset countered.

> . . . Dans le siècle où nous sommes,
> Je n'ai que trop connu ce que valent les hommes.
> Le monde, chaque jour, devient plus entêté,
> Et tombe plus avant dans l'imbécillité.
>   ("Dupont et Durand")

Whereas Musset's discontent with his age was often bitterly expressed, his scorn of contemporaries' optimism was more often revealed in smirking sarcasm. Through satire Musset attempted to destroy the debate over progress. As in the above quotation, a dialogue between two complaining tramps,

Musset frequently resorted to comic devices such as irreverence, false naïveté, or flippancy to spoof the doctrine. In "Histoire d'un merle blanc," whose title stresses the individuality Musset cultivated, for the subject was supposedly autobiographical, a mocking history of his encounter with the Romantic Movement, Musset speaks of his first literary endeavor. Using the Romantic formula of revealing one's private being publicly, the poet supposedly achieved great success, for he neglected no fact, no matter how intimate about himself. To insure a good market for his timely work, the author hastily appended a comment on progress and a solution for man's problems. The casualness with which he mapped the road to the future reveals the author's disbelief in the validity of any of the theories of the believers in progress. No panacea had yet been found, Musset suggests. Furthermore, he intimates man will never discover the key to perfection.

> Bien entendu d'ailleurs que je ne négligerais pas de traiter en passant le grand sujet qui préoccupe maintenant tant de monde: à savoir, l'avenir de l'humanité. Ce problème m'avait paru intéressant; j'en ébauchai, dans un moment de loisir, une solution qui passa généralement pour satisfaisante.[4]

The readiness with which others had produced a master plan for salvation greatly irritated the writer. In 1830, twelve years prior to the satirical "Histoire," Musset had expressed mock astonishment at the mad fervor of his contemporaries for perfection and their certainty in achieving it. To those "deluded" optimists, Musset preferred "realists" who recognised man's degeneracy.

> Dans un siècle comme le nôtre . . . où chacun vise à l'originalité, où dans la clameur universelle qui proclame à tout moment ce qu'elle appelle les besoins du temps, chacun s'écrie: "C'est moi! c'est moi qui l'ai trouvé;" et, tandis que l'esprit humain s'en va tombant d'une ornière dans une autre, bien digne d'être comparé par Luther à un paysan ivre qu'on ne peut placer d'équilibre sur son cheval et qui chavire de droite si on le relève de gauche, il est

---

[4] Musset. *Prose complète*. Texte établi et annoté par Maurice Allem. Ed. de la Pléiade. (Paris: Gallimard, 1950), pp. 721–722.

bien doux, bien précieux [de voir] le petit nombre de gens tranquilles qui ne voient les choses ni à travers des verres de couleur, ni en fermant les yeux à moitié. ("Exposition au profit des blessés," *Mélanges*)

Musset's most biting satire, and perhaps his funniest, of human progress is to be found in the "Lettres à Dupuis et Cotonet" of 1836.[8] Written in imitation of Pascal's *Lettres provinciales*, the correspondence takes place between a country bumpkin and his city cousin, the latter writing the former of the latest Parisian fashions, especially the literary mode, Romanticism, and the philosophical fad, Progress. With disarming naïveté the city dweller, puzzled by such words as *perfectibilité, l'humanitairerie* and *l'avenir*, sets forth on an investigation of them and passes his finding on to the provinces. He is unsure if perfection is to apply only to material objects or to man himself. He concludes that the latter would be dangerous. To improve humanity one would have to adopt the methods of the inquisition, he thinks. In any case, he concludes, the results would not be successful.

Perfectionner les choses n'est pas nouveau; rien n'est plus vieux; tout au contraire, mais aussi rien n'est plus permis, loisible, honnête et salutaire. . . . Mais s'attaquer aux gens en personne et s'en venir les perfectionner, oh! oh! l'affaire est sérieuse, je ne sais trop qui s'y prêterait, mais ce ne serait pas dans ce pays-ci. Perfectionner un homme, d'autorité, par force majeure et arrêt de la cour, c'est une entreprise neuve de tout point. . . . Mais croyez-vous qu'on réussira? quand on tournerait cent ans autour de mes pieds, on ne perfectionnerait jamais que mes bottes; la raison seule doit nous assurer.[6]

The proponents of progress, Musset remarks elsewhere, are

[5] An interesting fact concerning these letters is that the names Dupuis and Cotonet were suggested to Musset by Stendhal, at the time a close friend of the poet. During the publication of the satire the two authors corresponded signing the names of the Parisian or the provincial. For a while critics were led to believe that Stendhal was co-author of the "lettres," but this theory has been subsequently disproved. Musset. *Oeuvres complètes*. Revues et corrigées par Philippe Van Tieghem. (Paris: Aux Editions du Seuil, 1963), p. 872.

[6] Quoted by Fernand Baldensperger. *La Critique de l'histoire littéraire en France au dix-neuvième et au début du vingtième siècles*. (New York: Brentano's, 1945), p. 88.

merely windbags, "ceux qui ont les poumons assez pourvus de vent pour raisonner sur la perfectibilité." ("De l'indifférence en matières publiques et privées—Revue fantastique, Mélanges)

Aesthetic Independence

Particularly in matters pertaining to art did Musset most forcefully assert his independence. He was determined to remain free of the "rhyming school of Hugo" and repudiated most of its doctrines. Specifically Musset disagreed with Hugo's alliance of art and progress. Instead he believed in "la poésie pure" whose only purpose was to create beauty and to produce pleasure. Here again the poet reveals an affinity with Stendhal whose theory of aesthetics was based on the principle of pleasure.

Philippe Van Tieghem in his work on Musset remarks that the poet had no clearly defined literary doctrine but that his many ideas on the nature of art were all commonly rooted in his personal temperament.[7] Indeed Musset's motto could well have been "to thine own self be true." Unlike Lamartine, Musset did not feel he was a spokesman for humanity, only for himself.

Toujours le coeur humain pour modèle et pour loi!
Celui de mon voisin a sa manière d'être,
Mais morbleu! Comme lui j'ai mon coeur humain, moi!
(Quoted by Moreau, p. 382)

Jealousy doubtless played a part in Musset's coolness toward Hugo. The "Father of Romanticism" wielded enormous influence over his times and was surrounded by an adoring circle. His school was a powerful one; its war on classicism a popular issue. Unwilling to become one of the faithful followers, Musset rationalized that literary schools had been meaningless since the Renaissance and that artistic

---

[7] Philippe Van Tieghem. *Musset, l'homme et l'oeuvre*. (Paris: Boivin et Cie, 1944), pp. 118–119.

149

quarrels were sterile pastimes. Once in a conversation with Delacroix he scoffed at the warring factions of his day, saying that discussions have never made art progress, only the act of creation. (Van Tieghem, p. 120) During the revival of classical theatre due to the popularity of a lovely young actress, Mlle Rachel, the quarreling became particularly heated, for it seemed temporarily that *Hernani* would be forgotten for *Horace*. At that time Musset wrote a poem "sur les Débuts de Mesdemoiselles Rachel et Pauline Garcia," the latter a singer and not an actress, in which he reiterated his disbelief in the value of such debates.

Discourons sur les arts, faisons les connaisseurs;
   Nous aurons beau changer d'erreurs,
   Comme un libertin de maîtresses;
Les lilas au printemps seront toujours en fleurs,
Et les arts immortels rajeuniront sans cesse.

Discutons nos travers, nos rêves et nos goûts,
   Comparons à loisir le moderne à l'antique,
   Et ferraillons sous ces drapeaux jaloux!
Quand nous serons au bout de notre rhétorique,
Deux enfants nés d'hier en sauront plus que nous.

Believing beauty to be the prime requisite of art, Musset was shocked by Hugo's theory of the grotesque and the sublime, the juxtaposition of ugliness and beauty to emphasize the latter. Unlike Stendhal who believed a novel should be a mirror traveling along a highway, Musset thought art should ignore that part of reality which was not pleasing. Realism did not appeal to him.

Il faut la beauté à la littérature, à la peinture, à tous les arts.
. . . Les portraits seuls ont le droit d'être laids.[8]

---

[8] Musset, "Un Mot sur l'art moderne," (*Mélanges*, p. 854) Musset also expressed the same idea poetically:

Or la beauté, c'est tout. Platon l'a dit lui-même:
La beauté sur la terre est la chose suprême.
Rien n'est beau que le vrai, dit un vers respecté;
Et moi, je lui réponds, sans craindre le blasphème:
Rien n'est vrai que le beau, rien n'est vrai sans beauté.
(Quoted by Moreau, p. 384)

With beauty the poet's only concern the incursion of political and social theories into art outraged Musset. Since he believed mankind incapable of improving, he also thought that the poet's efforts in that direction, besides being a perversion of his art, were a waste of time. By combining politics and verse, the poet had stooped to journalism. A reaction should be forthcoming from the public which surely was tired of seeing rehashed in poetry daily events it had first read in the newspapers. A complete separation of poetry and politics would be the only salvation for either, Musset believed.

> Si la pensée veut être quelque chose par elle-même, il faut qu'elle se sépare en tout de l'action; si la littérature veut exister, il faut qu'elle rompe en visière à la politique. Autrement toutes deux se ressembleront. ("De la Politique en littérature, et de la littérature en politique— Revue fantastique" (*Mélanges*)

Musset chided his Romantic colleagues for their double duty as poet and leader. He sarcastically remarked that they obviously felt insecure, perhaps inferior as poets alone and had taken on new duties to augment their status. Perhaps a poet is good for nothing in the utilitarian sense. Still he is capable of producing beauty. That alone is adequate justification for his existence, Musset maintained.

> Il faut être franc dans ce siècle-ci: lorsqu'on est bien persuadé qu'on ne peut être ni médecin, ni avocat, ni banquier, ni évêque, ni courtiermarron, ni ministre, enfin lorsqu'on a l'intime conviction qu'on n'est bon à rien, on peut se faire poète: mais pour l'amour de Dieu pas autre chose. (*Ibid.*)

A poet should stick to poetic subjects in his verse: wines, mistresses, his friends, and himself—things he knows well. That excludes governmental and social questions, for the poet "ne sait pas faire de politique."

Not only did Musset advise, but he also gave an example. Unlike his politically ambitious fellow Romantics, Hugo, Vigny, and Lamartine, he did not seek election to the assembly. He for one was content with being merely a poet. All other matters but art and love disinterested him.

> Je ne me suis pas fait écrivain politique,
> N'étant pas amoureux de la place publique.

151

D'ailleurs, il n'entre pas dans mes prétentions
D'être l'homme du siècle et de ses passions.
(''Dédicace à M. Alfred Tattet,
Un Spectacle dans un fauteuil,'')

It is interesting to note, however, that once Musset spoke as did Vigny of the poet as a soldier marching ahead of his unit. For a moment he seemed tempted to assign the poet the position of leadership others were so willing to award. Musset managed, however, to remain consistent with his theory of disinvolvement. He spoke of the poet as detached from the group, isolated, yes, but in no way a leader. More often the poet is the abdicator of responsibility, the deserter. He should take no orders except from his heart. (''Dédicace à M. Alfred Tattet, La Coupe et les Lèvres,'' *Poésies*)

Temporary Involvement: Arbitration of the Quarrel

Musset becomes involved in the quarrel of the classicists and Romantics only on the question of theatre. As mentioned before, the plays of seventeenth-century France underwent a revival of popularity when performed by Mlle Rachel during the 1840's. Coinciding with the failure of Hugo's *Les Burgraves* which threatened Romanticism's claim to have found the way of the future in drama, the renewed public favor of Corneille, Racine, and Molière rekindled the bickering between traditionalists and innovators.

Musset's intervention in the quarrel was more as a mediator than as a participant. He recognized the merits of both sides and sought a harmonious peace. Despite his own dissatisfaction with certain Romantic theories, he acknowledged their contribution to drama.[9] Romantic playwrights, he admitted, had created pleasurable masterpieces which opened an immense new way for drama. In this instance it seems that Musset, like Hugo, believed that by expanding literary hori-

---

[9] Musset. ''De la tragédie, à propos des débuts de Mlle Rachel,'' *Mélanges de littérature et de critique.* Nouvelle éd., revue, corrigée et augmentée par Edmond Biré. (Paris: Garnier frères, libraires-éditeurs, 1908), I, 184.

zons, art had progressed. Classicism, and not its servile imitations, would always have its place, he acceded. A masterpiece is eternal. It was the imitators whom he attacked, for they wished to see literature's advance frozen. These ancients, not the admirers of the past but the denigrators of the present, were the object of criticism. With resignation, he admitted that the French would always have those who opposed the new, calling it decadent. "Nous avons quelque chose d'attique dans l'esprit." (Biré, p. 185)

The occasion of Mlle Rachel's triumph prompted the poet to write an essay in which he reviewed the history of tragedy to the present and ended by making suggestions for its future course. It is ironic that Musset who so bitterly denounced Hugo's efforts would so obviously imitate him and produce his own Cromwellian preface. No explanation is given by the author for this inconsistency. Rivalry could have played a major role in his decision. Musset probably felt that from his detached position outside the quarrel, he better than Hugo, who was too deeply involved to be subjective, could write an accurate appraisal of the status of drama.

Musset concentrates his discussion of tragedy on two authors, Sophocles and Corneille, whom he chooses as representatives of ancient and modern drama. The two are dissimilar, he explains, because of their emphasis. During the time of the Greeks the tragic situation came from outside of man and was due to fate. In modern times tragedy's source lay within man. His passion, not a vengeful god, created dramatic tension. Corneille, according to the writer, was the first to recognize the change and to employ it in his works. Thus, he is the father of modern tragedy.

> Corneille fut le premier qui s'aperçut de la distance qui, sous ce rapport, nous sépare des temps passés; il vit que l'antique élément (la fatalité) avait disparu, et il entreprit de le remplacer par un autre (la passion). (Biré, p. 190)

Musset's analysis was far from original. He like Chateaubriand credited Christianity with having awakened the conscience of man, thus producing a new dramatic source. Mme de Staël had denoted the increased use of psychology in mod-

153

ern works which she claimed rendered them superior. It is Hugo, however, to whom Musset is most indebted, for he goes on to choose neither Sophocles nor Corneille as the better tragedian but Shakespeare, the true modernist. Despite his reverence for the classical past, Musset remained a Romantic. Comparing Shakespeare to other writers he concludes that he is often as good as the best classicist and sometimes unsurpassed.

> Qui oserait dire que . . . Shakespeare ou Calderon . . . ne sont pas aussi glorieux que . . . Sophocle et Euripide? Ceux-ci ont produit Racine et Corneille, ceux-là Goethe et Schiller. . . . *Hamlet* vaut *Oreste, Macbeth* vaut *Oedipe*, et je ne sais même ce qui vaut *Othello*. (Biré, p. 185)

Despite his admiration for Shakespeare, Musset did not believe that the English playwright should be placed upon a pedestal to be worshipped and imitated. It is every writer's duty to express himself alone. Imitation has no place in art.

Musset rejects imitation because he, like Stendhal, believed art should be timely. The writer must always consider his milieu and his moment when creating. "Quel que soit donc notre respect pour les écrivains du grand siècle, nous sommes dans d'autres conditions qu'eux." (Biré, p. 196)

The neo-classicists' greatest failing was that they did not recognize the need of timeliness. Musset shows only contempt for these unthinking copiers who cheapened art.

> C'est ainsi que la tragédie grecque, cet océan majestueux et sublime, après avoir donné naissance à Racine et à Alfieri, ces deux fleuves au flot pur comme le cristal, engendra ces ramifications indécrottables de petites mares d'eau qui se desséchant encore çà et là au soleil, et qu'on nomme . . . l'école de Campistron (vulgairement les *classiques*).

> Imitateurs, troupeau d'esclaves! Quel soleil vous dessèchera jamais et pompera vos cervelles oisives? Un de nos peintres vous appelait hier la poussière que soulèvent les pas du maître. ("Revue fantastique," *Mélanges*, pp. 77–78)

Dissatisfied with either the restoration of classical theatre or the efforts of the Romantics, Musset called for a new drama which would synthesize elements of both. From the Greeks he wished to borrow terror. He called for reacceptance of the rules to produce simpler works. Subjects should be modern and French. Like Stendhal, Musset thought the story of Jeanne d'Arc a suitable subject for modern tragedy. (Biré, pp. 201–202) The classical playwright Musset seemed least inclined to criticize was Molière, who he felt remained as timely in the nineteenth century as he had been in the seventeenth. In 1830, when Racine and Corneille were considered outdated, Musset then agreed and remarked that "Molière, seul, inimitable, est resté amusant." ("Au lecteur, Contes d'Espagne et d'Italie," *Poésies*) During the 1840s when he praised the beauties of seventeenth-century tragedy, Musset once again extolled the undiminished virtues of Molière. Musset's admiration was for Molière's keen knowledge of mankind, his love of truth, and common sense. Unfortunately the public did not share Musset's enthusiasm, and Molière's plays received little attention. The poet joked about the playwright's unpopularity, making it clear that the public, not the author, was misguided. The satirical poem is entitled "Une Soirée perdue," or an evening "lost" at the theatre viewing Molière.

> J'étais seul, l'autre soir, au Théâtre Français,
> Ou presque seul; l'auteur n'avait pas grand succès.
> Ce n'était que Molière, et nous savons de reste
> Que ce grand maladroit, qui fit un jour *Alceste*,
> Ignora le bel art de chatouiller l'esprit
> Et de servir à point un dénouement bien cuit.
> Grâce à Dieu, nos auteurs ont changé de méthode,
> Et nous aimons bien mieux quelque drame à la mode
> Où l'intrigue, enlacée en feston,
> Tourne comme un rébus autour d'un mirliton.

A Hint of Optimism: Encouragement for Artists

Although Musset more frequently criticized his own era and mocked the excesses of Romanticism, he did not totally condemn his times and occasionally displayed optimism about the future of literature. In contradiction with the sentiments expressed in "Rolla" or "Les Voeux stériles" Musset in "Sur la poésie" defends the nineteenth century against attack by

155

maintaining that art is not in decline, for its source, the human soul, is eternal. If the times appear unsatisfactory, then it is man's duty to improve them, he counsels.

Serait-ce par hasard que le siècle et ses hommes,
Messieurs les écrivains, soient trop petits pour vous?
Ce siècle, c'est le nôtre; il est ce que nous sommes.

Musset denied the validity of the concepts of progress and decadence in art mainly to assert his individuality. He rejected them for they applied a common effort between many artists, a kind of team work where one carries on where the other left off. Musset believed each artist to be an individual whose merit came not from his debts to others but from his originality. Thus, the establishment of a progressive or regressive series between unrelated units struck him as an impossibility. One could speak of rebirths and declines only among imitators, he argued, as in the case of nineteenth-century neo-classicists, where there seemed to be a regression since the apex reached by Corneille and Racine. ("Un Mot sur l'art moderne," *Mélanges*, p. 852)

It would be possible to accept Musset's belief in the uniqueness of each artist and still believe in progress, however, for the total artistic effort, even if made up of unrelated units, could either stride forward or slip backward, depending upon the talent of each contributor and the quality of his works. There are debts among artists which do not necessarily imply imitation. The accomplishments of one artist may well inspire another to do even more, to innovate, or to expand his discipline, whereas without knowledge of the past the second artist may not be induced to try to surpass his predecessor. Musset himself later admitted this. Much of Musset's denial is due to his determination to remain free from the Romantic, or more honestly Hugo's, label. Rivalry prompted him to deny being exactly what he was, perhaps the most Romantic personality of the entire *Cénacle*.

As mentioned before Musset shared the moderns' belief in the value of timeliness. Again he strayed from the common path, however, and gave an individualistic interpretation to this theory. Timeliness alone assures nothing for art, he maintained. The circumstances which are reflected in a work can either become meaningless in the future or gain new importance. Timeliness then is a two-edged sword, offering either immortality or oblivion to creative works. (*Ibid.*, p. 853) The work most likely to endure, according to the poet, is the one which is both timely and timeless. The artist can fulfill these two conditions by pleasing two groups of admirers, the crowd and the connoisseur, he advised. The crowd seeks out elements which are relevant to its times and gives a work immediate popularity. The connoisseur looks beyond for enduring qualities common to all masterpieces. His approval suggests future appreciation. In fulfilling both requirements, the artist must remain loyal to his own sentiments and not prostitute his beliefs for either judge's approval. (Biré, "Salon de 1836," pp. 125–126) Raphaël as an artist was clever enough to satisfy self, the public, and the connoisseur, Musset suggests. By expressing his religious beliefs during an age of devotion, he was timely and pleasing to the crowd. By his use of form and color, he won approval of the critic. Thus, Raphaël's paintings are as admired today as they were during the Renaissance. (*Ibid.*, p. 128)

In the last analysis more important to Musset than progress, decadence, timeliness, or timelessness, was originality. An artist could seek inspiration from others but the source of his art must come from within.[10] If artists followed their own inclinations, Musset was confident that the future status of art would take care of itself.

---

[10] "Pourquoi imiter tel peintre lombard, espagnol ou flamand, mort il y a deux ou trois cents ans? Non pas que je blâme l'artiste qui s'inspire du maître; mais à dire vrai, copier certains fragments . . . voir la nature avec d'autres yeux que les siens, gâter ce qu'on sent par ce qu'on sait, est-ce là s'inspirer? Un pareil travail sur soi-même détruit l'originalité, tandis que l'inspiration véritable la ravive et la met en jeu. Il faut que l'enthousiasme pour le maître soit comme un huile dont on se frotte, non comme un voile dont on se couvre." ("Salon de 1836," *Mélanges*, éd. Biré, p. 131)

Chapter Nine
Gautier

Théophile Gautier's views on progress are often contradictory, for he was fond of paradoxes and in his later life was noted for his fairness—"le bon Théo" who spoke ill of no man.[1] In general, Gautier, like Baudelaire to come, found no reason to accept the doctrine of human perfectibility. Man is not irrevocably degenerate, the author argued, but neither is he destined to reach perfection. But Gautier did believe in aesthetic amelioration, which he qualified by saying that although the arts do progress, they are not fated to do so, and with every step forward in the sphere of aesthetics there can be equal retrogression. Most importantly he believed that when aesthetic progress does occur, it does not negate what has come before. Ninetheenth-century art and literature may be superior in many aspects to the creations of antiquity but the former can never replace the latter. Gautier's attitude towards progress can be better understood by considering the doctrine

---

[1] An earlier version of this chapter, entitled "Théophile Gautier on Progress in the Arts," appeared in *Studies in Romanticism,* spring 1973, Vol. 12, No. 2, pp. 530–550.

of Art for Art's Sake. In the tenets of this artistic credo, of which he was the author, one recognizes a fierce desire for independence. Gautier loved beauty, ancient and modern, and hated ugliness regardless of its epoch. He was not prejudiced *a priori* by the date at which a work was produced. Thus he did not champion one artistic manner at the expense of all others.

The Doctrine of Art for Art's Sake:
Abhorrence of Art for Progress

The slogan *l'art pour l'art* now associated mainly with Gautier was previously used in nineteenth-century France by such diverse personalities as Benjamin Constant, Victor Cousin, and Victor Hugo. Constant, perhaps the first to employ it, applied the phrase to Kant's aesthetic in his *Journal intime* in 1804. Cousin also used the slogan in his Sorbonne lectures, the famous "Cours de philosophie" of 1818. He maintained that Beauty's only duty was to itself, not to Goodness or Truth. The inclusion of Hugo's name among the "originators" of the cliché is ironic, for his own philosophy of "art for progress" conflicts with the ideal of disinvolved, pure art. Nevertheless, it was probably he who passed the phrase on to Gautier when discussing one of Voltaire's plays which he considered overly moralizing.[2]

Gautier took up the idea of art for art's sake in the early 1830's and championed it with youthful vigor in the prefaces to *Albertus* (1832) and *Mademoiselle de Maupin* (1835). He then contended that art was autonomous, that the artist who proposes any goal but the creation of beauty is not a true artist, and that the idea cannot be separated from the form. In time Gautier's ideas were to have far reaching effects. Baudelaire, Banville, and Flaubert were to join him in their championing of the liberty of art from external alliances and in their search for perfect formal expression. One sees the result of the theory in

[2] F. Vial et L. Denise. *Idées et doctrines littéraires du XIXe siècle.* 10e éd. (Paris: Librairie Ch. Delagrave, 1937), p. 155.

Baudelaire's quest to express the horrible artistically, in the Parnassians' attempts to create verse of perfect form, and in Flaubert's worship of style. By its desire for perfection, as well as its encouragement of innovation, which to most Romantics was essential to artistic progress, art for art's sake was not hostile to the idea of artistic progress. By its opposition to the utilization of art in the service of morality and politics, the doctrine also appears anti-progressive.

Wellek in his *History of Modern Civilization* emphasizes the negative aspects of the doctrine—its reaction against didacticism, government control of literature, and socialist demands that art improve man. In fact he minimizes the importance of the doctrine by saying it did not give birth to a real movement, for the manifestoes of Gautier were never taken seriously. They were simply an adolescent outburst against the art-for-progress school of thought. They were a means of venting spleen on utopians, Fourieristes, Saint-Simonians, and other believers in progress which the early nineteenth century had in abundance. Such partisans of progress deserved mocking, Gautier thought, for their efforts had come to naught.[3]

The Saint-Simonians were particularly a target of Gautier's wrath, for they insisted that art have a social utility and contribute to the progress of civilization. Art for its own sake was unmerited luxury, they believed. Artists were to forsake their former, unidealistic tasks of amusing the idle to take up with missionary zeal a more glorious work, that of arousing noble sentiments which would benefit society.[4] This doctrine is quite similar to Mme de Staël's and Lamartine's and reflects an eighteenth-century moralistic point of view.

Gautier also criticized those who would subjugate art to religion. He denounced Chateaubriand's call for return to the

---

[3] Vol. III, *The Romantic Age.* (New Haven: Yale University Press, 1955), p. 29.

[4] Albert Cassagne. *La Théorie de l'Art pour l'Art en France chez les derniers romantiques et les premiers réalistes.* Thèse. (Paris: Librairie Hachette et Cie, 1906), p. 45.

faith for attempting to make beauty Christian and virtuous, when art and beauty should be above religious differences. In opposition to the author of *Le Génie du christianisme*, who felt that art progressed by becoming more moral, Gautier could see no connection between beauty and morality, and professed stupefaction at those who did. "Alors on est chrétien, on parle de la sainteté de l'art, de la haute mission de l'artiste, de la poésie du catholicisme, de M. de Lamennais, des peintres de l'école angélique, du concile de Trente, de l'humanité progressive et de mille autres belles choses," but one does not talk about beauty, he retorted.[5]

Art for progress, be it social, religious, or physical, is a nonsensical doctrine. Literature cannot serve politics or morality nor can it improve man's physical lot, Gautier scornfully pointed out.

> Non, imbéciles, non crétins et goîtreux que vous êtes, un livre ne fait pas de la soupe à la gélatine;—un roman n'est pas une paire de bottes sans couture, un sonnet, une seringue à jet continu;—un drame n'est pas un chemin de fer, toutes choses essentiellement civilisantes, et faisant marcher l'humanité dans la voie du progrès. (*Mlle.*, p. xxx)

Poets, according to such believers in progress as Vigny and Lamartine, were supposed to at least provide sympathy for suffering humanity, whether or not they could bring about material improvement. Even this minor contribution is scoffed at by the author. "Des poètes philanthropes!" he mocks, "ce serait quelque chose de rare et de charmant!" They do not exist. (*Mlle*, p. xxix)

Gautier countered that art can be useful only in fulfilling an aesthetic need. It is useful to a poet that his rimes are correct but not that they serve an exterior purpose. (*Mlle*, p. xxxii) He goes so far as to say that anything which has a use is ugly, an extreme position from which he will later retreat.

> Il n'y a de vraiment beau que ce qui ne peut servir à rien; tout ce qui

---

[5] Gautier. *Préface de Mlle de Maupin.* Ed. critique par George Matoré. (Paris: Librairie Droz, 1946), p. x.

est utile est laid, car c'est l'expression de quelque besoin, et ceux de l'homme sont ignobles et dégoûtants, comme sa pauvre et infirme nature. —L'endroit le plus utile d'une maison, ce sont les latrines. (*Mlle*, p. xxxiv)

Kant's idea of art as an end in itself, transmitted through Constant, had not been as extreme. The German aesthetician spoke of autonomy, not purposelessness. Even Cousin in his famous treatise of 1836, *Du Vrai, du Beau et du Bien*, envisioned an abstract ideal which was quite dissimilar from *le beau sexuel* adored by Gautier. (Wellek, p. 30)

Gautier's extreme reaction was perhaps due to his growing consternation over society's rejection of the poet. Vigny, Lamartine, and Musset were highly aware of the public's view of the poet as useless and traced the antipathy as far back as Plato who had banished the poet from his utopia.[6] These three writers approached the problem differently from Gautier, however, for they denied the charge. Vigny and Lamartine believed themselves socially useful. Musset felt that the pleasure his verses gave others was justification enough for his existence.

Gautier's condemnation of humanitarian art was his form of retaliation for society's disinterest in, if not scorn of, the artist. Like the other Romantics, he believed the early eighteen-hundreds were negligent of the exceptional being, the aristocrat, the artist, and overly solicitous of the average and untalented man. Democracy and utility were favorite slogans of the day. Consequently a dilemma developed. The schism between public and artist grew and yet the artist, no longer patronized by a wealthy and aristocratic clientele, had to sell to the new public, the money-oriented bourgeoisie whose values were opposed to his own. Instead of being the

---

[6] Cf. Vigny, *Stello* (Paris: Ch. Delagrave, s.d.), pp. 274–275), for a discussion of Plato's banishment of the poet. A similar reference to Plato's antipathy can be found in Lamartine, ''Des Destinées de la poésie,'' seconde préface de *Premières Méditations poétiques*. (Paris: Hachette et Cie, éditeur, 1895), p. lx. Musset turns the bourgeois' insult that the poet is good for nothing into a compliment in ''De la politique en littérature et de la littérature en politique— *Revue fantastique*,'' *Mélanges de littérature et de critique*. (Paris: Alphonse Lemerre, éditeur, 1909).

center of society, the superior being, the artist discovered he was the outcast, the inferior being, in the eyes of the public. As a defense the artist has two choices—either to come to terms with his unsympathetic and ignorant public or to repudiate it. In his youth Gautier chose the latter. With age he became less recalcitrant. Initially, however, he fought back, hurling diatribes not only at the philistines but also at those unprincipled artists who catered to their vulgar taste. He deemed despicable the mercenary *feuilletonistes* who bowed to the masses' ideals of democracy, positivism, and progress.[7]

Gautier's attitude softened with the passing of time. Violently anti-bourgeois in his early years, he later came to accept middle class standards. Moreau even suggests that Gautier's obsession with matter, the marble and gold so revered in *Emaux et Camées* (1853), reveals a growing materialism.[8] Having earlier attacked the sold-out *feuilletonistes*, Gautier later joined their ranks, earning his living for years as a journalist.

With such an about-face borne in mind, one is not surprised by Gautier's changing attitude concerning the relationship of the artist to society, of art to the philosophy of progress. In an essay entitled "Du Beau dans l'art" of 1847 he maintained that the artist served humanity more than any moralizer. While remaining independent of philosophical alignments, he brought man closer to the ideal.

Que les artistes . . . croient avoir fait autant pour le perfectionnement de l'Humanité que tous les utilitaires par une strophe harmonieuse, un noble type de tête, un torse aux lignes pures où se révèlent la recherche et le désir du beau éternel et général. Les vers d'Homère, les statues de Phidias, les peintures de Raphaël ont plus élevé l'âme que tous les traités des moralistes. Ils ont fait concevoir l'idéal à des gens qui d'eux-mêmes ne l'auraient jamais soupçonné et introduit cet élément divin dans des esprits jusque-là matériels.[9]

---

[7] H. Van der Tuin. *L'Evolution psychologique, esthétique et littéraire de Théophile Gautier.* (Paris: Libraire Nizet et Bastard, 1933), pp. 124–125.

[8] Pierre Moreau. *Le Romantisme.* (Paris: J. de Gigord, éd., 1932), p. 400.

[9] Gautier. "Du Beau dans l'art, Réflexions et menus propos d'un peintre

This new attitude leads Gautier closer to Musset's position. Another parallel between the two writers' thinking can be noted in Gautier's "Le Poète et la foule" (1845) where he depicted the poet sacrificing himself for humanity as Musset's pelican had done for its young.

Laissez mon pâle front s'appuyer sur ma main.
N'ai-je pas de mon flanc, d'où mon âme s'écoule,
Fait jaillir une source où boit le genre humain?

Art could have served mankind, Gautier came to believe. At the same time as the preface to *Mademoiselle de Maupin* Gautier argued that it is better to have made a beautiful clock which serves a purpose than a bad statue which is good for nothing. Art cannot afford to be entirely divorced from reality, like Narcissus, or it will suffer the same fate as he. Art should be brought into the home and improve bourgeois taste.[10] The refinement of public taste, the encouragement of artistic production were worthy tasks for the artist. Gautier himself worked to win government commissions for others. He was concerned with the design of locomotives and of fashions. With increasing tolerance towards his own age, Gautier recognized new possibilities for artistic depiction provided by nineteenth-century culture. He no longer sought to impose classical ideals on the modern world. The ancient art of azure and marble is but one type of beauty, he wrote in *L'Evénement* in 1848; it is not superior to the modern art of steel and gas, which in its activity, rivals the serenity of the former in beauty. (Richardson, p. 133)

Gautier's Ambivalent Attitude on Progress: First Negativism

Bearing in mind Gautier's initial view that beauty was to be venerated regardless of its era or source and his evolution

---

genevois, ouvrage posthume de M. Töpffer," *La Revue des Deux Mondes,* le 9 sept., 1847.

[10] From *La Presse,* le 27 déc. 1836, cited by Joanna Richardson. *Théophile Gautier: His Life and His Times.* (London: Max Reinhardt, 1958), p. 132.

from extreme hostility toward the bourgeois values of materialism and utilitarianism to his subsequent tolerance of them, let us consider his specific pronouncements on the subject of progress, first viewing his opposition and then his agreement.

The matter of human progress can be dismissed in a few statements. Gautier never accepted the doctrine of mankind's indefinite perfectibility. In the 1830s he shows only scorn for the idea. Later he will simply ignore it. In the preface to *Mademoiselle de Maupin* one finds an example of his early condemnation of the idea. Perfectibility, in his estimation, could not even be physical, much less moral, or intellectual.

> Mon Dieu! que c'est une sotte chose que cette prétendue perfectibilité du genre humain dont on nous rebat les oreilles! On dirait en vérité que l'homme est une machine susceptible d'améliorations et qu'un rouage mieux engrené, un contre-poids plus convenablement placé peuvent faire fonctionner d'une manière plus commode et plus facile. (*Mlle*, pp. xxxv-xxxvi)

If man could be physically improved, then the idea would have some merit. Man could use a double stomach so that he could ruminate as a cow; eyes in the back of his head would be beneficial; wings would spare taxi fares, etc. Gautier's mockery borders on the obscene as he lists possible physical improvements man could enjoy. (*Mlle*, p. xxxvi)

Charles Fourier (1772–1837), founder of the economic doctrine of social reform which bears his name, epitomized for Gautier the deluded soul who had been won over to the doctrine of perfectibility.[11] Among Fourier's many sugges-

---

[11] Fourier's ideas are contained in his *Théorie des quatre mouvements* (1808) and elaborated in his *Traité de l'association domestique et agricole* (1822) and in *Le Nouveau monde industriel* (1829–30). In these works he proposed agricultural and economic reforms designed to better the lot of the common man. His view of the progress of civilization is most interesting, revealing a fertile imagination. He prophesied that the universe would exist for 80,000 years following a curve leading from chaos to the apogee of happiness and back to chaos. During the era of complete harmony which was to occur during the last 8,000 years, the earth would be transformed into paradise. The North Pole would be milder than the Riviera. The seas would be turned into lemonade. Each woman would have four husbands or lovers simultaneously. The arts especially would benefit. There would be thirty-seven million dramatists as good as Molière, etc.

tions for improving the lot of man, Gautier thought that of the *phalanstère* to be the most striking. Fourier had envisioned a communal village where all was to be shared, including love, by those working to establish a utopia. The word *phalanstère*, coined from *phalange* and *monastère*, suggested an earlier utopian cooperative society, Rabelais' Abbaye de Thélème, whose guiding principle, "Fay ce que vouldras," Gautier thought equally applicable to Fourier's group. Progress in hedonism was noted by Gautier since the days of the Rabelaisian paradise, however, in Fourier's concept of utopia.

> Le phalanstère est vraiment un progrès sur l'abbaye de Thélème et relègue définitivement le paradis terrestre au nombre des choses tout à fait surannées et perruques. Les *Mille et une nuits* de Mme d'Aulnoy peuvent seules lutter avantageusement avec le phalanstère. Quelle fécondité! quelle invention! Il y a là de quoi défrayer de merveilleux trois mille charretées de poèmes romantiques ou classiques: et nos versificateurs, académiciens ou non, sont de bien piètres trouveurs, si on les compare à M. Charles Fourier, l'inventeur des attractions passionnées.—Cette idée de se servir de mouvements que l'on a jusqu'ici cherché à réprimer est très assurément une haute et puissante idée. (*Mlle*, p. xl)

In the 1850s one finds Gautier no more disposed to a belief in man's ability to improve himself. Although less dramatic in his denial, he remains as firm. Speaking of Baudelaire, Gautier agrees with that poet and his source, Poe, that man can never change, he is destined to remain the "self-same."[12]

Concerning the arts Gautier did recognize both progress and regression. Man's creativity was not subject to universal law, he maintained. It depended on individual circumstances and moved forward or backward without regard to pattern.

Generally Gautier felt that classical antiquity and its revival in the modern era, the Renaissance, represented the highwater marks of artistic creation, never equalled in intensity or scope. Greek and Latin plastic art was superior because it achieved the highest degree of feeling for form. This judgment reflects of course Gautier's philosophy of art for art's

---

[12] Gautier. "Baudelaire," *Portraits et Souvenirs littéraires*. (Paris: Bibliothèque Charpentier, 1892), p. 177.

166

sake. Worship of the body encouraged by an anthropomorphic religion brought the art of sculpture to a summit which had never again been reached. During the Romantic era, for example, sculpture seemed woefully lacking. In fact Gautier explained that a sculptor is by definition classical, for sculpture is the art of a youthful society. Here one should note that Gautier shared the Romantic view that man and his artistic expression passed through ages, from youth to senility. To some the process of maturation afforded the opportunity for artistic progress by exploitation of each successive *Zeitgeist*; to others aging will mean decline.

> De tous les arts celui qui se prête le moins à l'expression de l'idée romantique, c'est assurément la sculpture. Elle semble avoir rêvé de l'antiquité sa forme définitive. Développée sous une religion anthropomorphe où la beauté divinisée s'éternisait dans le marbre et montait sur les autels, elle a atteint une perfection qui ne saurait être dépassée. Jamais, l'hymne du corps humain n'a été chanté en plus nobles strophes, la force superbe de la forme a resplendi d'un éclat incomparable pendant cette période de la civilisation grecque qui est comme la jeunesse et le printemps du génie humain. [13]

Thus as far as statuary is concerned there has been no artistic progress in over 2,000 years, and Gautier adds, some believe there has been only retrogression. [14]

For this retrogression Gautier held the Judeo-Christian tradition largely responsible. The Jews prescribed images, the plastic arts, as pagan and idolatrous, thus associating beauty with sin. They shared no love of form with the Greeks and thought of the body as a prison, not a palace. Early Christians continued this tradition, which resulted in artistic sterility. ("Civ.," p. 229)

By the time of the Renaissance, however, Catholicism's attitude towards physical beauty softened. It turned from the

---

[13] Gautier. *Histoire du Romantisme, suivie d'un Rapport sur le Progrès de la poésie française depuis 1830*. (Paris: Aux Bureaux de l'Administration du Bien Publique, 1872), p. 11.
[14] Gautier. "Civilization and the Plastic Arts," from the *Works of Théophile Gautier*. Trans. and ed. by Prof. F. C. de Sumichrast. (New York: The Jenson Society, 1905), XVI, 227.

Jewish philosophy that images are sinful to an appreciation of the plastic arts. The body was relieved of its curse and a new art, half-pagan, half-Catholic, was born. In some respects the mingling of the two traditions created the most ideal conditions for art, Gautier thought, and produced beautiful works depicting a God-Jupiter, a Mary-Venus, a Christ-Apollo, etc. But with the Reformation, the anti-art tradition was revived. Protestantism's austerity resembled the Jewish position that beauty, luxury, and art were evil and to be hated. Beauty must be sacrificed to utility, these philistines argued. Ever since the two factions, here represented by the pagan-Catholic and Jewish-Protestant traditions, have been at war. ("Civ.," pp. 230–232) The seventeenth and eighteenth centuries suffered the influence of the Reformation. In the nineteenth century polytheism and pantheism were slowly being revived but had won little support from the public. The utilitarians seemed to have won out. (Cassagne, p. 405) Gautier was speaking of the art for art's sake movement when he announced that a revival of Greek ideals was taking place. He found solace in contemplation of the "perfect" beauty of antiquity and escape from the "barbaric" tradition of gothic medieval art. In the poem "Bûchers et tombeaux" he remarks:

> Reviens, reviens, bel art antique,
> De ton paros étincelant
> Couvrir ce squelette gothique;
> Dévore-le, bûcher brûlant.

Gautier was not speaking of nineteenth-century neo-classicism, which he considered too confined by rules. He wished to rediscover true antiquity, not an imitation. (Van der Tuin, p. 129)

Like Musset before him Gautier laments being born too late in a world too old. [15] He declares that he is at odds with the

---

[15] The "Ode à Jean Duseigneur, sculpteur" of 1831 best presents Gautier's nostalgia for classical antiquity and his hostility to the contemporary scene. The nineteenth century is bad for all men, he states; it is a disenchanted, faithless era. The future seems no brighter. Man is being led to the abyss; art especially suffers:

world in which he must live. He is pagan in a Christian century. In *Mademoiselle de Maupin* he writes:

> Je suis un homme des temps homériques . . . aussi païen qu'Alcibiade ou que Phidias. . . . Mon corps rebelle ne veut point reconnaître la suprématie de l'âme et ma chair n'entend point qu'on la mortifie. . . . La spiritualité n'est pas mon fait. . . . Trois choses me plaisent: l'or, le marbre et la pourpre: éclat, solidité, couleur. (Moreau, p. 400)

With such a negative attitude toward his own epoch Gautier's rejection of the idea of artistic progress is not surprising. Speaking as a true *ancien* he declares that there is nothing new under the sun, that "progress" is only the rediscovery of the forgotten past. "Il n'y a pas de choses nouvelles," he once said to Emile Bergerat, his son-in-law and future biographer, "ce qu'on appelle progrès n'est que la remise en lumière de quelque lieu commun délaissé. J'imagine qu'Aristote en savait aussi long que Voltaire, et Platon que M. Cousin." (Van der Tuin, p. 140) Indeed in some instances Gautier's pessimism is so extreme that he seems to purport there has been only retrogression. The Renaissance at least had Raphaël and Michelangelo, he wrote in the preface to *Mademoiselle de Maupin*, but the nineteenth century has only Paul Delaroche, "le tout parce que l'on est en progrès."[16] He goes on to say that

---

L'Art et les dieux s'en vont.—La jeune poésie
Fait de la terre au ciel voler sa fantaisie,
Déplie à tous les tours sa pure et chaste voix.
On ne l'écoute pas. Ses chants que rien n'égale
Sont perdus comme ceux de la pauvre cigale,
Du grillon du foyer ou de l'oiseau des bois.

The sculptor and the painter trying to capture beauty in their art are misunderstood and neglected by the money-oriented public. The days when art and the artist were worshipped, the times of Raphaël et Michelangelo are over. It is not a time for art. Oh, to have been born earlier!

Si trois cents ans plus tôt Dieu nous avait fait naître,
Parmi tous ces hauts noms, l'on en eût mis peut-être
D'autres qui maintenant meurent désavoués;
Car nous n'étions pas faits pour cette époque immonde,
Et nous avons manqué notre entrée en ce monde,
Où nos rôles étaient joués.

[16] Gautier has Raphaël in "La Vie dans la mort" (part II of "La Comédie

Jupiter was a superior seducer to Don Juan. In sum, there has been no progress; nothing new has been invented and the old has not been perfected.

A particular strain of Gautier's argument against progress in the arts is concerned with size. Everything is not bigger, much less better, now than in the past. Using the opera as an example, Gautier complains that it is only one-tenth as large a spectacle as a Roman circus and that its singers are puny substitutes for the more heroic gladiators. The theatre is nothing in comparison with the spectacles of the ancients. Parisians brag that plays last until two in the morning, whereas in antiquity there were games which lasted one hundred days, real naval battles produced for entertainment with hundreds of men cutting each other to pieces. To have substituted plays and operas for these grandiose and fierce spectacles was the opposite of progress Gautier believed. One cannot help but wonder how Gautier, even in the enthusiasm of his youth, could have sustained such an argument. No mention of quality is made in the comparison and armed combat is declared superior to music. The illogical nature of the statement is the best grounds for its dismissal.

Gautier went so far as to declare that man had retrogressed because he had substituted one god for many and in destroying that richly imaginative world of pagan divinities he had only half-heartedly accepted its substitute. (*Mlle*, p. lii)

---

de la mort'') regretfully admit that no artist exists who can carry on his tradition. Imitators can copy his colors or his poses, but the lack of love and faith which characterizes this century of science prevents them from copying the spirit of his works. Indeed it seems to be the twilight of civilization. Humanity is moribund. The argument that only technical tricks can be passed on from artist to artist and not the essence of his talent is reiterated in the late 1840's when Gautier writes that ''chaque poète, chaque peintre, chaque sculpteur emporte son secret avec lui; il ne laisse pas de recettes'' (''Du Beau,'' p. 133). The individuality of artistic creation made it impossible to speak of continuing progress from one artist to another. Gautier will later extensively modify this statement and claim that every artist is another's son, that all artists contribute to a common stock of beauty which is passed intact from generation to generation.

Such a view serves as a rebuttal to Chateaubriand's glee over the downfall of Olympus and the triumph of Calvary. Remembering that Gautier himself was to become an active contributor to the newspapers of his day, one finds his initial antagonism to that profession ironic. He first felt that journalism was wrong because it was mercenary. It catered to public opinion, encouraging stereotyped thinking, for it reinforced generally accepted ideas without challenging them. Newspapers were also dangerous tools, in Gautier's estimation. They could control public opinion, overthrowing governments and destroying an artist's reputation. Gautier hints that the present hostility of the public towards the artist was due in part to bad publicity. (*Mlle*, p. 1)

Because information became so abundant, the public lazily relied upon the press to spoon-feed it, he argued. Scholarship, the personal search for truth, had been curbed. Not only was the public to be blamed for its passive receptiveness to *les opinions toutes faites* but, more reprehensible, it then repeated these opinions with great authority and was encouraged to draw erroneous conclusions from its feeble sources. In essence, every man felt himself a competent critic on all subjects, including art. Gautier was incensed to have the average man democratically demand an equal voice in praising or condemning a matter as elevated and esoteric as art. Only the favored few were capable of judging art, Gautier contended, but thanks to newspapers, every fool spoke his mind. (*Mlle*, p. li)

Gautier's irritation with the average man's pretense at being an art critic was based on his low opinion of the philistine or bourgeois as compared with his idealized view of the artist. Gautier maintained that the distance separating philistine and artist was the same as that dividing animals and humans. The average man has but five senses—touch, taste, sight, smell, and hearing. The artist has a sixth, aesthetic sensitivity. Most men experience nature as animals would, i.e., through their five senses, in a most rudimentary way. Others, the more intellectual ones, not only perceive more but are startled by similarities and differences in objects. They sense a rapport between sky and field, blue and green. But the artist, whose sense is not intellectual, but higher, goes beyond and realizes there is a common element in the blue sky and green field, beauty, an idea contained in both but not a part of either. ("Du Beau," p. 132) Only this type of man, semi-divine if you wish, fully understands art and should be allowed to speak of it. Democracy has no place in art. It is aristocratic by nature.

In that the sixth sense, the distinguishing factor between philistine and artist, is God-given, it puts art's development in an unregimented and uncontrolled sphere of action to which regular laws, such as progress, are foreign. This is the main difference between science and art, Gautier concludes. Voicing one of the most basic objections to the extension of the concept of progress to the arts, he writes:

> L'art, différent en cela de la science, recommence à chaque artiste. Hors quelques procédés matériels de peu d'importance, tout est toujours à apprendre, et il faut que l'artiste se fasse son microcosme de toutes pièces. En art, il n'y a pas de progrès: si le bateau à vapeur est supérieur à la trirème grecque, Homère n'a pas été dépassé, Phidias vaut Michel-Ange, auquel notre âge n'a rien à opposer. ("Du Beau," p. 133)

In science, on the contrary, a chemist or mathematician takes up where his predecessor left off and carries the whole body of scientific knowledge as far forward as he is capable. In this way science is perfectible by addition. Beauty cannot be kept intact from the past and to its sum perfections added. Parts of beauty die with its creator, only the inferior aspects—technical knowledge—can be passed on. Thus art is not capable of progress because it is not additionally perfectible. (*Ibid.*)

The idea of progress in art is a delusion of critics and artists alike according to Gautier. Critics, sated with bad art, look to the future for perfection. They have invented "la critique d'avenir" or "la critique prospective" which states that the perfect work is that which has not yet appeared. Whatever appears has faults but tomorrow's work will be faultless. Unfortunately tomorrow never comes; it is always today. (*Mlle,*

172

pp. xlv-xvli) Artists have also been duped by this belief. They naïvely think that they will produce the long awaited perfect work. To insure the critic's recognition of it, they cater to his tastes, making themselves socialists, progressivists, moralists, etc., thinking these qualities will insure their success. They, too, await a day which will never come. (*Mlle*, p. xlvi)

Yet, Gautier concedes, to look forward toward the future for better art is healthier than to look backward into the past, convinced that the best is over and as one grows further distant from the Golden Age one is increasingly inferior. "Cette recette est bien supérieure à celle que l'on pouvait appeler rétrospective et qui consiste à ne vanter que des ouvrages anciens qu'on ne lit plus et qui ne gênent personne aux dépens des livres modernes, dont on s'occupe et qui blessent plus directement les amours-propre." (*Mlle*, p. xlvii) Here one finds Gautier's basic opinion on progress. It is not inevitable nor probable. In the arts progress may occur but complete perfection will never be achieved. For what improvements that have come about man should recognize his good fortune. If there has been no progress, man cannot complain, for he has no reason to expect such a gift.

Recognition of Artistic Progress Outside of Literature

Turning to more optimistic statements concerning the development of art, one finds Gautier's admission that certain progress has occurred. No uniform progress has taken place, as explained above; instead there has been a series of flowerings and fadings, unrelated and unconnected. Gautier theorizes that the sum of genius which exists in the world has been constant except during four exceptional periods—the eras of Pericles, Augustus, Leo X, and Louis XIV. These moments all represent high points in art's development. Gautier cautiously does not rank one above the other.

It is well known, the author states, that the conditions necessary for the full development of art move from country to country. A nation may rule supreme for a while, then produce nothing. Italy serves as an example. For three centuries it was the leader of the arts. In the nineteenth century it creates nothing. It has become a museum. France has taken up where Italy left off. It has become the artistic leader of nations. Paris is the metropole of art. Gautier does not prophesy who shall replace the French as the cultural vanguard nor does he explain the reasons for the rise of his country and the descent of his neighbor on the artistic scale.[17] Interestingly he credits France with being eclectic in its art, a quality responsible for progress according to Balzac, whereas other nations stress but one dominant characteristic, he thought, e.g., the English individuality, the Germans ideas, and the Belgians savoir-faire. ("Expo.," p. 9)

In an article on civilization and the plastic arts Gautier gives a panoramic view of the development, and to some extent, the progress of art from its beginnings to the present. Typically, he credits the earliest stages with being among the best, for the Greeks, he believed, attained beauty in everything. His reason for such adulation was, as mentioned before, that the greatest feeling for form existed in their day. The Middle Ages were like a long night which followed a brilliant day. The feeling for beauty disappeared for many centuries in that chaotic time. ("Civ.," p. 253) With such a prejudiced view of medieval culture Gautier shared none of the nostalgia of the majority of the Romantics for that "pure and religious" age. The Romantic view was a distortion, a myth, he claimed, not recognizing his own to be equally biased. In *Mademoiselle de Maupin* he spoke out against Romantic veneration of the medieval epoch, saying: "Donc, à bas le moyen âge, tel que nous l'ont fait les faiseurs (le grand mot est lâché; les faiseurs)! Le moyen âge ne répond à rien maintenant, nous voulons autre chose."[18]

The lamp of beauty which went out in medieval times

---

[17] Gautier. "L'Exposition universelle de 1855" from *Les Beaux-Arts en Europe*. (Paris: Michel Lévy, libraire-éditeur, IIème série, 1856), pp. 3–5.

[18] (*Mlle*, p. xxii). Gautier did come to appreciate the art of the Middle Ages, even if he generally rejected the era and the Romantics' reconstruction of it. In literature, he was attracted to Villon, whose reputation he tried to restore, and in architecture, he was impressed by the lonely airiness of gothic cathedrals.

was relit, according to Gautier, during the Renaissance. ("Civ.," p. 254) Having returned to the source of true beauty—away from gothic barbarity to Greek purity—sixteenth-century artists were able to produce masterpieces and in certain instances to achieve progress in art. Leonardo da Vinci is a good example of a continuer and innovator, one who achieved aesthetic progress. Da Vinci's ideal possessed the purity, grace, and perfection of form found in antiquity, but in addition it had a totally modern feeling. He expressed a finesse, suaveté, and elegance unknown to the ancients. The Greeks had produced lovely sculptured heads of irreproachable correctness, Gautier believed, but they were merely serene. Da Vinci's painted heads had a sweetness which revealed intellectual superiority. He portrayed intelligent beauty, not just physical attractiveness. ("Civ.," pp. 261–262) Progress was clearly made by the Italian painter in Gautier's estimation, for his "Mona Lisa" is the most perfect of all paintings. It fuses reality and revery. (Richardson, pp. 135–136)

Raphaël is also singled out as a milestone in the development of art. He, too, brought painting to a degree of perfection never again equalled. Gautier was especially impressed by his painting "The Holy Family" which he enthusiastically praised, saying:

> Raphaël alors arrivé à l'apogée de son talent, n'a rien produit de plus parfait; la peinture n'est pas allée au-delà, et il est douteux qu'elle puisse jamais dépasser cette limite suprême, où les moyens humains font défaut au génie pour exprimer un idéal supérieur.[19]

As mentioned before, Gautier thought the combination of pagan mythology and Catholicism had produced an ideal set of conditions for the production of art. The pre-Reformation Renaissance flourished under its benign reign. Raphaël is an example of this happy combination of traditions. He re-clothed antiquity in Christian terms. He brought Christian art out of the melancholic darkness of the medieval tradition into the light of classical culture. Raphaël's Madonna has become

---

[19] Gautier. "Guide de l'amateur au Louvre," *Pages choisies des grands écrivains*. 4e éd. (Paris: Librairie Armand Colin, 1905), p. 229.

the symbol of the Virgin, the modern ideal of feminine beauty, the modern equivalent of Venus.

Il a fixé à jamais le type de Madonna, et c'est toujours avec les traits d'une Vierge de Raphaël que l'idée de "Marie pleine de grâce" se présente au dévot, au poète, à l'artiste. Il lui a ôté la tristesse, la souffrance et la laideur du moyen âge; il l'a revêtue de toutes les délicieuses perfections que lui prêtent les litanies: Etoile du matin, Rose mystique, Porte d'ivoire, et il en fait l'idéal de la beauté antique[20]

The next era to have made significant contributions to art was the eighteenth century. Watteau was greatly admired by the author for his representation of that special quality of the century—the rococo. The invention of rococo style represents a kind of artistic progress, for such a complete innovation in the history of art is a rare if not unique occurrence.[21]

It is Gautier's own era which receives his fullest attention, however. The growths and decays in the arts are carefully noted. In the discipline of painting Gautier was impressed by the sudden and remarkable development of landscapes, a genre which he associated with Romanticism. Here is an instance of literature creating a corresponding progress in another realm of art. Gautier suggests that nature owes its discovery to Rousseau. The nineteenth-century man living in an urbanized and skeptical world remembers Rousseau's admiration for tranquil and beautiful nature and turns to it for consolation. Thus he has created a demand for landscapes, encouraging the development of a neglected art form. (Richardson, p. 144)

Since the time of Louis Philippe, French art had found new freedom of expression resulting in a diversity of subject

---

[20] ("Guide," p. 230). As was the case with most authors considered in this study, Gautier frequently contradicted himself. In the poem "Melancolia" he condemns Raphaël's pagan-Christianity and especially his Madonna for being too worldly. In fact, he states, one feels the model for the portrait could have been a courtesan. In this instance he declares a preference for the German Catholic painters such as Dürer who were more spiritual, less worldly, who in his estimation created true Christian types. *Poésies complètes.* (Paris: G. Charpentier et Cie, éditeurs, 1889), I, 215ff.

[21] *Le Moniteur universel,* le 20 avril 1866, cited by Richardson, p. 138.

matter, Gautier believed. From the era of Louis XV until the bourgeois king, art was restricted to the reflection of clearly defined subjects. By the mid-nineteenth century the restraints had ended. The sphere of art had grown to encompass a multitude of subjects and techniques. In Gautier's opinion specialization was a thing of the past, eclecticism was the road of the future. The costly quarrels of academicians and rival schools had ended. Diversity was not acceptable.[22]

Turning from general traits of nineteenth-century art noted by the author to his statements on individual artists, one finds his optimism continued. Ingres, the epitome of classicism in the Romantic era, was highly esteemed by Gautier. In answer to the reproach that Ingres was not inspired by the spirit of modernity, that he refused to be of his times, Gautier maintained that Ingres was correct in doing so, for his was a timeless beauty. Timely beauty has many merits, but it is inferior to the eternal.

Loin de nous l'intention de blâmer les artistes qui se pénètrent des passions contemporaines et s'enfièvrent des idées qu'agite leur époque. Il y a, dans la vie générale où chacun trempe plus ou moins un côté ému et palpitant que l'art a le droit de formuler et dont il peut tirer des oeuvres magnifiques; mais nous préférons la beauté absolue et pure, qui est de tous les temps, de tous les pays, de tous les cultes, et réunit dans une communion admirative le passé, le présent et l'avenir.[23]

[22] *Le Moniteur universel,* le 18 mai 1864, cited by Richardson, p. 145.

[23] (*Beaux-Arts,* I, 143). It would be in order at this point to consider Gautier's beliefs concerning absolute and relative beauty. He often speaks of eternal (absolute) beauty as the goal of art, denigrating transitory (relative) beauty which pleases for the moment but has no lasting value. Yet Gautier's position is far more complex, as is revealed in one of the key articles of his aesthetic criticism, "Du Beau dans l'art."

In this article Gautier maintains that Beauty in its absolute essence is God, existing only in the divine sphere which houses all absolutes, such as Goodness and Truth. Beauty being divine, utterly spiritual, does not consist of sensorial images, it is not materialistic. Beauty in its celestial storehouse is rather an idea, untouchable, unattainable. But Beauty descends to man from time to time, leaving its absolute dwelling place and entering into the non-absolute, transitory, and material world of man. Descending to man, it adjusts to his image, becomes sensorially perceptible and manifested through temporal and finite objects. Beauty which descends to earth then is relative Beauty, the only Beauty man is capable of possessing. Thus human Beauty,

Art which ignores fad may have less appeal for the masses, for it appears cold to them, but "c'est . . . le grand art, l'art immortel et le plus noble effort de l'âme humaine: ainsi l'entendirent les Grecs, ces maîtres divins dont il faut adorer la trace à genoux." (*Beaux-Arts*, I, 143) Ingres then is Gautier's idol for he is an amateur of true antiquity. He carries on the torch passed from the Greeks to the Renaissance when so many have tried to extinguish it.

> Merci, maître invaincu, prêtre fervent du beau,
> Qui de la forme pure as conservé le moule,
> Et seul, resté debout dans ce siècle qui croule.
> De l'antique idéal tiens toujours le flambeau!
> (*Poésies*, II, 248)

Vernet, on the other hand, is a timely artist, who broke away from the tradition of depicting the cavalry nude and painted them in modern costume. Although Gautier preferred antique beauty, he did not ignore its modern counterpart nor disparage it. "La poésie des temps modernes n'est pas toute faite comme celle des temps anciens; il faut la deviner, la dégager et inventer des formes pour la rendre," which is really the more difficult task. (*Beaux-Arts* II, 11) Vernet's glory lies in his timeliness. He is original, spiritual, modern, and French.

Gautier prefigures Baudelaire in his enduring and audacious enthusiasm for Delacroix, the epitome of Romantic art. It was in fact that painter's Romanticism and modernity which most appealed to him. Gautier declared in an article published in *La France Littéraire* in March 1833, that together with Ingres, Delacroix had revolutionized French art. (Richardson, p. 139) Delacroix, like Ingres, he remarked in 1860, was not afraid of

---

inspired by an unchanging ideal, is moulded by the particular set of external influences which are present at its apparition. The work of art, the temporal expression of the eternal, bears the mark of the manners, habits, modes, and even the barbarity of the times. If civilization is at a low point, the relative expression of Beauty will be inferior. If culture is well developed, it will be of superior quality. But no matter how poorly Beauty is contained in its temporal clothing, it is still part of the one and ideal Beauty which exists eternally. The ideal may be denatured but never destroyed. Gautier's theory owes much to Plato as well as to Victor Cousin.

²⁴ *Le Moniteur universel*, le 6 fév. 1860, cited by Richardson, p. 145.

being original, of deviating from the norm. By never fearing boldness, by pushing to the limit of his faculties, he attained the goal of becoming a true artist. Delacroix's appearance on the French artistic scene was well timed, for he began producing during an era of decadence. Even the classicists had become bored by the disciples of David. (*Hist.*, p. 38) Delacroix was a fresh new talent sorely needed. He introduced color and movement into an art which had degenerated into line drawings closely resembling sculpture or bas-relief. In this case too much love of antiquity had been harmful to art. Acceptance of modernity's role in art ended the degeneration. (*Beaux-Arts* I, 267) When Delacroix borrowed from the past he transformed his material. "Il sait inventer même dans la mythologie et donner un aspect nouveau aux dieux de la Fable, sans toute fois s'écarter trop visiblement du type." (*Beaux-Arts* I, 270)

Turning from painting to a new art form considered by some a rival to the pictorial arts, photography, one discovers great tolerance in Gautier's attitude. Indeed he is much more progressive, more eager to accept the new in art than Baudelaire who is generally known for his modernity. Perhaps Gautier's friendship with Nadar had prepared him to appreciate that fledgling art form. In any case he displayed no fear that it would harm painting but instead thought that it would release artists to greater freedom. Gautier spoke of photography as a servant of art as well as an art in itself in the review of Eugène Piot's "L'Italie Monumentale." (Richardson, p. 146)

Gautier's modernism is best expressed in his view on architecture. Surprisingly for a man who earlier declared an abhorrence of medieval art, Gautier nonetheless recognized a new gothic art form possible through the use of cast iron construction. Railway stations, those composites of iron and glass, would become the new cathedrals of the future, he remarked in an article for *La Presse* of January 1848.[25] Stations

---

[25] The locomotive was considered a modern Pegasus by the author indicating his willingness to accept even the most modern and ironically the most utilitarian beauty. Gautier looked for science to give a new purpose to art. He did not think the two incompatible. (Richardson, p. 145)

would dictate the styles of other buildings and create an entirely new architecture which would be functional as well as beautiful. [26] Gautier had come a long way since the recalcitrance of *Mademoiselle de Maupin*. As Joanna Richardson has pointed out, Gautier's art criticism is marked by a practical, progressive, and idealistic character. (Richardson, p. 148)

Acknowledgement of Literary Progress

Gautier, more than any other Romantic, because of his talents as both painter and poet, was deeply interested in all aspects of art. His love of beauty, especially the antique, but also the modern, expressed in his statements concerning the fine arts, is carried over in his discussion of literature. In this discipline, however, certain notable changes of attitude occur. There is no enthralling model in antiquity or the second antiquity, the Renaissance, to which Gautier can be fiercely loyal. Instead it is modern literature, Romanticism, which to him represents the summit of literary achievement. Progress is more likely to be admitted in the verbal art than in the graphic or plastic ones.

Leading up to the Romantic era, French literature of the preceding two centuries elicited varied comments from the author. Classical drama of the seventeenth century, for example, was thought a poor substitute for the original Greek plays. The works of Aeschylus, Sophocles, and Euripides were of grandiose proportions employing choirs, making the most of scenic decor, in sum, resulting in dazzling spectacle. The Greek Theatre was more like modern opera, Gautier precedes Wagner in saying, for it represented a synthesis of the arts into an ideal dramatic form. [27]

Poor imitations of the original that Corneille and Racine's plays were, the playwrights deserved certain admiration in his opinion. Of the two Gautier preferred Corneille, whom he named the Homer of Paris, ''le fier dessinateur, le Michel-

---

[26] *Le Moniteur universel*, le 13 juillet 1868, cited by Richardson, p. 147.
[27] *La Presse*, le Ier jan. 1849, cited by Richardson, p. 64.

Ange du drame."[28] His esteem for the author of *Le Cid* would have been greater, had he developed further the Spanish elements of his theatre, indeed the Romantic characteristics, rather than the classical aspects. Had Corneille continued in the tradition of *Le Cid*, Gautier once remarked, he would have become the equal of Shakespeare.[29]

Racine received less praise from Gautier's pen. His *Phèdre* however, was deeply admired. Gautier had been made aware of its merits during a revival of classical drama in which the actress Rachel took part. She interpreted the title role so well that Gautier was moved to say that Phèdre was indeed the finest female character in tragedy. True to his classical taste, he also noted that this play was the most classical of all of Racine's, that Phèdre was the most Greek of his characters, more pagan than Christian. Thus it is Racine's classicism which won Gautier's praise.[30]

Molière appealed to Gautier because of his whole-hearted humor. He represented Romantic audacity carried to the extreme, and thus by his freedom from convention he prefigured Hugo in his quest for total dramatic license. (Richardson, p. 67)

In general, Gautier felt that the theatre more than any other literary genre must be timely. Thus French Classicism regardless of its merits or its announcement of Romanticism was part of a past age and should be forsaken for a new form. Exclusive love of Corneille and Racine had indeed harmed the development of drama. Modernity of feeling and expression were essential to a progressive theatre, and in Gautier's opinion, the theatre must progress to stay alive. In an article written for *La Presse* in 1844 he noted that painters no longer created in the same manner as Masaccio, nor writers like Jodelle or Du Bartas, nor sculptors like the religious image-makers of the thirteenth century. Thus in drama, one cannot

---

[28] Gautier. "Pierre Corneille pour l'anniversaire de sa naissance," *Théâtre, mystère et ballets.* Nouvelle éd. (Paris: G. Charpentier, éditeur, 1882), p. 216.
[29] *Le Moniteur universel*, le 20 juillet 1857, cited by Richardson, p. 65.
[30] *La Presse*, le 23 jan. 1843, cited by Richardson, p. 66.

181

continue to produce the same play that the classicists did. One must progress, "marcher en avant," or die. (Richardson, p. 63)

Gautier supported every new poetic attempt in the theatre. One has only to remember his fierce defense of *Hernani*. He, as an artist, felt the importance of decor and the need for innovation in scenic art. Absolute freedom must be the playwright's legacy, he wrote. Art is a religion unto itself, free from politics, religion, or morals. With this understanding the playwright should be able to awaken the presently dormant dramatic art and bring about a new theatrical renaissance. Gautier hoped a dramatic flowering would soon occur. Until then he would wait patiently and confidently for great progress in drama.[31]

Gautier often expressed his belief that art must progress with the times if it were to survive. A work of art belonged not only to an author but to an age, reflecting a period's color. (Richardson, p. 69) The nineteenth century could be the source of great works of art, he contended, if artists would make the effort to extract its beauties from surrounding ugliness, if they would seek the necessary perspective to view their times. (Richardson, p. 134) The classical religion of beauty should be inspired by a contemporary spirit. One should take up the work of the Greeks and continue the hymn to human beauty with modern feeling and modern ideals, Gautier once wrote.[32] Timeliness is essential as the poem to Claudius Popelin written on the back of a copy of the magazine *La Mode* points out:

> Sous ce petit format commode
> Un grande problème est agité:
> On y cherche si la beauté
> Peut arranger avec la mode.
> Notre art, à tort, répète l'ode
> Que, dans sa blanche nudité
> Chanta la jeune antiquité;
> Il faut qu'au temps l'on s'accomode.

Romanticism was a timely art form, highly conscious of

---

[31] *Le Moniteur universel*, le 21 juillet 1862, cited by Richardson, p. 74.
[32] *La Presse*, le 3 avril 1844, cited by Richardson, p. 135.

being modern. It was a second Renaissance, a time in which the ideal of poetry was resurrected. In Gautier's opinion the era was also a second Elizabethan Age, for drama looked back to Shakespeare, not to Racine and the Greeks. Romanticism was an example of the occasional flowering of the arts with which history is marked. For a while at least Gautier felt its contribution, its progress, so important that he might have called it the fifth age of genius, following the times of Pericles, Augustus, Leo X, and Louis XIV.

It was Romanticism's freedom to explore the new in art which most captured Gautier's imagination. He frequently refers to the expansion of the artistic sphere during that period to embrace concepts previously considered non-aesthetic. Looking back on the era from his old age, Gautier, in the *Histoire du Romantisme* and in its appendix which significantly bears the title *Le Progrès de la poésie française* (1872), still viewed this movement with the enthusiasm of the supporter of *Hernani*.

> Ces jeunes bandes [the Romantics] . . . combattaient pour l'idéal, la poésie, et la liberté de l'art. Les générations actuelles doivent se figurer difficilement l'effervescence des esprits à cette époque; il s'opérait un mouvement pareil à celui de la Renaissance. Une sève de vie nouvelle circulait impétueusement. Tout germait, tout bourgeonnait, tout éclatait à la fois. Des parfums vertigineux se dégageaient des fleurs: l'air grisait, on était fou de lyrisme et d'art. Il semblait qu'on vînt de retrouver le grand secret perdu, et cela était vrai, on avait retrouvé la poésie. (*Hist.*, p. 1)

One of Romanticism's principle merits was that it had encouraged an inmixture of art in poetry. Thus its first adherents were often men like Gautier himself, painter and poet. By synthesizing, or at least by encouraging a cooperation between two art forms, an entire, new vista was opened to both writer and painter, affording the opportunity of immense progress in both their disciplines.

> Une foule d'objets, d'images, de comparaisons, qu'on croyait inéluctable au verbe, sont entrés dans la langue et y sont restés. La sphère de la littérature s'est élargie et renferme maintenant la sphère de l'art dans son orbe immense. (Cited by Vial, p. 158)

Language especially made progress. The restricted vocabulary of French classicism was no longer sufficient to express the great variety of new images and new sensations. By incorporating the fine arts into literature, one also had to incorporate their terminology. "Notre plus grand plaisir a été de transporter, dans notre art à nous, monuments, fresques, tableaux, statues, bas-reliefs, au risque souvent de forcer la langue et de changer le dictionnaire en palette."[33]

In the *Histoire* Gautier reviews the birth, growth, and regretfully the decline of Romanticism, speaking with first-hand knowledge of its members and their accomplishments. He sees as one lasting effect the influence of those great giants Hugo, Lamartine, Vigny, and Musset on the poets of the mid-nineteenth century. Reversing a previous opinion that each artist is so individual that he lea . es nothing of importance to those who follow him and that each creator must begin anew, Gautier here states that each succeeding artist contributes to a common stock of beauty which has been amassed over the ages by all creative men. In art, he states, one is always another man's son. (*Progrès*, p. 240)

Gautier singles out the important contributions to the stock of beauty of the Romantics writers. His inventory is so vast and complete that it would be impossible to recapitulate it here, but one can observe a sampling of his comments on better known figures to demonstrate his conviction that these men caused progress in art.

Chateaubriand is credited with many accomplishments of note but is praised mainly for his invention of melancholy, the modern passion, in his *René*. Gautier, like the other Romantics, was particularly struck by the addition of this new sentiment to literature, which contributed, he felt, to its progress. (*Hist.*, p. 19) Lamartine's discovery of the soul and its outpourings as a poetic theme was also an important innovation in the history of literature, hence a kind of progress. The appearance of his collection *Les Méditations* had great impact

---

[33] From *L'Artiste*, 1851, cit d by J. Giraud, *L'Ecole romantique française.* 6e éd. (Paris: Librairie Armand Colin, 1953), p. 94.

on literary thought because of its novelty. "Ce volume fut un événement rare dans les siècles. Il contenait tout un monde nouveau, monde de poésie plus difficile à trouver qu'une Amérique ou une Atlantide. . . . Il avait découvert l'âme."[34] Hugo, it will be remembered, was the Romantic par excellence for Gautier. He epitomized the freedom of the movement, daring to do what had never been done before. "Jamais l'inexprimable et ce qui n'avait jamais été pensé n'ont été réduits aux formules du language articulé, comme dit Homère, d'une façon plus hautaine et plus superbe," Gautier wrote of the "Légende des siècles," a comment he thought generally applicable to Hugo's total effort. (*Progrès*, p. 32)

The two authors who receive the greatest praise from Gautier were not members of the Romantic *Cénacle*, however, but the late-comers Balzac and Baudelaire who do bear the movement's imprint. Again, it is the timeliness, the extreme modernity of these writers which Gautier finds to be their most important and laudable characteristic, for it enables them to achieve literary progress.

In an article about the author of *La Comédie humaine* which appeared in *Portraits contemporains* in 1858 Gautier puts emphasis on Balzac's modernity.

On a fait nombre de critiques sur Balzac et parlé de lui de bien des façons, mais on n'a pas insisté sur un point très-caractéristique à notre avis;—ce point est la modernité absolue de son génie. Balzac ne doit rien à l'antiquité;—pour lui il n'y a ni Grecs ni Romains, et il n'a pas besoin de crier qu'on l'en délivre. On ne retrouve dans la composition de son talent aucune trace d'Homère, de Virgile, d'Horace, pas même du *de Viris illustribus*; personne n'a jamais été moins classique.[35]

To have started from scratch, so to speak, owing nothing to the past was an extremely difficult undertaking. When one has a model and explicit instructions to follow, the task of recreating beauty is much simpler. Usually one's models come

---

[34] Gautier. "Lamartine," *Portraits et souvenirs littéraires*, p. 171.
[35] Gautier. "Balzac," *Portraits contemporains*. 5e éd. (Paris: G. Charpentier et Cie, éditeurs, 1886), p. 107.

185

from the far-distant past, and time has allowed the important to disengage itself from the unimportant. An author like Balzac who ignores this easier way and sets off to explore on his own has only his genius as a guide and must himself impose perspective on all that surrounds him, doing in a moment the task of many years.

> Etre de son temps,—rien ne paraît plus simple et rien n'est plus malaisé! Ne porter aucunes lunettes ni bleues ni vertes, penser avec son propre cerveau, se servir de la langue actuelle, ne pas recoudre en centons les phrases de ses prédécesseurs! Balzac posséda ce rare mérite. ("Balzac," p. 107)

Unfortunately Balzac's talent had negative side effects. His profound comprehension and appreciation for the modern made him insensitive to antique beauty. Gautier remarks that Balzac in the Louvre was more attracted to the pretty young Parisian standing before the Venus de Milo than by the statue itself. Classical beauty was too serene and pure, too cold and simple, to appeal to a man of complicated and varied genius like Balzac. Still it must be remembered these faults were also the author's principle merits, and one cannot wholly criticize them. Sad as this blindspot may be to one who does appreciate classical art, one should admit that often great admiration for an artistic tradition becomes a stumbling block in the creation of the new. Thus Balzac was fortunate not to view reality through the lenses of antiquity. His freshness allowed him new discoveries, prepared him to make progress in art. ("Balzac," p. 109)

Important accomplishments of Balzac which Gautier considered a form of artistic progress were the new elements which he introduced to the genre of the novel: philosophical analysis and detailed descriptions of characters and decor. Because of their novelty they were not immediately understood by the public, more used to swift-moving plots than to word-pictures. Readers were irritated by the needless, they thought, interruption of the action. Only later did they understand the function of Balzac's analysis.

> Plus tard on reconnut que le but de l'auteur n'était pas de tisser des intrigues plus ou moins bien ourdies, mais de peindre la société

dans son ensemble du sommet à la base, avec son personnel et son mobilier, et l'on admira l'immense variété de ses types. ("Balzac," p. 78)

Gautier suggests that one may apply Alexandre Dumas' statement concerning Shakespeare to Balzac, "l'homme qui a le plus créé après Dieu," for never before had so many characters sprung from the brain of one man.

Baudelaire is admired by Gautier for his modernity which finds expression in "le style décadent."[36] In a principal essay on the poet of *Les Fleurs du mal* written in 1862 Gautier reiterates Hugo's observation that Baudelaire had indeed created "un frisson nouveau," but in a later *Portrait* (1875) Gautier expressed apprehension that perhaps Baudelaire had gone too far in his worship of strange and severe beauty. Here is an unusual manifestation of a Romantic fearing innovation which was generally accepted as a means to progress. Gautier in his more "reasonable" old age had perhaps grown too bourgeois for the decadent poet and thought excess, whether in the veneration of the past or in fascination with the future, to be dangerous to the health of art.

As Gautier had thought sculpture more suited to the "youth" of civilization, Baudelaire thought previous literature appropriate only for earlier ages. Mid-nineteenth century writing must reflect the values of the day, its sophistication and decline, not naïveté and vigor. Gautier explains Baudelaire's rejection of his predecessors' standards by a theory of the ages of man which owes much to the earlier doctrines of Pascal and Hugo. The ancients, he notes, lived in the youth of

---

[36] Van der Tuin traces the concept of "le style décadent" back to the German writer Otto Mann who spoke of an "Aesthetischer Spättypus," literally a late-comer or epigone, which Van der Tuin merely translates "type esthétique décadent." Van der Tuin defines decadence as the decline of an organism just after it has reached the culmination of its development. Gautier's own style is decadent, according to the critic, but it is Baudelaire and Verlaine who more fully develop the concept. Two of the main characteristics of decadence are negativism and isolation of the author which is usually expressed as hostility to his epoch. In Gautier traces of decadence are found in the poems "Melancolia" of 1834, "L'Ode à Jean Duseigneur" of 1831, and "La Comédie de la mort" of 1838.

the world when all was yet to be done. Simple geniuses spoke to simple, childlike peoples. Their utterances were then profound. Today, however, after centuries of development, evolution and/or progress, man and his civilization are much more complicated. The pronouncements of the past seem unfitting. By dint of their repeated use they have become worn-out clichés. A new and complicated genius is required to speak to modern, complex man. Art, reflecting this change, is now characterized by complexity, nuance, and subtlety.[37]

Gautier himself shared Baudelaire's belief in the ages of man and art as demonstrated by his article "Du Beau dans l'art" of 1847. Reviewing a number of leading aestheticians' statements on the nature of beauty, he devoted significant space to Winckelmann's theory that "l'unité et la simplicité sont les véritables sources de la beauté." Gautier felt that the German theorist was mistaken, at least in regards to modern art. Ancient art alone submitted to this standard. Modern creations sought the opposite qualities: richness, variety, ornateness, complexity, and affectation. These works were far from simple and yet they possessed beauty, equal, if not superior, to those of the past. As if speaking for Baudelaire as well as himself, Gautier contended:

[Winckelmann's theory] est fautive relativement à la peinture, à la poésie et surtout à la musique moderne, dont beaucoup de chefs-d'oeuvre sont compliqués et splendides. A ce point de vue, que deviendraient Rubens, Michel-Ange, Shakespeare et Beethoven, qui assurément ne sont pas si simples? ("Baud.," p. 168)

Simplicity alone is no virtue, he adds. If Winckelmann meant by it naturalness, again he was mistaken. "Beaucoup de gens

---

[37] Gautier, "Baudelaire," *Portraits et souvenirs*, pp. 168–169. By using the argument that each age of man had a peculiar literary expression Gautier took his place in a long tradition. To Pascal's theory of the ages of man Hugo had added that of corresponding ages of literature to justify Romantic drama. Baudelaire himself will make continued use of this reasoning to defend his decadence as appropriate for the twilight of civilization. It is with Baudelaire that the association of progress with increased complexity receives its fullest expression.

ont cette qualité dans une organisation médiocre et alors ils sont naturellement plats, voilà tout."[38] Gautier does not go so far as to say that nineteenth-century art is the greatest ever.[39] But he does admit it represents a high point possible only at times of extreme maturity as seen in the art of comparable periods such as the late Roman Empire, the Byzantine era, and late Greek history.[40] Decadence occurs when the factitious life replaces the natural life, when new seeds spring up within man. In trying to satisfy these new longings, art by invention does make progress. "Il exprime des idées neuves avec des formes nouvelles et des mots qu'on n'a pas entendus." ("Baud.," p. 172) In opposition to the classical, decadent style adds shadows, superstition, phantoms, remorse, and nightmares to the artist's storehouse. The negative, an extension of Hugo's grotesque, is allowed expression in art. Baudelaire especially developed these traits,

---

[38] In an earlier essay, however, Gautier maintained the opposite point of view. In "Civilisation et les arts plastiques" he explained that art, like nature, develops by passing from the complex to the simple, citing as an example of this strange comparison a Hindu god and a Greek one. Perfection, he claims, aims at economy of material and harmony of lines. Art's goal is to make the most out of the least. This point of view obviously reflects Gautier's philosophy at the most intense period of his support of art for art's sake.

[39] Gautier is less committed to the idea of the superiority of being timely than Baudelaire. He adopts the poet's view that civilization passes through phases corresponding to the times of day and that art should be appropriate for its epoch, e.g., innocence in a sophisticated world is out of place. But Gautier refuses to say a later era is superior to a former one. "Sans disserter vainement pour savoir si l'on doit préférer l'aurore au crépuscule," he writes, "il faut peindre à l'heure où l'on se trouve et avec une palette chargée des couleurs nécessaires pour rendre les effets que cette heure amène. Le couchant n'a-t-il pas sa beauté comme le matin? . . . [Its colors] n'offrent-ils pas autant de poésie que l'Aurore aux doigts de rose, que nous ne voulons pas mépriser cependant?" ("Baud.," p. 169)

[40] Gautier saw a direct resemblance between Latin and French decadence. "Ne semble-t-il pas au lecteur, comme à moi, que la langue de la dernière décadence latine—suprême soupir d'une personne robuste déjà transformée et préparée pour la vie spirituelle—est singulièrement propre à exprimer la passion telle que l'a comprise et sentie le monde poétique moderne?" ("Baud.," p. 174) Gautier also notes a certain improvement in modern decadence over the Latin form, at least in comparing Baudelaire to Catullus. The latter knew only sensuality and brutality, whereas the former displays a keener sense of beauty and heightened sensitivity.

he believed. He pushed back the frontiers of artistic expression. He devised a language of extreme richness which was composed of borrowings from every form of art in order to express the inexpressible, to capture the neurotic mood of the times.

> [His style forced itself] à rendre la pensée dans ce qu'elle a de plus ineffable, et la forme en ses contours les plus vagues et les plus fuyants, écoutant pour les traduire les confidences subtiles de la névrose, les aveux de la passion vieillissante qui se déprave et les hallucinations bizarres de l'idée fixe tournant à la folie. Ce style de décadence est le dernier mot du Verbe sommé de tout exprimer et poussé à l'extrême outrance. ("Baud.," p. 171)

Gautier's enthusiasm for Baudelaire's triumphs with "le style décadent . . . le dernier mot du Verbe sommé de toute exprimer et poussé à l'extrême outrance"—doubtless evidence of literary progress—confirms the author's belief in the phenomenon. Thus Gautier must be counted among the moderns in the continuing quarrel. Although Gautier recognized in the achievements of other writers and artists further proof that art can progress, he did not believe improvement had been universal or regular. Sculpture had remained a peculiarly Greek form, he would have noted, and the Middle Ages contributed little to art's advance. Thus artistic progress has been uneven and sporadic. Nevertheless Gautier took special pride in the unparalleled contributions of his age to the arts brought about in the main through the newly encouraged cooperation of heretofore separate disciplines. Keenly aware of the importance of artistic reciprocity—photography's service to painting, literature's encouragement of landscape painting, the fusing of palette and dictionary, uniquely nineteenth-century accomplishments—Gautier believed the status of art to have recently been significantly elevated. In addition, the nineteenth-century artist, that curious combination of martyr and god, seemed to Gautier especially capable of profiting from the increased aesthetic opportunities this second Renaissance afforded. Thus Gautier prefigures Baudelaire as champion of "le beau moderne," the new beauty which only such a rich, complex, artificial, and sophisticated age could produce. Yet Gautier was never chauvinistic nor fanatically anti-ancient in his preferences. His appreciation of beauty remained universal. New art, even if superior, can never replace what has come before, he had argued; it can only complement the masterpieces of the past. By doing so, the progress of art will be assured.

Chapter Ten
Balzac

Balzac's optimism concerning the progress of mankind and the arts unequivocably ranks him among nineteenth-century moderns, for he believed both man and art perfectible to a degree, if not continuously and indefinitely.[1] Balzac's statements on progress are not consistent, however, nor do they form an organized treatise on the subject. At times the novelist appears to damn his epoch and its art as much as he lauds them. Yet one discovers that for every loss he takes note of in the history of man, Balzac can point out more than compensating additions.

Balzac's faith in progress is derived from an overwhelming self-confidence. His enormous ambition—to do what had never been done before, to erect a literary monument of immense proportions which would house an entire epoch, an entire society—attests to the fact that Balzac believed in artistic, i.e., literary, progress because he thought himself capable of accomplishing it. Balzac's view of man's perfectibility was

---

[1] An earlier version of this chapter entitled "Balzac on the Novel or An Immodest Proposal of Literary Progress," appeared in *WSU Research Studies*, September 1980, Vol. 48, No. 3, pp. 152–161.

not as certain. He recognized an intellectual advance, but with it came moral corruption, he believed. Yet in his optimistic way he felt that Good with the aid of religion would triumph over Evil, and perhaps from learning the moral lessons contained in his works, mankind could create a better future. Representative statements revealing Balzac's divided opinion concerning human progress are to be found in the preface to the first edition of *La Peau de chagrin* of 1830 and in the *Avant-propos de la Comédie humaine* of 1842. In the first instance there is only pessimism that man is eternally condemned to retrace the footsteps of his ancestors, never rising from the rut, "le cercle éternel dans lequel l'esprit humain tourne comme un cheval de manège."[2] A more cheerful view is expressed in the *Avant-propos* where Balzac argues against Rousseau's thesis that innocent man is corrupted by evil society. Here Balzac claims that man, neither good nor bad but a mixture of the two, is perfected by social institutions, especially the Church. He writes:

L'homme n'est ni bon ni méchant, il naît avec des instincts et des aptitudes; la Société, loin de le dépraver, comme l'a prétendu Rousseau, le perfectionne, le rend meilleur mais l'intérêt développe alors énormément ses penchants mauvais. Le christianisme, et surtout le catholicisme, étant, comme je l'ai dit dans le *Médecin de campagne*, un système complet de répression des tendances dépravées de l'homme, est le plus grand élément de l'Ordre-Social.[3]

It is also each man's task to perfect himself in this life and the next as well, Balzac believed. Society as a whole is neither good nor bad, it merely reflects the vice or virtue of its members. "Je ne partage pas la croyance à un progrès indéfini, quant aux Sociétés," he once remarked, "je crois aux progrès

---

[2] Balzac. *La Comédie humaine*. Texte établi par Marcel Bouteron. Ed. de la Pléiade. (Paris: Gallimard, 1955), XI, 176. In this instance the circle which symbolized progress for both Goethe and Vigny is employed by Balzac to signify the opposite, man's unchanging imperfection. Balzac's circle is fixed in size, neither rising heavenwards nor expanding. It is the "vicious circle" of human history, the expression of an early but profound pessimism.

[3] Balzac. *Oeuvres complètes*. Texte révisé et annoté par Marcel Bouteron et Henri Longnon. (Paris: Louis Conard, libraire-éditeur, 1935), I, xxx.

de l'homme sur lui-même." (*O.C.*, I, xxxiv) Balzac nevertheless believed that civilization had followed a progressive path. He wrote to Mme Hanska in 1833 that recent political turmoil threatened to halt this advancement. "Et puis," he lamented, "les événements sont si sombres autour de moi et de mes amis! La civilisation est menacée; les arts, les sciences, les progrès sont menacés."[4]

Balzac saw the work of art as an instrument of progress. Adopting the socialistic attitude of other Romantics, he felt it his duty to bring man to a better life. Turning again to the *Avant-propos* one finds him speaking of the artist as a prophet and a priest. (*O.C.*, I, xxx) The novelist especially was to point the way to progress by creating artistically the utopia which man had not yet been able to achieve in reality, an idea borrowed from Mme de Staël.

> L'histoire n'a pas pour lui, comme le roman, de tendre vers le *beau idéal*. L'histoire est ou devrait être ce qu'elle fut; tandis que *le roman doit être le monde meilleur,* a dit Mme Necker, un des esprits les plus distingués du dernier siècle. (*O.C.*, I, xxxiii)

Balzac hoped that his works by reflecting the imperfections of present-day society would induce men to correct them. By mirroring vice he would encourage virtue. "Parmi les ambitions de ce prodigieux créateur," writes Pierre Moreau, "la plus chère a peut-être été d'agir sur le monde réel."[5]

The key to Balzac's view of aesthetic progress is his belief that by pioneering new endeavors in the arts one made progress, a typically Romantic belief. Balzac himself felt that he had perfected literature by filling in lacunae which existed in the tradition. Whoever forges ahead, be he pioneer, explorer, discoverer, or military leader, is an artist in Balzac's opinion. The true creator is one who goes beyond others' limitations and conquers the new. An early indication of this philosophy is contained in the essay "Des Artistes" of 1830.

Ainsi de Guttenberg, de Colomb, de Schwartz, de Descartes, de

---

[4] Balzac. *Lettres à l'Etrangère.* (Paris: Calmann-Lévy, éditeurs, 1906–1950), I, 4.

[5] *Le Romantisme.* (Paris: J. de Gigord, éditeur, 1932), p. 4.

Raphaël, de Voltaire, de David. Tous étaient artistes, car ils créaient; ils appliquaient la pensée à une production nouvelle des forces humaines, à une combinaison neuve des éléments de la nature, ou physique ou morale. Un artiste tient par un fil plus ou moins délié, par une accession plus ou moins intime, au mouvement qui se prépare. Il est parti nécessaire d'une immense machine, soit qu'il conserve une doctrine, soit qu'il fasse un progrès de plus à l'ensemble de l'art. (*O.C.*, XXXVIII, 351–352)

Applying this logic Balzac could say that Napoleon was the equal of Homer, for both created great battles. Chateaubriand was called as great a painter as Raphaël, despite differences in their materials. (*O.C.*, XXXVIII, 354) In turn Balzac compared himself with Napoleon, hoping to achieve by the pen what the emperor had done with the sword.[6] The artist then was a great achiever. He was also a prophet, and like the latter was a man who suffered. Balzac pictured the writer as a Christ figure, drawing many parallels. First of all he was misunderstood and rejected by his times and could only hope for future vindication. (*O.C.*, xxxviii, 357) Like the Christ, the artist had to die to be reborn, forsaking ordinary existence for a more elevated one, sacrificing everyday pleasure for an immortal reputation. Like the Messiah, the artist was to lead men to perfection. Both were called by God to communicate truth to their fellow men, to lift man's gaze beyond his limited horizons, to show him the path of progress.

En effet, avant tout, l'artiste est l'apôtre de quelque vérité, l'organe du Très Haut qui se sert de lui, pour donner un développement nouveau à l'oeuvre que nous accomplissons tous aveuglément.(*Ibid.*)

The dichotomy of the artist's situation —his intellectual superiority, his semi-divinity on the one hand, his social inferiority, his persecution on the other—troubled Balzac like other Romantics. Not only in the essay on artists but throughout the author's writings recur complaints that the artist was unappreciated and unprotected. Balzac nostalgically remem-

---

6 "Lettre adressée aux écrivains français," 1834, *O.C.*, XXXIX, 648. In *César Birotteau*, 1838, Balzac writes "Troie et Napoléon ne sont que des poèmes." Plé., V, 367.

bers pre-Revolutionary France, when the Monarchy and the Church ruled supreme, for then the artist was patronized and honored. (*O.C.*, XXXVIII,352) On the contrary, in the industrial and bourgeois society of early nineteenth-century France, Balzac complained, the artist seemed forced to exert as much effort in eking out a living as he did in the creation of art. As late as 1840 in the preface to *Pierrette* he points this out:

> [J'ai] déjà fait observer que nous ne sommes plus dans ces époques où les artistes pouvaient s'enfermer, vivre paisiblement, à l'écart, et sortir de leur solitude armés d'un ouvrage entièrement fait, et qui se publiait en entier, comme les oeuvres de Gibbon, de Montesquieu, de Hume, etc. Au lieu de vivre pour la science, pour l'art, pour les lettres, on est obligé de faire des lettres, de l'art et de la science pour vivre, ce qui est contraire à la production des belles oeuvres. (Plé. XI, 393)

Even worse than forcing the artist to work for a living, Balzac added, the public now thinks of his profession as a trade, his creations as products. Industrialism is the culprit in the cheapening of art, Balzac frequently asserted, as in *Béatrix* in 1839. Mass production has replaced craftmanship, revealing the incursion of a manufacturing mentality among artists themselves. (Plé. II, 320)

Ambivalence Toward the Times; Confidence that Progress Is Possible

Balzac's complaints against his era should be viewed in the light of a statement by Lamartine, one of the most fervent supporters of progress. All thinking men disparage the present, Lamartine had remarked to the Academy. Critics of the nineteenth century merely followed a tradition of preferring what is not to what is. It is much easier to idealize the past or future, whereas the present with its faults and assets must be seen more objectively. Lamartine had added that despite its failing the nineteenth century should be granted preeminence over preceding epochs. Its accomplishments were great, its array of talent vast. Balzac adheres to this point of view. Not blindly optimistic, his nature was nevertheless sanguine.

In a series of articles in 1830 Balzac vented his spleen against the failings of the era. Far from proclaiming that literature was enjoying unparalleled success, he lamented its sterility and lack of authors. The crisis was to be blamed in part on political events which had distracted the writer and involved him too much in contemporary affairs. *Engagement* should be held within proper limits, he advocated: the artist is primarily a creator of beauty, then a prophet and moralizer. A second cause of sterility was the lack of new plots and characters. In the essay "De la mode en littérature" he states that "nous avons fatigué toutes les situations, et nous voulons du drame." (*O.C.*,XXXIX, 41)

If one takes literally Balzac's comments that plots have been used up, the theory of progress is seriously questioned. The ancients had long argued that there was nothing new under the sun, that all plots, all characters had long ago been created. If one must grant that this is true, then to preserve a belief in progress, one must argue that even if the artist is forced to use the same material, he can possibly surpass his predecessors by his more skillful handling of it. Balzac later claims to have done just that. On the other hand he did not really believe that there are no new subjects in art. He felt that by portraying modern society he had found new plots and characters to be exploited, not heretofore dealt with by writers.

In the case of repetition of characters and plots Balzac displays confidence in having improved on his model in the "Note de la première édition des *Scènes de la vie privée*" of 1830. Balzac had been attacked for expropriating another writer's plot. He defended himself by counter-attacking that too much insistence on the new in art can be as harmful as doggedly maintaining the status quo. The thirst for novelty had caused some writers to seek the extraordinary, the bizarre, the weird simply for the sake of being different. They had gone beyond the boundaries of clarity and naturalness, the unchanging limits of art, Balzac then argued. (Plé., XI, 164) Restricting oneself to the logical bounds of innovation, one can still improve on what has come before. Thus, as in this particular case, the use of another's plot is inconsequential, if the borrower improves its quality. Balzac justified his plagiarism by claiming to have done just that. By giving more attention to details he had improved upon his model. How ironic that personal pique motivated Balzac to draw attention to his use of detailed descriptions, thus obliquely announcing the way to realism.

La marque distinctive du talent est sans doute l'invention. Mais aujourd'hui que toutes les combinaisons possibles paraissent épuisées, que toutes les situations ont été fatiguées, que l'impossible a été tenté, l'auteur croit fermement que les détails constitueront désormais le mérite des ouvrages improprement appelés *Romans*. (Plé. XI, 165)

A second example of Balzac's conviction that he could improve on older works by changing the emphasis in them or by adding new elements is to be found in his comments on Molière. This playwright was Balzac's chief mentor, his most venerated predecessor. In 1825 in *La Vie de Molière* Balzac had written that no writer had ever surpassed Molière in the creation of comedy. Molière is more natural and gay than Aristophanes, more decent than Terrence in the comedy of manners, better than Plautus in the comedy of situations, he eulogized. (*O.C.*, XXXVIII, 144)

The lack of comedy in nineteenth-century French literature elicited constant complaint from the novelist. In a note attached to *La Fille aux yeux d'or* of 1835 Balzac criticized the Romantics for neglecting both tragedy and comedy to create a genre which had the merits of neither. He blamed society's metamorphosis into a classless amalgam for having removed a vital source of the comic. (Plé. XI, 199) He felt that writers neglected other comic elements in their preoccupation with the grotesque.[7] As late as 1845 he complains that there are now only comic possibilities among criminal types, justifying his inclusion of the prostitute in his literary panorama. (Plé. XI, 418) Thus Molière's achievements had certainly not been surpassed.

---

[7] From *Complaintes satiriques*, cited by Geneviève Delattre. *Les Opinions littéraires de Balzac*. (Paris: Presses Universitaires de France, 1961), p. 82.

In matters not related to the comic, however, Molière's works could be improved upon. The earlier writer's characters needed perfecting, he remarked. In a letter to Mme Hanska in 1837 he spoke of a play then in process entitled "La Première Demoiselle ou l'Ecole des Ménages." The very title suggests Molière. In this work Balzac would present a female Tartuffe and portray the husband as the adulterer, two important innovations in his opinion. By making the hypocrite a woman the author felt her power over the character representing Orgon would be more credible. He brags to Mme Hanska:

> Personne n'a encore pensé à mettre à la scene l'adultère du mari, et ma pièce est basée sur cette grave affaire de notre civilisation moderne. . . . Personne n'a encore songé à faire un Tartuffe femelle, et [la] maîtresse [du mari] sera Tartuffe en jupons; mais on concevra bien plus l'empire de la première demoiselle sur le maître, qu'on ne conçoit celui de Tartuffe sur Orgon, car les moyens de domination sont bien plus naturels et compréhensibles. (*Etr.* I, 381)

A further improvement of Tartuffe is suggested some years later when Balzac states his intention to expose the hypocrite in all situations rather than in one alone as Molière had done. With the growth of society had come a proliferation of hypocrisy, Balzac explained to Mme Hanska, offering more opportunity for depiction. His work *Le Grand artiste* would present the more complex modern equivalent, the "Tartuffe-Démocrate-Philanthrope." Balzac also intended to incorporate in his work material Molière had relegated to the *avant-scène*, a fault which needed correcting, in his opinion. (*Etr.* II, 258) Balzac's "superior" version of the play is referred to a third time in the dedication to the *Bourgeois de Paris* of 1844. Here Balzac speaks of having bettered the work by ridding it of religious overtones which were offensive and distracted from its merit. (*Etr.* II, 270)

The mixed opinion of Balzac toward his time is further substantiated in the preface to *La Peau de chagrin* of 1830. In keeping with his remarks on Molière, Balzac first laments the incompleteness of the literary atmosphere of the day, then suggests how it can be rectified. He indicates that the modern cannot only correct the mistakes of his time but surpass his predecessors in achievement.

Frequently Balzac's claims to progress were sparked by criticism of his works. In the preface mentioned above Balzac defends his *Physiologie du mariage* against the accusation that it was immoral. Its ribald gaiety can be justified in remembering the prevalence of such a tone in the eighteenth century, he explains. Balzac claims to have turned back to a century to recapture this spirit lost since the Revolution. Literature was better then in many respects, he remarks, for authors were not so preoccupied with discoursing on their art as with creating. Balzac's complaint against most Romantics' noisy impotence is contrasted with his own sense of achievement. He especially found Romantic theatre to be substandard and Hugo more a theoretician than an accomplished playwright.

> L'auteur de ce livre cherche à favoriser la réaction littéraire que préparent certains bons esprits ennuyés de notre vandalisme actuel, et fatigués de voir amonceler tant de pierres sans qu'aucun monument surgisse. (Plé. XI, 176)

Here Balzac is attacking the public's taste for horrors and the grotesque which he thought an inacceptable innovation in literature, novelty for its own sake. He preferred satire to sadism.

Balzac's opinion of his contemporaries was never very high. Certainly his personal knowledge of the authors colored his estimation of their works, this being particularly true of Hugo and Sainte-Beuve.[8] As a result of his pessimism concerning the contemporary scene Balzac stated that if the masterpieces of the past had not been created already, it would be impossible to produce them now, for an artist must be inspired by beauty in order to create, and the nineteenth century was singularly lacking in this quality. Poetry had already fallen victim to the ugliness of the age. It had forsaken the bourgeois, workaday world and taken refuge in a more glorious past,

---

[8] He speaks disparagingly of Hugo, Lamartine, and Musset in a letter to Mme Hanska in 1838. They are only "la monnaie d'un poète, car aucun d'eux n'est complet." (*Etr.* I, 503)

Balzac, like Musset before him, complained. Consequently the artist instead of creating beauty now only mocks the ugliness about him. Mockery is characteristic of the literature of a dying society, the novelist believed.[9] Literature as well as society was moribund, Balzac warned in the *avertissement des Contes drôlatiques* of 1830. The introductory remarks to this collection, credited to the publisher but actually penned by the author, epitomize the most pessimistic pronouncement of any ancient.

Aussi, plus nous allons vers le terme auquel meurent les littératures, mieux nous sentons le prix de ces oeuvres antiques où respire le parfum d'une naïveté jeune et où se trouvent le nerf comique dont notre théâtre est privé, l'expression vive et drue qui peint sans périphrase, et que personne n'ose plus *oser*. (Plé. XI, 433)

In his usual manner Balzac quickly qualifies his pessimism, however. By writing the *Contes* he had proven that naïveté and comedy were not impossible in the nineteenth century. If other artists like Balzac would " dare to dare," the lacunae of the era could be filled and present literature rid of its inferiority.

It is interesting to note that Balzac is not referring to classical antiquity in the quotation above but to the late Middle Ages of France and Italy. It is more often Rabelais and Boccacio who win his praise than Homer or Virgil. His concern was with modernity, the present. Gautier had noted an absence of feeling for antiquity and had remarked that Balzac went to the Louvre not to view the Venus de Milo, but the pretty young Parisian who admired the statue. The living being was Balzac's model, with its imperfections and variety, not an idealized replica of beauty preserved through the ages.[10]

---

[9] Accepting the fact that the present is unpoetic, Balzac can nevertheless work within this limitation and create art from his environment. "A une époque comme celle-ci," he wrote in the preface to *La Femme supérieure* in 1838, "où tout s'analyse et s'examine, où il n'y a plus de foi ni pour le prêtre ni pour le poète, où l'on abjure aujourd'hui ce qu'on chantait hier, la poésie est impossible. [L'auteur] a cru qu'il n'y avait plus d'autre merveilleux que la description de la grande maladie sociale, elle ne pouvait être dépeinte, le malade étant la maladie." (Plé. XI, 361)

[10] Balzac even preferred modern sculpture to the Greeks'. He wrote to

Because of this overwhelming love for modernity and corresponding lack of appreciation for antiquity, one can readily understand Balzac's preference for relative beauty, which he credits the Chinese with having originated, instead of absolute beauty, whose origin was Greek. By breaking away from a limited concept of one true form to recognizing at least some elements of beauty in a variety of form, the modern artist has a richer source for art than the ancient. Balzac's antipathy for the Greeks' narrowness of view is evident when, reviewing a book on China in 1842, he wrote:

> L'art grec était réduit à la répétition d'idées, en définitive très pauvres, n'en déplaise aux classiques. . . . Le Beau n'a qu'une statue, il n'a qu'un temple, il n'a qu'un livre, il n'a qu'une pièce; l'*Iliade* a été recommencée trois fois, on a perpétuellement copié les statues grecques, on a reconstruit le même temple à satiété, la même tragédie a marché sur la scène avec les mêmes mythologies, à donner des nausées. (*O.C.*, XXXX, 545)

The Chinese had dismissed the idea of one beauty and recognized the immense possibilities for art in the exploitation of the ugly or the grotesque, as Balzac preferred to call it. European adoption of this point of view allowed for the variety of medieval art which Hugo wished to recapture by mingling the sublime and the grotesque. It also prefigures Baudelaire's determination to exploit the artistic possibilities of the ugly. This extension of artistic boundaries, the awakening of modern man's sensitivity to all sorts and conditions of beauty, fragmented and unequilibrated as they may be, is an example of re ent progress in art, Balzac like Gautier believed.

Balzac's coolness towards classical antiquity is reflected in his disdain of Greek mythology. Somewhat more tolerant than Chateaubriand, for Balzac did admit the eternal verity of the myths, he was in full agreement with the author of *Le Génie* that they had no place in modern literature. One could not

---

Mme Hanska in 1834 that a contemporary statue, *La Pudeur*, "écrasait l'antique." (*Etr.* I, 158) In 1845 he repeated his preference by declaring that the ancients were in no way superior to contemporaries such as David and Etex in the art of sculpture. (*Etr.* III, 27)

impose the point of view of earliest man on the citizen of the nineteenth century, for life had changed too much, he felt, to express the soul of modern Christian man in terms of pagan antiquity. (*Etr.* I, 203)

Preparation of *La Comédie humaine:*
Improvement Through Innovation

It was not until 1842 that Balzac presented to the public a concise statement of his aims in creating the mass of works which he entitled *La Comédie humaine*, although prefigurations of his manifesto were numerous in the preceding decade and a half. These statements which comprise his literary theory help to explain his belief in artistic progress.

Balzac took credit for having personally caused progress in literature. He felt that in being a secretary to his epoch he was bringing up to date literary depiction of social history. In that his era was more civilized and more complex than any of the past, showing the result of progress in other fields, his portrait of it would have the same qualities.

Balzac did not claim to be creating a new genre but saw himself as a continuer and improver of a long tradition. As early as 1833 he had begun to recognize his task and to envision his course of action. In *La Théorie de la démarche* of that year, he wrote:

Il y a dans tous les siècles un homme de génie qui se fait le secrétaire de son époque: Homère, Aristote, Tacite, Shakespeare, L'Arétin, Machiavel, Rabelais, Bacon, Molière, Voltaire ont tenu la plume sous la dictée de leurs siècles. (*O.C.*, XXXIX, 625)

To this series his own name was to be added. Balzac's self-esteem was considerable to have ranked himself with the most eminent representatives of both the ancients and the moderns. It reveals an ego which fully believed that if literary progress were possible, it would be accomplished by his own hand. Balzac, like Hugo, considered himself elected to his task. Modesty could have no place in the accomplishment of a divine duty, both seemed to have believed.

As secretary to nineteenth-century France, Balzac envisioned his undertaking as different from his forerunners'. To keep abreast of the times, he would have to make certain innovations. He contends, for example, that no previous writer had fully utilized the literary potential of the French provinces and provincials. Having created a work such as *Eugénie Grandet* he had corrected this omission. Writers had overlooked this vast source because they had assumed that life outside of Paris was too tranquil, too monotonous, too humdrum to be of interest to literature. Little did they realize the possibility that "tumultuous passion" could be at play beneath a placid surface. "Aucun poète n'a tenté de décrire les phénomènes de cette vie qui s'en va, s'adoucissant toujours. Pourquoi non?" he asks. There is poetry in Touraine as well as in the Ile de France. (Plé. XI, 200)

With the passing of the years Balzac's conception of his total masterpiece became increasingly clear. He adds to his list of predecessors Petronius, who described the private lives of the Romans, although partially Balzac adds, and L'Abbé Barthélemy, who in the eighteenth century tried to reconstruct Grecian customs in his *Voyage du jeune Anarchasis en Grèce* (1788), also an incomplete attempt. More successful than either of these writers was Dante, who came to represent for Balzac a chief model and rival. Dante's universe was complete. It housed the most prominent figures of antiquity and the Middle Ages. He had portrayed the vices and virtues of his times in greatest detail.

Because of his admiration for the Florentine, Balzac came to view his own work as the modern equivalent of the *Commedia*. Paris—smoky, crowded, and above all wicked—was a new inferno. Vautrin and Père Goriot's daughters revealed the same evil, the same lack of human compassion which characterized certain of Dante's condemned. In the early pages of *La Fille aux yeux d'or* of 1835 Balzac makes the comparison most clearly: "Nous sommes arrivés au troisième cercle de cet enfer, qui, peut-être un jour aura son Dante."[11]

---

[11] (Plé. X, 262) The idea of surpassing Dante is even more clearly expressed in *Splendeurs et misères des courtisanes* where Balzac refers to Esther

Just as Dante had encompassed his age in the *Divine Comedy* Balzac wished to incorporate nineteenth-century France in his human one. The vastness of the ambition is striking. Balzac was not deterred by the enormity of the task, however. "Souvenez-vous seulement," he wrote in the preface to the *Scènes de la vie parisienne*, "que l'auteur veut tout peindre du XIXe siècle et faire en quelque sorte un état de situation de ses vices et vertus." (Plé. XI, 253) The totality of the work is stressed once again in the preface to *Père Goriot.*

> Le plan général qui lie ses oeuvres les unes aux autres . . . l'oblige [Balzac] de tout peindre . . . enfin de saisir la paternité tout entière comme il essaie de représenter les sentiments humains, les crises sociales, tout le pêle-mêle de la civilisation. (Plé. XI, 263)

Balzac's tendency to see himself as a second Dante was only reinforced by his mystical leanings. His study of Swedenborg and its reflection in his works, e.g., *Louis Lambert, Séraphita, La Recherche de l'absolu,* indicate a desire to recreate *il Paradiso* as well as *l'Inferno* by portraying the search for higher reality, for the absolute, which possessed so many of his characters. Balzac's mystical interests primarily reflect a peculiar bent of his personality; nevertheless he spoke of exploiting them in literature to fill a long-neglected gap, another indication of progress to be achieved. In the preface to *Le Livre mystique* of 1835 Balzac reveals his determination to bring mystical literature up to date.

> L'auteur n'a pas cru qu'il fût honorable pour la littérature française de rester muette sur une poésie aussi grandiose que l'est celle des Mystiques. La France littéraire porte depuis cinq siècles une couronne à laquelle manque un fleuron, si cette lacune n'était remplie même imparfaitement comme elle le sera par ce livre. Après de longs et de patients travaux, l'auteur s'est donc hasardé dans la plus difficile des entreprises, celle de peindre l'être parfait dans les conditions exigées par les lois de Swedenbourg sévèrement appliquées. (Plé. XI, 270)

Gobseck's face as she falls victim to Vautrin as having "une expression que Dante a oubliée, et qui surpassait les inventions de son Enfer." The interior conflict of Honorine's husband is called "un cercle oublié par Dante dans son Enfer." (Delattre, p. 19)

By writing *Le Livre mystique,* Balzac pointedly remarks, he had created a work "comme une nouvelle divine comédie." (Plé., XI, 271)

The Balzacian ego which accounts for the grandiose quality of his works also explains his tendency to magnify a personal situation into a historical phenomenon. His work was the history of an epoch; his book on mysticism a long overdue necessity. Therefore one is not surprised to discover that he considered his personal misfortunes great enough to slow the march of all humanity, and he defended himself against critics in the name of progress:

> Quoique mes adversaires ne méritent pas cet honneur, leurs attaques forment une page trop curieuse dans l'histoire littéraire, et prouvent trop contre les progrès de l'esprit humain en mettant nu les passions misérables qui, de tous les temps, ont assailli les artistes, pour ne pas me faire souhaiter que le livre soit beau afin que la vengeance soit éternelle. (Plé. XI, 283)

When ridiculed for pretentiously signing his works "de Balzac," he justified himself by naming Molière and Voltaire, his models, who had abandoned such drab names as Arouet and Poquelin when they chose to depict their times. As their equal, Balzac belonged to that special status of artist, the genius who lives above human laws and standards. One should understand that such men are entitled to "toutes les audaces." (Plé. XI, 291) One is immediately reminded of Hugo and his egotism. That both writers compared themselves to Napoleon or suffered from a Promethean complex was not by accident. They epitomize the idealized image of the artist as a god, the most cherished myth of the Romantics.[12] Thus one can understand some of their contemporaries' acceptance of

---

[12] In Maurice Schroder's *Icarus, the Image of the Artist in French Romanticism* (Cambridge, Mass.: Harvard University Press, 1961) much attention is paid to the Romantic concept of the artist as a deity. He cites as an example Hugo's belief that the poet reigns over humanity when he has succeeded in portraying it, expressed in "Les Souffrances de l'inventeur" of 1843. Likewise, Balzac expressed his power complex by shaping the lives of his characters when unable to control humanity directly. Both associated themselves with Prometheus, the symbol of human progress, for being a god they could bring light to humanity and liberate him from error. (Schroder, pp. 97–98)

the idea of progress. Humanity now had gods capable of achieving it.

Besides having included provincial life and characters in literature Balzac claims to have made another innovation in the art of letters, that of including the bourgeoisie, heretofore dismissed as too unexciting to be of interest in fiction. Not only had he introduced the social class as a whole into literature but he had even chosen certain of its members as heroes.[13] In the novel *César Birotteau* of 1838 Balzac draws attention to this progress.

Puisse cette histoire être le poème des vicissitudes bourgeoises auxquelles nulle voix n'a songé, tant elles semblent dénuées de grandeur, tandis qu'elles sont au même titre immense: il ne s'agit pas d'un seul homme ici, mais de tout un peuple de douleurs. (Plé. V, 367)

One's attention is drawn to Balzac's emphasis on size. Not only does he vaunt his additions to literature but adds that they are grander and more inclusive than other writers'.

Increased Belief in the Superiority of the Century and of Its Literature

Balzac's concern for, and sensitivity to, size was rooted in his conception of nineteenth-century civilization. He was most impressed by its grandeur, its determination to make things bigger and better than before. Extending this feeling to the artistic realm he felt that literary creations of the nineteenth century were also greater in scope and number than ever before. It must be remembered that at the same time Balzac blamed his times for crassness and materialism which led to the neglect of art and the artist. But more frequently he lauded his times, joining the Romantic chorus which spoke of a new Renaissance. One finds a very clear example of his dual attitude in the "Lettre addressée aux écrivains français" of 1834 where first complaining that "à nulle époque l'artiste ne fut moins protégé" he ends by boasting that "nul siècle n'a eu de masses plus intelligentes; en aucun temps la pensée n'a été si puissante." (*O.C.*, XXXIX, 644) As a result of man's intellectual progress, artistic output had also increased. "Notre siècle en produit autant qu'en produit le plus littéraire des siècles passés, n'en déplaise à la critique," he wrote referring to the "belles oeuvres littéraires" of his time. (O.C., XXXIX, 650) When Mme Hanska showed a preference for the past he was quick to rebuke her. "Notre dix-neuvième siècle sera bien grand," he wrote in 1835; "il y a un déluge de talents." (Etr. I, 245) Three years later he scolded her for having called the century stupid and for having remarked that only Napoleon was great. Balzac drew up an enormous list of important figures in the arts, sciences, and military to convince Mme Hanska that the nineteenth century was far from stupid. (Etr. I, 503)

Unashamedly crediting his work with greater grandeur than his predecessors', Balzac attributed this to the basic character of his era. He named his *Un grand homme de province à Paris* (1839) superior to works of the preceding two centuries because it reflected a superior age.

Le sujet a l'étendue de l'époque elle-même. Le Turcaret de Lesage, le Philinte et le Tartuffe de Molière, le Figaro de Beaumarchais et le Scapin du vieux théâtre, tous ces types s'y trouveraient agrandis de la grandeur de notre siècle. (Plé XI, 338–339)

Balzac goes beyond French literature and considers himself superior to the author of the *Arabian Nights* because his task was greater, French society being more vast and complex than its Middle Eastern counterpart. Acknowledging Chris-

---

[13] Not only is César the person a hero, but *César* the novel is to be an epic account of the bourgeois life. Raymond Giraud in his *The Unheroic Hero* (New Brunswick, N.J.: Rutgers University Press, 1957) refers to Balzac's double pride for having filled a literary lacuna and for being a modern Homer. "The shopkeeper hero of this novel was chosen with a purpose. *César Birotteau* was to be a sort of modern middle-class epic, a bourgeois *Iliad*. . . . Balzac will dare to initiate a new kind of epic poem, the epic of bourgeois humanity." (pp. 105–106)
    Balzac will later claim to have given not just the bourgeoisie but also the mediocre man a place in literature when others had passed him by for more dramatic characters. In the preface to *Un Grand homme de province à Paris* of 1838 he insists that the average man can be transformed by art into " ne belle peinture." (Plé. XI, 339) Similarly he had rehabilitated the prostitute to literary

tianity's influence, Balzac explains how under this religion women have gained greater liberty. Their role has expanded; their personalities have greater dimension. Man moves more freely in Western cultures. The author of the *Arabian Nights* had only two locales to depict, the bazaar and the sultan's palace. Balzac's settings are countless. Life is more complicated now, thanks to civilization's progress. In essence Balzac is reiterating Mme de Staël's and Chateaubriand's arguments when he contends that modern western European man has a new viewpoint which must be reckoned with in literature and that greater civilization and greater complexity in life require a richer, more detailed and varied literary expression. (Plé. XI, 372)

Having moved strictly into the realm of the novel, whereas before we have been considering Balzac's statements on all of literature, one finds his claims of progress more numerous and proud. The novel as a genre being relatively new and undeveloped, it afforded authors more opportunity for progress than older, more established forms of writing. The creation of new works, rather than the modernization of older ones, represented a greater potential for progress, Balzac believed.

The arguments for progress do not necessarily change when applied to the new genre, for Balzac's two key criteria are complexity and size, but when considering the work of earlier novelists, Balzac developed them more fully and advanced them with greater passion. Turning from his Arabian rival to his English one, Sir Walter Scott, Balzac continues to maintain that modern characters are infinitely more difficult personalities to portray. He reasons that in earlier times, life being simpler, man tended to reflect the nature of his peer group, restricting the latitude of his individuality. Even throughout the Middle Ages one could deal with types,

---

status. Most writers had ignored this character from prudish fear. As Balzac was wont to put it, he dared to dare. "Faire les *Scènes de la vie parisienne* et y omettre ces figures si curieuses, c'eût été le fait d'une couardise de laquelle nous sommes incapables. D'ailleurs personne n'a osé aborder le profond comique de ces existences." (Plé. XI, 4'5–417)

whereas in the nineteenth century no two human beings seemed alike. Walter Scott chose the easier type of depiction by choosing a simpler age.

> Chez nous autrefois, le roman rencontrait aussi des éléments fort simples et peu nombreux. Le seul roman possible dans le passé, Walter Scott l'a épuisé. C'est la lutte du serf ou de la bourgeoisie contre la noblesse, de la noblesse contre le clergé; de la noblesse et du clergé contre la royauté. (*Ibid.*)

The novel had been stereotyped and one-dimensional through the Age of Louis XIV, the author adds. Even the great love novels of the eighteenth century so admired by Mme de Staël are disdained as inferior by Balzac for their incompleteness. Writing to Mme Hanska in 1838 he found fault with the entire tradition:

> Je n'ai jamais lu de livre où l'amour heureux ait été peint. Rousseau est trop imprégné de rhétorique; Richardson est trop raisonneur; les poètes sont trop adorateurs des faits, et Pétrarque est trop occupé de ses images, de ses *concetti*. Il voit bien la poésie [plutôt] que la femme. Il n'y a que Dieu qui ait peint l'amour autour de l'Ile de Saint-Pierre. Pope a donné trop de regrets à Héloïse. Nul n'a décrit les jalousies hors de propos, les craintes insensées, ni la sublimité du don de soi-même. (*Etr.* I, 476)

In contrast, the modern novel, because of society's metamorphosis from rigid class structure toward relative equality, has richer resources which in turn have added countless nuances to art. An advance in the depiction of love is now possible because modern man has the profounder understanding of the human heart. Balzac allied with other Romantics who spoke of the greater sensitivity now present in literature. Art now sought out "les émotions les plus délicates du coeur humain," he wrote in the preface to *Une Fille d'Eve* (Plé. XI, 372). This, too, he traced to social causes. Balzac, like Stendhal, was a social scientist.

Society's richness as a literary source was not a general phenomenon, according to the author. In fact, France alone enjoyed the celebrated fecundity which made the superior novel possible. Balzac dismissed English society as being oppressed by its sense of duty, Italian by its lack of liberty (the only possible novel to come from this source of inspiration was Stendhal's *Chartreuse de Parme*, a further tribute to the glory of French novelists), German society (surprisingly) for being without firm character, still in the process of becoming, and Russian as autocratic, admitting only the rich a place in literature. (Plé. XI, 372–373) Thus progress was being made in France alone, thanks to the leveling process of the Revolution. That progress was being accomplished almost single-handedly by Balzac, for Stendhal had limited himself by choosing an inferior society (artistically speaking) to depict. Balzac goes so far as to praise himself for his perspicacious appraisal of the phenomenon, overlooked by his colleagues.

L'auteur ne sait encore aucun observateur qui ait remarqué combien les moeurs françaises sont, littéralement parlant, au-dessus de celles des autres pays comme variété des types, comme drame, comme esprit, comme mouvement. . . . Ainsi n'est-ce pas par gloriole nationale ni par patriotisme qu'il a choisi les moeurs de son pays, mais parce que son pays offrait, le premier de tout, l'*homme social* sous des aspects plus multipliés que partout ailleurs. La France est peut-être la seule qui ne soupçonne pas la grandeur de son rôle, la magnificence de son époque, la variété de ses contrastes. (*Ibid.*)

So high was Balzac's opinion of his era that he claims that even second-rate writers are better in the nineteenth century than in any previous age. This extreme sort of optimism and pride can be found in no other author considered in this essay. They had each limited their discussion of progress to the best writers each century produced. In the *Lettre sur la littérature* of 1840 Balzac goes beyond such bounds.

Je ne suis pas de ceux qui méprisent leur époque, qui accablent les écrivains modernes par des comparaisons avec les sept ou huit génies des dix-septième et dix-huitième siècles; je pense que les talents secondaires de notre temps sont tellement au-dessus des talents secondaires d'autrefois, que les conditions de la gloire sont devenues plus difficiles pour les écrivains du premier ordre. (Plé. XI, 272)

Balzac ranked but four of his contemporaries among the writers of the first order—Hugo, Gautier, Musset, and Vigny, for they were equally capable of writing either prose or verse.

(Plé. XI, 279) Hugo was considered the greatest of this group, despite his failings in drama, for he was the finest poet France had ever produced, Balzac believed, pointing to the delicacy, simplicity, and grandeur of his works. In the essay on literature Balzac even places Hugo above Racine, reversing his usual opinion, because of the perfection of Hugo's "Fonction du poète."

> Sans vouloir prendre Racine pour modèle, [Hugo] l'a de beaucoup surpassé. Ce qui, jusqu'à présent, a été l'arche saint de la poésie française, est assurément les choeurs d'*Esther* et d'*Athalie* . . . mais le premier morceau, intitulé Fonction du poète, est bien supérieur comme pensée, comme image, comme expression, à ces chants que Voltaire proclamait inimitables. [14]

Complete Victory over Rivals; Literature's Culmination in *La Comédie humaine*

Balzac's important critical treatise, "Etudes sur M. Beyle" of 1840, proves to be more pertinent to an understanding of the novelist's aesthetics than even the better known *Avant-propos*. In fact it can be considered a superior document of literary criticism. In the *Avant-propos* the novelist at best summarizes his view of himself as secretary to his epoch and his desire to be the all-inclusive curator of a literary museum,

---

[14] (Plé. XI, 293) In an article on Stendhal Balzac lavishly praises the modern novelist to the detriment of Racine. He even prefers the Duchess Sanseverina to Phèdre for being a more complete female character, a woman of varied emotions, a living being of flesh and blood, rather than a symbol which lacked harmony in its makeup, stressing but one side of its character to the neglect of all others. "La Phèdre de Racine," he writes, "ce rôle sublime de la scène française, que le jansénisme n'osait condamné, n'est ni si beau, ni si complet, ni si animé [as that of the Duchess]." (*O.C.*, XXXX, 382) Yet one finds that in most instances Balzac held Racine in highest esteem, refuting any preference for Hugo as a poet or Stendhal as a creator of characters. The strongest example of this opinion can be found in a letter to Mme Hanska in 1842 where he described an argument with Hugo over Racine. He quotes himself as saying to the poet, "jusqu'à mon dernier soupir, je tiendrai pour Racine . . . car c'est la perfection. *Bérénice* ne sera jamais surpassée; *Athalie* est la pièce la plus romantique qui existe, la plus hardie; et Phèdre le plus grand rôle du temps moderne." (*Etr.* II, 94)

212

ideas which appear in his writings years before this statement. The work on Stendhal, however, represents a new departure for Balzac. It is concerned with literature, not the novel alone; it is grandly theoretical and historical in the manner of Hugo's *Préface de Cromwell*. It cannot be denied that the essays on Stendhal eventually become propaganda pieces which preach Balzac's own superiority, just like the *Avant-propos*; nevertheless, his massive egotism does not immediately color the treatise and one can respect Balzac for his attempt at self-effacement for the sake of historical perspective and literary truth.

Preceding the *Avant-propos* by two years, this work presents a long view of the development of literature. Like Hugo, Balzac interprets literature's development—one could say progress, for both felt its final form superior—as having passed through three stages. The final and superior stage is so because it has had the advantage of extracting the best from what came before, while at the same time adding new qualities lacking in earlier stages of growth.

The three kinds of literature are the literature of images, the literature of ideas, and the combination of the two, which Balzac misnames "eclectic literature," for he really spoke of a synthesis. According to the writer the literature of images is suited for the dreamer, the meditative man. It is lyrical and epic, dealing in great images and vast spectacles of nature. The literature of ideas appeals to the active soul, the lover of movement and drama. It is philosophical and dynamic. Yet both are incomplete. Their synthesis, "eclectic literature," represents a whole. It appeals to the complete man, who recognizes and wishes to nourish both natures within him. It is intended for the thinker and the doer, the lover of both odes and dramas, the man who realizes that life cannot be compartmentalized and wishes art to reflect its duality. (*O.C.*, XXXX, 371)

Balzac classifies—and one must admit rather arbitrarily —contemporary writers in these three categories. Hugo, Lamartine, Chateaubriand, Gautier, and Sainte-Beuve have created literature of images. Musset, Mérimée, Nodier, and Stendhal have written literature of ideas. Only Walter Scott and Balzac have produced eclectic literature, that is, superior works. Balzac interprets the conflict between Classicists and Romanticists in light of these divisions. The seventeenth and eighteenth centuries encouraged the production of philosophical literature to the neglect of lyrical works, assuming their preferred genre contained all that was necessary to art. Despite its incompleteness the literature of ideas, classical literature, won recognition for the genius of France, Balzac concedes. But in the nineteenth century a reaction occurred. The literature of images was resurrected, giving poetry new aspects totally unsuspected by the classical age, with the exception of La Fontaine, Racine, and Chénier, who were imagists in an age of ideas. Yet the literature of images could not be superior to its predecessor, for it was equally incomplete. In fact Romanticism had failed, in Balzac's opinion, to continue many of the best qualities of Classicism. Its theatre was weak and comedy totally lacking.

> On peut dire que les Romantiques n'ont pas inventé de nouveaux moyens, et qu'au théâtre, par exemple, ceux qui se plaignaient d'un défaut d'action se sont amplement servis de la tirade et du monologue, et que nous n'avons encore entendu ni le dialogue vif et pressé de Beaumarchais, ni revu le comique de Molière, qui procédera toujours de la raison et des idées. Le Comique est l'ennemi de la Méditation et l'Image. (O.C., XXXX, 373)

By 1840 Balzac felt that the two opposing forces had agreed to a truce. Mutually respectful of each other, they now lived in harmony. But this solution did not go far enough. Instead of remaining separate, the literatures of ideas and images, Classicism and Romanticism, should be combined into eclectic literature. Therefore, credit should be given to Balzac and Scott who had risen above the warring factions and married the best of the two branches, giving birth to a stronger child, the novel, the superior genre. From the literature of images the novel had taken sentiment and imagery; from the literature of ideas, action. The novel is "la création moderne la plus immense." It continues comedy under a new form acceptable to a transformed society. The novelist is a composite writer. He has the talents of a La Bruyère, a Molière, and a Shakespeare. He must have moral insight and be capable of depicting the most delicate nuances of passion. In short, he is the writer par excellence.

Although there is but one French representative of eclectic literature, he and the talented authors of the other two branches have created a literary atmosphere of the finest quality in early nineteenth-century France. The activity of all three branches contributes to a new spirit not unlike that of the Renaissance. "Cette triplicité . . . est l'éloge du dix-neuvième siècle, qui n'offre pas une seule et même forme, comme le dix-septième et le dix-huitième siècles, lesquels ont obéi à la tyrannie d'un homme ou d'un système." (O.C., XXXX, 371) Balzac traces this diversity and its resulting enrichment to progress in other fields. Intellectually man has advanced. Education is more widespread, and as a result there is now a greater reading public. Contemporary men in fact are better readers than their ancestors, Balzac maintains, and progress in reading encourages progress in writing.

Because the "Etudes" were originally intended as a study of Stendhal it is amusing to note that Balzac went to such great length to prove himself superior to Beyle before even considering his rival's works. Balzac lavishly praises La Chartreuse de Parme but only as "le chef-d'oeuvre de la littérature à idées." Considering the limitations of this category and the inferiority, artistically speaking, of Italian society, Stendhal's source, the work nevertheless deserves admiration, Balzac concedes. In fact, La Chartreuse might be called the new Prince, Balzac generously proposes, the work Machiavelli would have written had he lived in the nineteenth century.[15] With Stendhal so cleverly dismissed, there remains but one rival, Walter Scott, to be dealt with. Balzac awaits the appearance of the

---

[15] (O.C., XXXX, 374) The same comparison was made to Mme Hanska in a letter of April 1839. "Beyle vient de publier, à mon sens, le plus beau livre qui ait paru depuis cinquante ans. Cela s'appelle la Chartreuse de Parme . . . si Machiavel écrivait un roman, ce serait celui-là." (Etr. I, 509)

215

Avant-propos de la Comédie humaine in 1842 to assert his supremacy over his sole competitor.

In the *Avant-propos* Balzac explains that until the present [Balzac], other writers [Scott] have been content with the creation of only one or two types of characters. He had created thousands. In addition, Scott in resurrecting the Middle Ages, for indeed he was a modern *trouvère*, had been content to leave his novels isolated from each other. No attempt to incorporate them into an overall scheme was made. Balzac, who recognized this failing, had then determined to correct it and in his portrait of the nineteenth century would present an integrated and cohesive literary edifice. Although Balzac kindly adds that Scott was no less great for having left a fragmented work, one seriously doubts his sincerity. (*O.C.*, I, xxvii) Furthermore, Balzac felt he had surpassed Scott by choosing the present as his model which he could know more completely. When one views the past, as did Scott, from such a great distance, one's knowledge is hindered and omissions and exaggerations tend to mar one's account of it. By reflecting present reality Balzac believed that he could better create living types who would move men of all eras. Timeliness would insure immortality, Balzac seems to say. (*O.C.*, I, xxviii)

By virtue of his creation the novelist becomes the supreme being, semi-divine, a god presiding over his universe. Previously Balzac had delighted in comparing himself to Napoleon, now he ventures to say that the writer is greater than any political leader. The writer shows absolute devotion to his principles and is more truly concerned with humanity. His work can have an immortality which empires never know.

Balzac concludes that the novel's eminence has increased since the days of Walter Scott. Novels are like diamonds in a nation's crown. Each year more have been added to the tiara which adorns the head of France. Writers like himself have increased the glory of their nation by achieving literary progress. That progress had occurred was an indisputable fact to Balzac. Was not the novel superlative in every degree? It is the work of modernity, the synthesis of literary efforts. It combines the poetry of antiquity with the drama of the present. It utilizes dialogues and portraits, landscapes and descriptions. It joins *le merveilleux* to the true, epic grandeur with humblest language. The novel then is proof of literature's progress; more specifically *La Comédie humaine* is the milestone marking aesthetic advance.[16]

---

[16] Balzac's vision announces the same quest for the absolute one finds later in Wagner and in Mallarmé. In the 1860's Wagner will announce that his musical drama is the great synthetic work, the culmination of art. Some years later Mallarmé will speak of capturing all of reality in *le Livre*. Cf. E. Hartman. "Baudelaire, Mallarmé, and Wagner: A Comparison of the German Musician's Influence on Two French Symbolist Poets." *Proceedings*, PNCFL, 1976, Vol. XXVII, Part I, pp. 27–30.

Chapter Eleven

Baudelaire

Baudelaire's attitude toward progress is two-fold. In broadest terms he categorically rejects the doctrine as "la grande chimère des temps modernes." On the other hand Baudelaire recognizes evidence of aesthetic progress in the works of his contemporaries, in particular Delacroix, whom he considered "la dernière expression du progrès dans l'art."[1] This ambivalence can be explained by studying Baudelaire's two definitions of progress. It is "la diminution progressive de l'âme et la domination progressive de la matière," he wrote in the "Salon de 1859." (*O.C.*, p. 1033) In this case Baudelaire narrowly confined progress to the material world as a concept too crass to be associated with art. Progress to him meant the accumulation of money, the growth of industry, the development of democracy—bourgeois and especially American values. Progress when abstractly taken as improvement,

---

[1] Baudelaire. *Oeuvres complètes*. Texte établi et annoté par Y.-G. Le Dantec. Ed. révisée, complétée et présentée par Claude Pichois. Ed. de la Pléiade (Paris: Gallimard, 1961), pp. 1131 and 899. Portions of this chapter, entitled "Baudelaire, Romanticism, and the Idea of Progress," previously appeared in *Papers in Romance*, UW, Seattle, Fall, 1983.

however, was an accepted term in his vocabulary. When the fine arts and/or literature achieved greater perfection, when an artist or writer surpassed all others in his rendition of beauty, then Baudelaire quite naturally spoke of this phenomenon as progress.

Baudelaire, because of this double attitude—rejection of the concepts of social, intellectual, and moral progress; defense of aesthetic advance—distinguished himself from other Romantic writers who were discussing the idea of progress and its application to man and his cultural activities. Unlike Hugo, Baudelaire thought society incapable of improvement and thus would not force art to work for a non-existent utopia. Unlike Mme de Staël, he recognized no intellectual advance; modern man seemed no wiser to him. Unlike Lamartine, he did not believe man could be made better morally either by the aid of art or religion because of the curse of original sin. At best man could only recognize his flaws, not erase them. Baudelaire did admit that greater material wealth and comfort now existed than ever before. Technically man had progressed, but in doing so he had paid an extremely high price, that of spirituality. The only progress which the poet joyously proclaimed was aesthetic advance. Any evidence which he found of it provoked a lyrical response.

Hostility Toward Nonartistic Progress

Baudelaire's hostility toward all but artistic progress was less pronounced before the Revolution of 1848. During the 1840's he hoped for a kind of cooperation between the poet and society based on mutual respect. In much the same manner as earlier Romantics, he felt the artist's worth to be so great that society could not fail to recognize it, according him proper honor. Baudelaire even went so far as to describe the Romantic Movement as a product of progress, in that it was the most timely expression of art, an idea stated earlier by Stendhal.

The poet's flirtation with bourgeois society and the doctrine of non-aesthetic progress was short-lived, however. Political events, first, then personal experiences, increasingly

219

alienated him from his fellow humans, encouraging his native pessimism and distrust. The events of the 1850's, his persecution by the public—in particular, the scandalized attitude of the bourgeoisie toward *Les Fleurs du mal* and their cry for legal vindication—convinced him that he was an alien member of the human race, that all mankind was so base that a belief in perfectibility was absurd.

Many critics speak of Baudelaire's "about-face" after 1848, perhaps with exaggeration. Cassagne, for example, in the *Théorie de l'Art pour l'Art* writes of a post-Revolutionary Baudelaire, "bien revenu de ses erreurs de 1848."[2] Marguerite Gilman in her *Baudelaire the Critic* deals in great length with the poet's abdication of his former heresy.[3] While it is true that Baudelaire's rancor against progress, i.e. materialism and human perfectibility, and its supporters, the bourgeoisie, increased with time, it is also evident that his initial acceptance of that doctrine had been so short-lived that one wonders if critics have not tried to make a "road-to-Damascus" experience out of a much less dramatic event. Baudelaire's appreciation of timeliness, represented by modern beauty, became more fervent, not less. He simply ceased to express his relative (à la Stendhal) point of view in terms of progress. Baudelaire had never favored the supremacy of the material world over the spiritual. There was no error to correct. At the same time he openly spoke of aesthetic progress before and after 1848. Again there was no recanting.

For what change there was Gilman puts great emphasis on the roles of Poe and de Maistre. (p. 110) Baudelaire felt such spiritual kinship with the American poet that he adopted unhesitatingly Poe's scorn of industry, democracy, and progress. America's neglect, if not persecution, of Poe symbolized for Baudelaire the fundamental antagonism of a materialistic society toward the artist. He felt his own mistreatment in 1847

---

[2] Albert Cassagne. *La Théorie de l'Art pour l'Art en France chez les derniers romantiques et les premiers réalistes.* Thèse. (Paris: Librairie Hachette et Cie, 1906), p. 113.

[3] (New York: Columbia University Press, 1943), p. 90 ff.

had been foretold by Poe's. Lack of appreciation for art and admiration for only the useful and profitable was an attitude of a common mind, Baudelaire conjectured. Thus a democracy which preferred quantity instead of quality could not avoid being philistine.[4]

An influence closer to home was that of Joseph de Maistre. In common with Poe, this French writer was fully convinced of the reality of original sin as well as unfavorably inclined toward rule by the people. An ardent Catholic, de Maistre stressed the consequences of sin, man's pain and suffering. He believed that Providence ruled the affairs of man, thus negating the freedom necessary for mankind's perfectibility. Baudelaire admitted both men's influence, once writing, "de Maistre et Poe m'ont appris à raisonner," which Gilman interprets to mean that Baudelaire's previous acceptance of progress was unreasoned, an emotional liberalism. (Gilman, p. 110)

A third explanation for Baudelaire's aversion to human progress is offered by Schroder in his *Icarus, the Image of the Artist in French Romanticism*.[5] This writer finds an answer in Baudelaire's Romantic inheritance, the negative traits of *mal du siécle* and satanism. Schroder points out that Baudelaire's fascination with evil, especially its beauties, follows the tradition of *Les Jeunes-France*. But he outdid his immediate predecessors in his Romantic posturing. Compared with René's melancholy, Baudelaire's ennui and spleen are infinitely more tragic and depressing. Previous Romantics may have been curious

---

[4] America was the land of the average man, Baudelaire must have thought. In this one-class mass, aristocrats sometimes came to the fore, but were hated for their superiority. Edgar Allan Poe, although not titled nor wealthy, was such an aristocrat in Baudelaire's eyes. He was refined, poor but elegant, a dandy. Poe was also a Virginian, a member of one of the few groups in America which cultivated class distinctions. Baudelaire's identification with this image, glorified by his own awe of Poe's talents, was total. Baudelaire cultivated his snobism, played the dandy, and thought of himself as a poet, therefore superior to the common man. To emphasize his superiority, Baudelaire stressed his originality. Talent demanded full expression of one's uniqueness, he maintained.

[5] Maurice Z. Schroder. (Cambridge, Massachusetts: Harvard University Press, 1961), p. 181 ff.

observers of evil in modern times, but none sat before Satan's temple enthralled by the beauty of sin as did Baudelaire. Be the reason Poe, de Maistre, or dark Romanticism, it is clear that Baudelaire did not possess the necessary optimism to champion the cause of human progress.

It is not surprising then to find Baudelaire violently opposed to a cooperation between art and progress as was sought by earlier writers such as Lamartine and Hugo. Baudelaire believed the Beautiful eternally separated from the Good and the True. In an essay on Gautier, whose opinion was much the same, Baudelaire wrote, "la fameuse doctrine de l'insolubilité du Beau, du Vrai, et du Bien est une invention de la philosophaillerie moderne." (*O.C.*, p. 683) Truth, he explains, is the goal of science, Goodness of morality, and Beauty of art. To have confused the three, as Cousin had done, was unthinkable.

Interestingly enough, however, Baudelaire recognized that sometimes art is not completely limited to a quest for beauty. Truth and/or moral edification can be by-products. If this occurs naturally, without a perversion of art's fundamental task, then it is acceptable. Baudelaire's tolerance is best expressed in "Les Notes nouvelles sur Edgar Poe" of 1857. (*O.C.*, p. 635) Poe had not been as liberal.

In "Les Drames et les romans honnêtes" of 1851 Baudelaire had argued that art even has a utility of its own. It satisfies an aesthetic need. But art is not necessarily useful or moral. It can sometimes be pernicious, upsetting the conditions of life, portraying vice as well as virtue. Since beauty exists everywhere, in evil as well as in good, one would lose a great portion of it in allowing only virtuous art.[6] This is the error of the believers of human progress, he explains.

---

[6] In a projected preface for a second edition of *Les Fleurs du mal* Baudelaire sought to justify his motives and to explain his poetic philosophy to the nonunderstanding public. He then put great emphasis on the separateness of beauty and morality. His task as a poet was not to improve man or to corrupt him, only to sharpen his aesthetic sensitivity. Baudelaire's insouciance rivals Musset's.

Quelques-uns m'ont dit que ces poésies pouvaient faire du mal; je ne m'en

In his review of *Les Misérables* published in *Le Boulevard* in 1862 Baudelaire criticized Hugo's sublimation of his role as creator of beauty to that of moralizer.[7] Baudelaire also believed that material progress had produced a lack of sympathy among men, the result of original sin. Hugo's *Les Misérables* itself served as an illustration of man's natural and unchanging perversity. (*O.C.*, p. 793) Baudelaire pessimistically concluded that modern man has not really progressed much beyond the primitive savage, his ancestor. It is interesting to note that Baudelaire's response to the novel was despair, while Hugo wished his work to serve as a stimulus to man to perfect himself.

Reservations and Superficial Hostility Toward Artistic Progress

Moving from the realm of material and human advance to the sphere of artistic progress, which Baudelaire generally believed did exist, one finds many serious reservations on his part which caused him to appear, at least superficially, no more optimistic.[8]

Baudelaire mainly objected to the concept of indefinite and continuous aesthetic improvement. He did not believe

---

suis pas réjoui. D'autres, de bonnes âmes, qu'elles pouvaient faire du bien; et cela ne m'a pas affligé. La crainte des uns et l'espérance des autres m'ont également étonné et n'ont servi qu'à me prouver une fois de plus que ce siècle avait désappris les notions classiques relatives à la littérature. (*O.C.*, p. 185)

[7] (*O.C.*, p. 788) Ironically Hugo never understood or admitted Baudelaire's position that art could not serve progress. In response to the article on *Les Misérables*, a rather laudatory review, Hugo stubbornly insists on the inseparability of the two. "C'est l'honneur des poètes de servir de la lumière et de la vie dans la coupe sacrée de l'art. Vous le faites et je l'essaye. Nous nous dévouons, vous et moi, au progrès par la Vérité." (*O.C.*, p. 1681)

[8] In 1861 in the proposed preface to *Les Fleurs du mal* Baudelaire scorns progress and mocks the present lack of appreciation of art by progressive society. He writes: "La France traverse une phase de vulgarité. Paris, centre et rayonnement de bêtise universelle. Malgré Molière et Béranger [whom he considered tainted by the doctrine], on n'aurait jamais cru que la France irait si grand train dans la voie du progrès. Questions d'art, *terrae incognitae*." (*O.C.*, p. 184)

223

that artistic achievement submitted to general laws, and thus one could not predict future production on the basis of present or past output. Cultural flowerings are spontaneous and individual events, he noted. There are no connections between succeeding renaissances. Likewise there are no inheritances between artists. Imitators may abound, but they cannot truly continue the quality of their master.

L'artiste ne relève que de lui-même. Il ne promet aux siècles à venir que ses propres oeuvres. Il ne cautionne que lui-même. Il meurt sans enfants. Il a été *son roi, son prêtre,* et *son Dieu. (O.C.,* p. 959)

The artist is the rarest of human beings, a gift from God to undeserving and usually unappreciative man. His appearance on earth is providential, i.e., beyond explanation by human law. Although the artist is divinely elected, he is not a messiah, Baudelaire, unlike the majority of the Romantics believed. He is neither the prophet of utopia nor a philanthropic social worker. His function is extra-human. (*O.C.,* p. 700)

As art and the artist are beyond human laws, so the cultural prominence of nations is beyond the realm of scientific explanations. A general pattern of cultural flowerings and fadings can be established, e.g. Greece, Rome, Florence, Paris, but the length of time each enjoyed supremacy or the reason for this particular pattern is inexplicable. Baudelaire, again reflecting the influence of de Maistre, suggests that the only possible answer is Providence, meaning none in human terms. (*O.C.,* p. 959)

More in agreement with his fellow Romantics who did espouse the doctrine of artistic progress, Baudelaire took note of an aging process in nations and their art—a kind of maturation from childhood to senility. Again Baudelaire breaks away from the group, however, for he insisted that the various stages of development are isolated segments, not members of a series. Youth does not inherit from childhood, nor maturity from youth, he argued. (*O.C.* p. 960)

A contemporary of Baudelaire, Chevanard, had developed the theory of humanity's aging in great detail. He illustrated the Platonic doctrine, which Pascal among others helped to popularize in France, by means of an emblematic calendar. Reviewing Chevanard's work in his *Art philosophique* of 1851, Baudelaire suggests he is in agreement with the finding of this "scientist."[9]

Chevanard's calendar divides humanity in the following manner. Childhood was the time from Adam to Babel, virility from Babel to Christ, the zenith of human life. Middle age set in after Christ and continued until the time of Napoleon. Since the time of the emperor, man has slipped into old age, if not senility. Chevanard's pessimism went well with Baudelaire's. Both felt that decadence of their own era was characterized by the supremacy of America, the anti-art nation, and industry, the anti-art endeavor. Chevanard, unlike Baudelaire, does not point out the special beauties available for artistic depiction in man's senility. Later the poet will accept the "decadence" of his age but vaunt its special advantages.

Before discussing the artistic assets of humanity's old age, let us consider its liabilities as Baudelaire envisioned them. Foremost was a pervading mediocrity. In the "Salon de 1859" Baudelaire complained that although mediocrity prevails in all epochs, in no other time had it so dominated man and his activities as in the mid-nineteenth century. As a result, the artist of that era seemed inferior even to his immediate predecessors, a fact all too evident in his works.

Baudelaire singles out several causes for the present low point in art. First he, like Balzac, blames a growing industrial mentality among artists who look upon their profession as a trade, a means of earning money. Secondly, he accuses the scientific spirit of the age of having preferred truth to fantasy, leaving imagination seriously handicapped. (*O.C.*, p. 1029)

An obvious result of science's expanding influence is

---

[9] Chevanard had maintained that humanity, analogous to the individual, has definite ages to which certain pleasures, work, and philosophies are best suited. The parallel with Hugo and his historical survey of mankind in the *Préface de Cromwell* is striking. Art especially adapts itself to man's stage of development in relation to the dominant passion of the age, Chevanard believed. Baudelaire's insistence on the necessity of modern art for modern man finds foundation at least in Chevanard's theories.

seen in his contemporaries' disportionate love of photography. The artist has been replaced by a machine, Baudelaire lamented. Photography should instead be the servant of art, not its supplanter.[10]

Je suis convaincu que les progrès mal appliqués de la photographie ont beaucoup contribué à l'appauvrissement du génie artistique français, déjà si rare. . . . La poésie et le progrès sont deux ambitieux qui se haïssent d'une haine instinctive, et quand ils se recontrent dans le même chemin, il faut que l'un des deux serve l'autre. (*O.C.*, p. 1035)

A third cause of artistic regression according to Baudelaire is the era's eclectic nature. Whereas Balzac believed that present literature had gone beyond eclecticism to a true synthesis of former traditions, Baudelaire saw only a hodgepodge of influences and characteristics, a lack of unity and harmony, in contemporary writing. Modern authors, by their desire to be all things, were nothing in particular.

These arguments written in 1846 reveal the author's displeasure over his contemporaries' inability to synthesize their rich and varied sources. Baudelaire, more cautious than Gautier, then even feared that Romanticism's encouragement of *les transpositions d'art*, i.e. synesthetic interplay, was but another example of unskilful eclecticism.

Le doute a conduit certains artistes à implorer le secours de tous les arts. Les essais de moyens contradictoires, l'empiétement d'un art sur un autre, l'importation de la poésie, de l'esprit, et du sentiment dans la peinture, toutes ces misères modernes sont des vices particuliers aux éclectiques. (*O.C.*, p. 930)

In the 1860's, however, Baudelaire expressed great pleasure over Wagner's combination of dance, music, scenic decor, and poetry into his music-drama. Ironically, he then

---

[10] It is interesting to note that Baudelaire's fear of photography—he does not stress the advantages it could bring to art, the new freedom it gave painters from having to depict reality to give vent to their imagination—is similar to Mme de Staël's fear of printing. Firm believer in progress that she was, she condemned printing as harmful to poetry, never pointing out the special advantages of having a printed text.

found himself alone in his defense of the German musician. In *Richard Wagner et Tannhäuser à Paris* Baudelaire approvingly noted:

> Dans la musique, comme dans la peinture et même dans la parole écrite, qui est cependant le plus positif des arts, il y a toujours une lacune complétée par l'imagination de l'auditeur. Ce sont sans doute ces considérations qui ont poussé Wagner à considérer l'art dramatique, c'est-à-dire, la réunion, la *coïncidence* de plusieurs arts, comme l'art par excellence, le plus synthétique et le plus parfait. (*O.C.*, p. 878)

Likewise, Baudelaire came to praise Gautier's use of aesthetic reciprocity. Obviously, Baudelaire, approved of *les transpositions d'art* if judiciously controlled. A work of art can be enriched by drawing from many sources, Baudelaire believed, but the whole must always be greater than the sum of its parts. Eclecticism must give way to synthesis.

Le Beau moderne:
Firm Conviction of Artistic Progress

Despite Baudelaire's bitter criticisms of his era and its shortcomings, he also lauded its unique achievements, especially the progress of its artists and writers. Baudelaire's basic philosophy of beauty makes him a potential adherent to the doctrine of artistic progress. His concern with finding the aesthetic expression most suitable for his times as early as the "Salons" of the 1840's, with allowing his epoch to depict beauty on its own terms, to do artistically what had never been done before, certainly makes Baudelaire an early and continued supporter of the concept.

In the "Salon de 1846" Baudelaire had first stated most clearly his belief in relative, not absolute, beauty. Each age, each people has its own expression of beauty and morality, he then wrote. Thus the nineteenth-century French have theirs, which in literature and the arts is called Romanticism. Like Stendhal, Baudelaire defines the movement as "l'expression la plus récente et la plus moderne de la Beauté." Implying that by 1846 Romanticism, as conceived in the earlier decades of the century, was no longer completely current, he suggested an alteration, a means of making it more timely and hence better, a way of achieving progress in the arts. Baudelaire contended that the time had come for a great artist to add naïveté to the basic stock of Romantic qualities. By doing this the artist would preserve the essence of the most recent tradition and at the same time give it a tone the specific era demanded. He would then create "le plus de romantisme possible." (O.C., p. 878)

Baudelaire's acceptance of the doctrine of aesthetic progress is qualified, however. Although artists and their creations can show signs of improvement over the works of predecessors, they can never reach absolute perfection. Yet modern art can move toward it by means of judicious innovations, for recent artists, the Romantics, have learned to exploit "des aspects de la nature et les situations de l'homme, que les artistes du passé ont dédaignés ou n'ont pas connus." This, of course, is one of the most fundamental arguments in favor of artistic progress advanced by nineteenth-century writers. Baudelaire follows in this tradition by speaking of a new awareness of nature—human and nonhuman—and of new plots either disdained or unknown in past times which in recent decades have found artistic expression.

The progress made by modern art is substantial, Baudelaire adds. Romanticism is characterized by an emphasis on the intimate—the development of *douleur* and *sensibilité*—and at the same time by a love of color and an aspiration for the infinite. These qualities have been achieved by the calling into play of all the resources available to the arts. (O.C., p. 879) The implication that these traits did not exist, at least in such intensity or so well synthesized, in the creations of earlier eras is made tacitly by the author.

Baudelaire's arguments against absolute beauty, it must be admitted, are more intense than his defense of relative beauty. Employing the same terms as in his arguments against human perfection, another absolute, he explains that should such an ideal exist, its cost would be greater than its value. It would reduce artists to imitators, constant repeaters of one perfect model. It would destroy individual expression. Romanticism in particular would be annihilated, for the artist would be compelled to ignore his *moi*, his *sui generis*. Thus absolute beauty is an impossibility. This false belief only serves as an escape for the artist's own shortcomings. It, like the belief in human progress, in which lazy men trust to rid themselves of their own responsibility for moral improvement, provides the unproductive artist with the perfect excuse. (*O.C.*, pp. 949–950)

In his attack on absolute beauty and its devotees, the Neo-Classicists, Baudelaire became increasingly articulate in his defense of relative beauty and its worshippers, the Romantics and the Modernists. By 1863 his theory is well defined and appears in the essay "Le Peintre de la vie moderne." This article reveals another evolution in Baudelaire's thought. Instead of denying the existence of absolute beauty, he now recognizes the dual nature of art, the simultaneous presence of absolute and relative elements in each creation.

C'est ici une belle occasion, en vérité, pour établir une théorie rationnelle et historique du beau, en opposition avec la théorie du beau unique et absolu; pour montrer que le beau est toujours, inévitablement, d'une composition double, bien que l'impression qu'il produit soit une. . . . Le beau est fait d'un élément éternel, invariable, dont la quantité est excessivement difficile à déterminer, et d'un élément relatif, circonstantiel, qui sera si l'on veut, tour à tour, ou tout ensemble, l'époque, la mode, la morale, la passion. Sans ce second élément, qui est comme l'envelope amusante, titillante, apéritive, du divin gâteau, le premier élément serait indigestible, inappréciable, non adapté et non approprié à la nature humaine. Je défie qu'on découvre un échantillon quelconque de beauté qui ne contienne pas ces deux éléments. (*O.C.*, p. 1154)

Baudelaire had first expressed this duality in the "Salon de 1846." There he spoke of the absolute versus the particular qualities of art, the eternal versus the transitory, the timeless versus the timely. At that point, however, he was more reluctant to admit the existence of absolute beauty. (*O.C.*, p. 950)

Baudelaire's definition of modernism is taken up again in his article of 1863 and expanded into a complete theory of the varieties of beauty which exist. Baudelaire then notes that nations, professions, social classes, and centuries have a distinguishable beauty, which is expressed by gestures, manners, and appearance. (*O.C.*, p. 1164) The nineteenth century, being different from the preceding, has an individuality which contains unique elements of beauty.

The elements of modern beauty are many. The city alone offers vast resources to art. Very similar to Balzac, Baudelaire thought of Paris as a fount of unexploited aesthetic potential. "La vie parisienne est féconde aux sujets poétiques et merveilleux. Le merveilleux nous enveloppe et nous abreuve comme l'atmosphère, mais nous ne le voyons pas." (*O.C.*, pp. 951–952) Baudelaire, of course, did see it as evidenced in the eighteen poems of "Les Tableaux Parisiens."

The Progress of Decadent Literature

Previously Baudelaire's statements have been concerned more with the plastic arts than with literature. His theory of modern beauty and its advantages over previous forms of aesthetic expression is developed extensively, however, in the realm of his own discipline.

Baudelaire's defense of the literary character of his era was sparked by the accusing label "littérature de décadence." Chaffed for a while by its derogatory connotation, Baudelaire came to accept and defend the label, as in the "Notes nouvelles sur Edgar Poe" where he does so most eloquently. There he cleverly turns the argument against his accusers and says, if it is true that the times and the arts are decadent, which his antagonists explained by natural law, the theory of the ages of man, then the artist is correct in obeying this law, in adapting himself to the spirit of the age and in seeking that beauty which is now left. (*O.C.*, p. 620)

Baudelaire then so describes decadence that he easily convinces the reader that it is more beautiful than the periods of infancy or virility. Drawing upon his own artistry, he paints a portrait of the twilight era of art which throbs with beauty. The poet compares the times of day to the ages of man. Virility is equated with noon, when the sun bears down directly with a crushing white light. Decadence is likened to evening, when the sun's rays are diagonal, creating shadows and half-tones. The pure whiteness of noon is broken into a myriad of colors. To some, Baudelaire chief among them, this period is preferable to noontime.

The poet's vocabulary depicting the twilight of man and art richly evokes visions of beauty. He speaks of "colonnades éblouissantes," of "cascades de métal fondu," of "paradis du feu." The approach of darkness, the opposing element which meets and blends with the light, adds overtones of melancholy—"une splendeur triste . . . la volupté de regret . . . les magies du rêve . . . [et] les souvenirs de l'opium." (*Ibid.*) Decadence then is both a highpoint—the culmination of day, the brilliant fireworks of the setting sun—and the beginning of the decline—the approach of night with its monsters lurking in shadows, harbingers of death. Teetering between the two, man looks back with satisfaction at the beauty of the fleeting moment, made possible only by the passing of an entire day, and glances onward into ever-increasing darkness and obliteration. His attitude can only be mixed, joy and satisfaction for what is, but fear and dread of what will be. Man could not help but feel that he is experiencing one of life's most dramatic moments, rivalled but perhaps unequalled even by that other great moment, the dawn, symbol of birth. Clearly such a period of decadence enjoys immense advantages. For Baudelaire, art which reflects the character of this moment will be superior to, and will evidence progress over, the art of less rich and dramatic epochs. [11]

---

[11] The poet in "Le Coucher du soleil romantique" of 1862 re-expressed his thoughts on the parallels between literary periods and the time of day. Romanticism is here described as sunrise, literature of decadence as sunset. Baudelaire suggests it is more difficult to appreciate waning day, for night/ death quickly pervades the atmosphere, filling the observing poet with fear. Because of day's fleeting presence, one must hurry toward the horizon to prolong the view of the sun/life. The pressure felt by the poet to capture this twilight civilization in art before it is destroyed is suggested by these verses. One cannot help but notice the similarity of metaphors in this poem and the prose argument found in "Notes nouvelles sur Edgar Poe."

To turn from statements about the general tone of decadent literature to observations concerning specific creators of it, one sees that Baudelaire found evidence of the new beauty in their works. He proudly signaled the unparalleled accomplishments of his contemporaries in capturing "le beau moderne."

Balzac is praised for his depiction of nineteenth-century life and characters. Who more than this novelist followed Baudelaire's beliefs that the lessons of the past are limited and that one must extract beauty from one's own times? It is Balzac's timeliness and rich variety which Baudelaire admired. (*O.C.*, p. 952)

Hugo received credit for having rejuvenated poetry. His arrival on the literary scene was "providential" interestingly enough and saved poetry from oblivion.

Quand on se figure ce qu'était la poésie française avant qu'il apparût, et quel rajeunissement elle a subi depuis qu'il est venu; quand on imagine ce qu'elle eût été, s'il n'était pas venu; combien de sentiments mystérieux et profonds, qui ont été exprimés, seraient restés muets . . . il est impossible de ne pas le considérer comme un de ces esprits rares et providentiels qui opèrent, dans l'ordre littéraire, le salut de tous, comme d'autres dans l'ordre moral et d'autres dans l'ordre politique.[12]

It is interesting to note that Baudelaire is willing to proclaim Hugo a literary messiah but not a human one. Consistent with his philosophy, Baudelaire believed aesthetic progress more easily attained than moral improvement.

Que le soleil est beau quand tout frais il se lève,
Comme une explosion nous lançant son bonjour!
—Bienheureux celui-là qui peut avec amour
Saluer son coucher plus glorieux qu'un rêve!
Je me souviens! . . . J'ai vu tout, fleur, source, sillon,
Se pâmer sous un oeil comme un coeur qui palpite. . . .
—Courons vers l'horizon, il est tard, courons vite,
Pour attraper au moins un oblique rayon.

[12] (*O.C.*, p. 708) Baudelaire was most impressed, not only with Hugo, but by the entire chorus of Romantic poets, with the exception of Musset, who, in his opinion, was frivolous and weak, and created no real doctrine. (*O.C.*, p. 682)

It is Gautier, though, who receives the highest praise from Baudelaire of any contemporary author. The master of art for art's sake, it will be remembered, was paid the tribute of having *Les Fleurs du mal* dedicated to him as "[le] poète impeccable, [le] parfait magicien ès lettres françaises . . . mon très-cher et très vénéré maître et ami." In an article published in *L'Artiste* in 1859 Baudelaire continues his praise (*O.C.*, p. 1167), and it was in reponse to this article that Hugo wrote his famous letter championing "L'Art pour le Progrès" and crediting Baudelaire with having created a "frisson nouveau" in literature.

Baudelaire's empathy with Gautier was manifold. They shared a similar hatred of the philistine and bourgeois ideal, material progress—"nous nous entretînmes également de la grande fatuité du siècle et de la folie du progrès." (*O.C.*, p. 680) Gautier's eventual softening toward things bourgeois—money, industrialism, democracy, and progress—is explained away by the poet on the grounds that "le bon Théo" wished to live in harmony with everything.

C'est sans doute ce même désespoir de persuader ou de corriger qui que ce soit, qui fait qu'en ces dernières années nous avons vu quelquefois Gautier faiblir, en apparence et accorder par-ci par-là quelques paroles laudatives à monseigneur Progrès et à très-puissante Dame Industrie . . . parce qu'il veut vivre en paix avec tout le monde, même avec l'Industrie et le Progrès, ces despotiques de toute poésie. (*O.C.*, p. 700)

A more positive reason for Baudelaire's admiration of Gautier was that poet's extreme love of physical beauty. Gautier transmitted his adoration of beauty to the public; he opened their eyes, and this most impressed Baudelaire, to new beauties, even those contained in objects heretofore considered ugly. This aesthetic kinship between master and pupil easily explains, more than their mutual hatred of human progress, their reciprocal esteem. Baudelaire says of Gautier's contribution:

Nul n'a mieux su que lui exprimer le bonheur que donne à l'imagination la vue d'un bel objet d'art, fût-il le plus désolé et le plus terrible qu'on puisse supposer. C'est un des privilèges prodigieux de l'Art que l'horrible artistement exprimé devienne beauté, et que la *douleur* rythmée et cadencée remplisse l'esprit d'une *joie* calme. (*O.C.*, p. 695)

Gautier had significantly contributed to literary progress, Baudelaire believed. He had perfected the negative aspects of beauty by continuing the melancholic tradition begun by Chateaubriand and by reintegrating antique elements in its expression. In addition, Gautier had contributed a new element to melancholy, a kind of artistic consolation.

D'un autre côté, il a introduit dans la poésie un élément nouveau, que j'appellerai la consolation par les arts, par tous les objets pittoresques qui réjouissent les yeux et amusent l'esprit. Dans ce sens, il a vraiment innové, il a fait dire au vers français plus qu'il n'avait dit jusqu'à présent. (*O.C.*, p. 698)

Delacroix, Paragon of Artistic Progress

Baudelaire's greatest appreciation of a contemporary was not, however, for a fellow poet, but for an artist. His praise of Delacroix is sustained longer, occurs more frequently, and is more intense than that of Balzac, Hugo, or Gautier. If Baudelaire recognized artistic progress in any contemporary's creations, he mainly saw it in the paintings of Delacroix.[13]

Baudelaire was impressed by two kinds of artistic progress, which one might call internal and external, i.e. in relation to oneself and to other artists. Internal progress is that which an artist achieves in his works over his creative lifetime, usually brought about by maturity. External progress is that which the artist contributes to the whole of art, representing an

---

[13] It is Delacroix who is ranked highest by Baudelaire in his poetic catalog of great artists, "Les Phares." After having paid homage to Rubens, da Vinci, Rembrandt, Michelangelo, Watteau, and Goya, Baudelaire culminates his praise with Delacroix. His characterization of that painter's works is flavored with morbidity. Strikingly he makes a comparison between painting and music, an early indication of Baudelaire's change in heart and growing belief in the reciprocity of the arts.

Delacroix, lac de sang hanté des mauvais anges,
Ombragé par un bois de sapins toujours verts,
Où, sous un ciel chagrin, des fanfares étranges
Passent, comme un soupir étouffé de Weber;

improvement over the accomplishments of predecessors or contemporaries. Baudelaire felt that Delacroix had notably progressed in both instances.

In the "Salon de 1845" Baudelaire first speaks of Delacroix's internal progress which he felt was evidenced in the artist's mastery of the science of harmony.

Dès longtemps, il a tout dit, dit tout ce qu'il faut pour être le premier—c'est convenu;—il ne lui reste plus—prodigieux tour de force de génie sans cesse en quête du neuf—qu'à progresser dans la voie du bien—où il a toujours marché. . . . C'est que M. Delacroix est plus fort que jamais, et dans une voie de progrès sans cesse renaissante, c'est-à-dire qu'il est plus que jamais harmoniste. (O.C., pp. 815–816)

Baudelaire cites the painting, "Le Sultan de Maroc," as an example of this kind of progress. Other references are made to Delacroix's internal progress in the "Exposition Universelle de 1855" (O.C., p. 968) and in a later article dated 1863, where he wrote: "Ce qui est justement la marque principale du génie de Delacroix, c'est qu'il ne connaît pas de décadence; il ne montre que le progrès." (O.C., pp. 1123–1124)

The second kind of progress, that made to the body of art as a whole, was also evident in Delacroix's creations. Baudelaire readily labels his favorite painter "le peintre le plus original des temps anciens et des temps modernes." His painting "Les Dernières paroles de Marc-Aurèle" represents absolute perfection. To illustrate the progress painting has achieved since the time of the Italian Renaissance, Baudelaire points out that in Delacroix's "La Madeleine dans le désert" one sees a perfection of design which Raphaël was never able to achieve. (O.C., pp. 815–817)

Delacroix's greatness was due to his timeliness, Baudelaire believed. The poet speaks of him as the "true painter of the nineteenth century." Delacroix, like Gautier and Chateaubriand, had depicted melancholy, the modern sentiment. It is interesting to note the great emphasis put on this emotion in the nineteenth century—happiness and self-containment seemed lost in the material advance of the century. Delacroix's visual rendition of *mal du siècle* was especially noted by

235

Baudelaire, for the painter had captured it in the faces, gestures, and colors of his portraits. Delacroix's particular brand of melancholy is "la douleur morale," according to the author. He is a great painter of human suffering in the manner of a Dante or Shakespeare. (*O.C., p.* 898) Delacroix's timely depiction of melancholy placed him squarely in the Romantic tradition. Heir to Dante, Shakespeare, Ariosto, and Byron, Delacroix had transferred their verbal pictures to graphic art, thus creating *transpositions d'art* à la Gautier, albeit in reverse.

If Delacroix had been only a continuer of a tradition, however, he would never have been the object of such lavish praise from Baudelaire. It was the new qualities—the progress —which Delacroix brought to painting which accounted for Baudelaire's esteem. In 1858 the poet drew attention to the painter's beneficial innovations.

> [Le] mérite très particulier et tout nouveau de M. Delacroix, qui lui a permis d'exprimer simplement avec le contour, le geste, de l'homme, si violent qu'il soit, et avec la couleur, ce qu'on pourrait appeler l'atmosphère du drame humain, ou l'état de l'âme du créateur, ce mérite tout original a toujours rallié autour de lui les sympathies de tous les poètes. (*O.C., p.* 1117)

Delacroix's portrayal of the human drama—that quality which made him most modern and akin to poets—went far beyond other painters' attempts. Although Rembrandt had also expressed by color and gesture human existence, his success was minimal compared to Delacroix's, Baudelaire believed. In the "Salon de 1845" the poet does not hesitate to speak of Delacroix's greater ability as evidence of artistic progress. As when speaking of Hugo's contribution to poetry, Baudelaire here announces that Delacroix's contribution to art is so valuable and unique that without it there would have been a serious lacuna.

> C'est à cause de cette qualité toute moderne et toute nouvelle que Delacroix est la dernière expression du progrès dans l'art. Héritier de la grande tradition, c'est-à-dire de l'ampleur, de la noblesse et de la pompe dans la composition, et digne successeur des vieux maîtres, il a de plus qu'eux la maîtrise de la douleur, la passion, le geste! C'est vraiment là ce qui fait l'importance de sa grandeur. —

En effet, supposez que le bagage d'un des vieux illustres se perde, il aura presque toujours son analogue qui pourra l'expliquer et le faire deviner à la pensée de l'historien. Ôtez Delacroix, la grande chaîne de l'histoire est rompue et s'écroule à terre. (*O.C.*, p. 899)

Delacroix is to France what Rubens is to Flanders and Raphaël and Veronese are to Italy, Baudelaire concludes. He is unrivalled. Neither Lebrun nor David approaches him in his fervent expression, in his completeness, or in his realization of the intangible on canvas. Art definitely has progressed since the time of David thanks to Delacroix, Baudelaire states as late as 1863.

Delacroix, le dernier venu, a exprimé avec une véhémence et une ferveur admirables ce que les autres n'avaient traduit que d'une manière incomplète. . . . Mais enfin, Monsieur, diriez-vous, sans doute, quel est donc ce je ne sais quoi de mystérieux que Delacroix pour la gloire de notre siècle, a mieux traduit qu'aucun autre? C'est l'invisible, c'est l'impalpable, c'est le rêve, c'est les nerfs, c'est l'âme, et il a fait cela . . . . Il l'a fait mieux que pas un; il l'a fait avec la perfection d'un peintre consommé, avec la vigueur d'un littérateur subtil, avec l'éloquence d'un musicien passionné. C'est, du reste, un des diagnostiques de l'état spirituel de notre siècle que les arts aspirent, sinon à se suppléer l'un et l'autre, au moins à se prêter réciproquement des forces nouvelles. (*O.C.*, p. 1116)

Synthesis, reciprocity, completeness—qualities of nineteenth-century art, recognized by Baudelaire as well as by Gautier—are the traits of this master painter. Delacroix, in addition to all these merits, possesses yet another, according to his fervent admirer. Delacroix gives birth to poetry in his viewers' souls. (*O.C.*, p. 117)

On this high note any comment would be anticlimactic. Yet for the sake of honesty one must be reminded of Baudelaire's unrelenting hostility to the doctrine of progress, per se—i.e. moral, social, or intellectual. In the very article in which he called to his readers' attention the progress achieved by Delacroix, Baudelaire ends by mocking the doctrine and stating that neither he nor Delacroix were disciples of it.

Ainsi, le causeur qui, devant M. Delacroix, s'abandonnait aux enthousiasmes enfantins de l'utopie, avait bientôt à subir l'effet de son rire amer, imprégné d'une pitié sarcastique, et si, imprudem-

237

ment, on lançait devant lui la grande chimère des temps modernes, le ballon-monstre de la perfectibilité et de progrès indéfinis, volontiers il vous demanderait: "Où sont vos Phidias? Où sont vos Raphaëls?" (*O.C.*, p. 1131)

Charles Lalo in his "L'Idée de progrès dans les sciences et dans les arts" suggests that one should have answered they are dead, while modern artists, like Delacroix himself, are living.[14] The old has given way to the new. Baudelaire, first of all men, recognized this. He knew the answer to Delacroix's question. His writings more than prove it, despite his reluctance to admit it.

[14] *Journal de Psychologie normale et pathologique,* XXVIIe année, Nos. 5–6, (15 mai–15 juin, 1930), p. 459.

Chapter Twelve

Sainte-Beuve

Sainte-Beuve's special position in the literary panorama of the first half of the nineteenth century makes him a suitable concluding author to be studied in this essay. His vast knowledge of the writers and works of the early 1800's as well as his erudition in the literatures of the past, both ancient and modern, grant him an authority to judge both the theory of progress in literature and his associates' claims to have accomplished it.

One must proceed with caution, however, while considering Sainte-Beuve's opinion of the state of health of nineteenth-century French literature. Despite his claims, he was not an impartial historian of his epoch. He was too closely associated with its authors to maintain such a point of view. Actually Sainte-Beuve judged his era by his personal preferences, often condemning a writer for his personality rather than for his lack of talent. In general, the critic's view of deceased authors rings truer than his comments on contemporaries. Implicit in his critical method was the belief that the man and his works are one, a notion which marred his appreciation of many works of his period.

Sainte-Beuve's disenchantment with the Romantics is

well known. His slight appreciation of Stendhal, his coolness towards Musset and Baudelaire, his hatred of Balzac are also common knowledge. Thus one expects no statements that these writers had achieved progress in literature. A richer area of investigation is Sainte-Beuve's pronouncements on general literary theory and aesthetics. When dealing with abstract ideas and not people, Sainte-Beuve came closer to being the objective critic he thought himself to be. In the area of theory, Sainte-Beuve does propose literary progress to be possible. Unfortunately for him, he could give few examples of it from his own generation.

In this chapter samples of Sainte-Beuve's opinions on the question of aesthetic progress as a general theory and as applied to the authors comprising this essay shall be investigated in an attempt to determine his personal convictions. First, let us consider his view of literary criticism in order to understand why he judged as he did, what was his goal, and what importance he attached to his work. Secondly, turning to the history of literature itself, let us study his appraisal of two periods—the time of the Quarrel of the Ancients and Moderns, when the idea of progress was first rigorously applied to the arts, and the first half of the nineteenth century, the time limit of this essay. From his opinions of the Quarrel and its echoes in his own day, we may determine his stand on the question of progress in the arts.

Sainte-Beuve's View of the Critic and Its Relationship to the Idea of Progress

Mustoxidi in his *L'Histoire de l'esthétique française 1700–1900* maintains that Sainte-Beuve had no well-defined theory of literature, which he explains by saying that the critic believed art to be relative, the result of complex forces only partially explicable in human terms. Thus no dogmatic statements could be expected from Sainte-Beuve.[1] If this be true,

---

[1] T. M. Mustoxidi. *Histoire de l'esthétique française 1700–1900, Suivie d'une Bibliographie générale de l'esthétique française des origines à 1914.* (Paris: Edouard

then the critic would have expressed no preference for any period or author and would have concluded that each epoch equaled the other, although differing in its style. Such scientific objectivity was Sainte-Beuve's theory but not his practice, particularly regarding his own era. Taking Sainte-Beuve at his word, however, let us consider his goal as he envisioned it.

In *Chateaubriand et son groupe littéraire* Sainte-Beuve leads us to believe that he was totally impartial. He writes: "Je ne prétends pas établir un rang, ni fixer la valeur des oeuvres, mais seulement mesurer les rapports apparents et l'étendue du rayon."[2] In an article on French poets he also praises eclecticism, that tolerance in a critic which allows him to see beauty in all types of literature and which condemns a narrow taste. "Non pas au moins que je veuille sacrifier une école à l'autre," he explains, "mon désir et mon voeu serait de les associer et de les combiner."[3]

To associate, to compare is the task of the historian, the image Sainte-Beuve chose for himself. The critic believed that by his numerous articles he was recording for posterity the main events of literary history. Like l'abbé Dubois et Marmontel in the eighteenth century, Sainte-Beuve pictured himself as a Buffon of literature.[4]

> Je n'ai plus qu'un plaisir; j'analyse, je suis un naturaliste des esprits. — Ce que je voudrais constituer, c'est l'histoire naturelle littéraire. . . . Aujourd'hui, l'histoire littéraire se fait comme l'histoire naturelle, par des observations et par des collections.[5]

Champion, 1920), p. 168. Portions of this chapter were presented at the Triennial Meeting of the American Comparative Literature Association, Santa Barbara, California, March 1983.

[2] Sainte-Beuve. *Chateaubriand et son groupe littéraire sous l'Empire, Cours professé à Liège en 1848–49.* Nouvelle éd. (Paris: Calmann-Lévy, éditeur, 1889), I, 45.

[3] Sainte-Beuve. *Portraits littéraires.* (Paris: Garnier frères, 1881), III, 145.

[4] (Mustoxidi, p. 168) One cannot help but be struck by the similarity of Sainte-Beuve's and Balzac's ambitions. Both wished to leave a record of their times for posterity and both believed that their task had never before been so completely performed.

[5] *(Por. litt.,* III, 546) And *Poésies complètes, Vie, poésies et pensées de Joseph Delorme.* (Paris: G. Charpentier et Cie, 1869), Pensée 21.

Sainte-Beuve could never attain his goal, for the artist did not submit himself to such scientific scrutiny as did the plants and animals classified by Buffon. The writer, being human, if not more so, because of his unaccounted for and unpredictable genius, defied complete analysis. A thorough investigation of his religion, his diet, and his secret vices could never produce all the answers. Sainte-Beuve admitted this when he wrote in the *Nouveaux Lundis*: "Il n'y a rien de plus imprévu que le talent, et il ne serait pas le talent s'il n'était imprévu, s'il était un seul entre tous." Sainte-Beuve concludes that the artist is the most individual of men. He views reality through a special set of lenses; he has his "monade unique et individuelle."[6] Sharing the common view that the artist was elected, raised above ordinary men, Sainte-Beuve, like Gautier, explains his talent as a kind of sixth sense:

Le sentiment de l'art implique un sentiment vif et intime des choses. Tandis que la majorité des hommes s'en tient aux surfaces et aux apparences, tandis que les philosophes proprement dits reconnaissent et constatent un *je ne sais quoi*, l'artiste, comme s'il était doué d'un sens à part, s'occupe paisiblement à sentir sous ce monde apparent l'autre monde tout intérieur qu'ignorent la plupart et dont les philosophes se bornent à constater l'existence: il assiste au jeu invisible des forces et *sympathise* avec elles comme avec des âmes; il a reçu en naissant la clef des symboles et l'intelligence des figures; ce qui semble à d'autres incohérent et contradictoire n'est pour lui qu'un contraste harmonique, un accord à distance, sur la lyre universelle. Lui-même, il entre bientôt dans ce grand concert, et, comme des vases d'airain des théâtres antiques il marie l'écho de sa voix à la musique du monde. (*Pensée* 20)

If artistic progress exists, it could not be explained by a scientific method. Sainte-Beuve's view of the creative genius was mystical, not rational.

Whether or not Sainte-Beuve could justify a belief in aesthetic progress, he did think it possible, for example, in his own field of endeavor. Despite his eventual disassociation

---

[6] Sainte-Beuve. *Les Nouveaux Lundis.* (Paris: Calmann-Lévy, éditeur, 1885), VIII, 87 and 93.

with the Romantics, Sainte-Beuve could not free himself from their influence. He reflects a typically Romantic ego in proclaiming that his form of literary achievement, "critical recreation," was in itself a form of progress. With the vanity of a Balzac he claims progress possible because he himself had accomplished it:

La critique est la seconde face et le second temps nécessaire de la plupart des esprits. Dans la jeunesse elle se recèle sous l'art, sous la poésie ou si elle veut aller seule, la poésie, l'exaltation s'y mêle trop souvent et la trouble. Ce n'est que lorsque la poésie s'est un peu dissipée et éclaircie, que le second plan se démasque véritablement et que la critique se glisse, s'infiltre de toutes les parts et sous toutes les formes dans le talent. Elle se borne à le tremper quelquefois; plus souvent elle le transforme et le fait autre. N'en médisons pas trop, même quand elle brise l'art; on peut dire de ce dernier, même lorsqu'il est brisé en critique, que les morceaux en sont bons. . . . Il y a aussi, au fond de la plupart des talents, un pis-aller honorable, (la critique), s'ils savent n'en pas faire fi et comprendre que c'est un progrès.[7]

The Quarrel of the Ancients and Moderns

Of special note is Sainte-Beuve's recognition of the importance of the Quarrel. In general his contemporaries overlooked the debate, dismissing it as either trivial or part of a dead past. Although they echoed many of its arguments, few, if any, gave credit for their ideas on aesthetic progress to the proper originators. Sainte-Beuve saw beyond the pettiness of much of the Quarrel and recognized the eternal nature of it. He felt that the fundamental question argued by Perrault and Boileau—whether recent artistic creations could be superior to those of the past or whether the ancients had once and for all achieved the ultimate—was the same question asked by the Hugos and Stendhals of his time. Although the Quarrel as a historical phenomenon lasted but a hundred years, Sainte-Beuve maintained that "sous des formes diverses [elle] s'est renouvelée depuis, querelle aussi vieille que le monde, depuis

---

[7] Sainte-Beuve. *Portraits contemporains*. Nouvelle éd., revue et corrigée. (Paris: Didier, libraire-éditeur, 1855), I, 516.

que le monde n'est plus enfant, et qui durera aussi longtemps que lui, tant qu'il ne se croira pas tout à fait vieillard."[8] The emphasis on the age of mankind is significant. For such a revolt against authority to have taken place, Sainte-Beuve believed, man had to have gained maturity. He needed the boldness of youth, its optimism, as well as the self-confidence experience brings. Old age, despite its comfort in past accomplishments, would doubtless be too pesimistic in realizing to what extent it fell short of its goal to cling to such a dream as that of progress.

With such a point of view in mind Sainte-Beuve states that two conditions are prerequisite for such a quarrel to occur. First, antiquity must be well known. Second, modernity must be brilliant and flowering enough to feel distinct and emancipated from the past. Applying these standards to French history, Sainte-Beuve believed that only the Age of Louis XIV met them. The Middle Ages was too uninformed of classical antiquity and its greatness to feel challenged. In addition, it lacked the necessary brilliance for revolt. The Renaissance, although meeting the second condition, was too involved in rediscovering antiquity to have the proper perspective for judging it. (*C.L.*, XIII, 134–135)

During the era of the Sun King, ripe as it was for insurrection, the revolt in literature would never have taken place without the stimulus of an outside force, Sainte-Beuve adds. Science was the catalyst. It had drastically and distinctly set modern man apart from his predecessors, giving him immense material advantage over them. This led him to conclude, although erroneously in the critic's opinion, that he was superior to his ancestors in all aspects, even artistically. (*C.L.*, XIII, 136) Sainte-Beuve did not deny that progress could occur in the arts, but he refused a facile explanation for it. He saw no relation between scientific and artistic advance.

---

[8] Sainte-Beuve. *Causeries du lundi*. 5e éd. (Paris: Garnier frères, libraires-éditeurs, s.d.), XIII, 133. This article was prompted by the publication of Hippolyte Rigault's definitive history of the Quarrel by Hachette in 1856. Sainte-Beuve does not review the entire debate but chooses to comment upon representative aspects.

To prove his contention that there have always been those who believed modernity superior to antiquity, Sainte-Beuve cites antique examples of the Quarrel. He mentions a similar debate in Greece prior to the reign of Alexander, another in Rome at the time of Seneca. Seneca's attitude, as revealed in a letter to Lucilius, is similar to that of both Perrault and Sainte-Beuve, as seen in the following excerpt:

J'honore les découvertes de la sagesse [des anciens] et leurs auteurs; j'aime à y entrer comme dans un héritage laissé à tous. C'est pour moi qu'ils ont acquis tout cela, pour moi qu'ils ont travaillé. Mais soyons comme un bon père de famille, accroissons à notre tour ce que nous avons reçu. Que ce patrimoine par moi agrandi se transmette à mes descendants. Il y a encore beaucoup à faire, et il y aura toujours beaucoup; et à *celui-là qui naîtra après mille siècles, l'occasion ne manquera jamais d'ajouter encore quelque chose de nouveau.* Mais quand même tout aurait été trouvé par les Anciens, il y aura toujours cette nouveauté, à savoir l'application, l'usage habile et la combinaison de ce que les autres ont trouvé. . . . Ceux qui nous ont précédés ont beaucoup fait, mais ils n'ont pu rien parfaire: Multi egerunt qui ante nos fuerunt, sed non peregerunt. (*C.L.*, XIII, 138)

Seneca's belief in the open-mindedness of the quarrel and in the possibility of improving on the works of others was shared by Sainte-Beuve. The critic saw his task as that of knowing the application, the use and the combination of what others had found. By recreating works in criticism he would be following Seneca's advice. To Sainte-Beuve this often meant perfecting them.

Of the many *querelleurs* Sainte-Beuve chose to discuss l'abbé de Pons, a supporter of La Motte and his translation of Homer. Houdar de la Motte had modernized the *Iliad* to appeal to genteel French society of his day, removing barbaric episodes such as noblemen doing their own laundry and rephrasing crude expressions, omitting unmentionable words. Sainte-Beuve points out that La Motte's translation was no longer Homer's work. While perhaps more polite and elegant in the opinion of the eighteenth century, it lacked the original's freshness and beauty, albeit somewhat primitive. La Motte and his defender, de Pons, were wrong, he thought, to have confused the orders of literary merit and social refinement and not to have appreciated a youthful language for its peculiar qualities. "Il s'agissait," Sainte-Beuve comments, "avec Homère des qualités vives, brillantes, harmonieuses et musicales, des langues adolescentes, souffle, véhémence, torrent, abondance, grandeur, feu et richesse. Voilà les caractères continus de l'*Iliade* que ni Pons ni La Motte ne soupçonnait pas." (*C.L.*, XIII, 154)

Pons' error, important because it is repeated by the Romantics, is his argument that modernity—its language and point of view—is superior to antiquity. In making such a comparison he had confused the ages of man and falsely weighted an older epoch against a younger one, when middle-age and youth have entirely different qualities. One should be able to appreciate the childhood of man which produced primitive art, closer to nature, while living in a more sophisticated and artificial age, Sainte-Beuve argued. (*C.L.*, XIII, 155)

Speaking as a critic and a scholar, Sainte-Beuve indicted the abbé and La Motte for their lack of knowledge of the ancients they had condemned. Neither possessed the background for comparing literatures. They were unaccustomed to placing themselves in different historical points of view. They lacked the ability to remain neutral, to view art as a relative phenomenon. One remembers Sainte-Beuve's own claim to impartiality and the wide gap between practice and theory in his relations with the Romantics.

Pons' worth lies in the fact that he tossed off the yoke of servility toward the ancients. Pons rejected authority and thought for himself. He was especially correct, in Sainte-Beuve's opinion, in refusing to accept the *Iliad* as the model for all epics to come. Pons is to be admired, the critic concludes, for having taught men to appreciate Homer with independence. (*C.L.*, XIII, 157)

A final important point made by Sainte-Beuve in his evaluation of the Quarrel in his stand against man's tendency to denigrate the present. Like Lamartine, Sainte-Beuve explains that it is a human trait to decry one's own times. A longing for a Golden Age, be it past or future, is natural but wasteful. Creativity can only flourish when the creator is at one with his environment—the basic tenet of his theory of the true classic, the ideal writer, which Sainte-Beuve develops at great length later.

Man's pessimism probably stems from his discouragement over the lack of moral progress, Sainte-Beuve suggests. Certainly modern man is no better than his ancestors, but also no worse. Intellectually, as well as scientifically and materially, he was advanced, Sainte-Beuve believed. The mere accumulation of ideas over the ages offers modern man a richer treasury from which to draw. He should be content with this. Modern man has a striking advantage over the ancients, Sainte-Beuve points out. Contemporaries, by virtue of being alive, possess the potential of improving on their lot, of creating a better work of art. The deeds of the ancients cannot become better or worse. Their limitations are fixed forever. Like Lamartine and Vigny, Sainte-Beuve betrays a belief in a cyclical view of history when he states that each generation rises to a summit for a moment and is able to view all else below it. The moment of triumph is brief and eventually each generation must yield to its successor. (*C.L.*, XIII, 133)

In general these remarks are optimistic. Sainte-Beuve does not wholly champion modernity but encourages its independence and self-esteem within limits. A more pessimistic note is sounded in an article entitled "La Grèce en 1863" when he laments that the moderns seem to be winning the battle. Pride in the present must always be tempered by a healthy respect for the past. He fears that the mid-nineteenth century had lost sight of past greatness.

Tôt ou tard, je le crains, les Anciens, Homère en tête, perdront la bataille,—une moitié au moins de la bataille. Tâchons, pour l'honneur du drapeau, nous qui soutenons la retraite, que ce soit le plus tard possible, et que la nouveauté en partie si légitime, ne batte pourtant pas à plate couture la tradition. (*N.L.*, V, 323)

Romanticism

Because of Sainte-Beuve's emotional involvement with

247

the Romantics his judgment of the movement must be questioned. While a budding poet, a newcomer to the *Cénacle*, Sainte-Beuve could not find high enough praise to bestow on the group of young authors whose future seemed so glorious. For a time Victor Hugo was a god, but unfortunately Adèle Hugo was also a goddess, and the unrestrained affections of Sainte-Beuve toward Mme Hugo quite reasonably cooled the friendship with her husband. Sainte-Beuve's abandonment of poetry for criticism also served to separate him from the Romantic fraternity. More and more he became their judge rather than their colleague. As his critical nature developed, the faults of his former friends became more apparent. Their initial claims to have set the literary woods on fire appeared to be childish exaggerations. In some instances—especially concerning Romantic poetry—Sainte-Beuve honestly recognized the important contribution of the group, but he also noted that the accomplishments often fell short of the claims. Keeping in mind the change of attitude undergone by the critic, one more easily understands his contradictory statements on Romanticism, his initial belief that each new work was evidence of great progress in art and his subsequent complaint that the Romantics were only conceited children.

Sainte-Beuve recognized the literary battle between Romantics and Classicists as another episode in the eternal Quarrel of the Ancients and Moderns. Those who attacked the new movement, he wrote as late as the 1850's, were the literary Tories who are always present to defend an exclusive taste and a fixed language. Such reactionaries repeatedly struggle to hold the line against artistic advance, claiming the outer limits of innovation to have already been set definitively. They fight a losing battle, however, for each generation gains new concessions. These Tories existed in the seventeenth and eighteenth centuries, he commented, and in the nineteenth had attacked Mme de Staël, Chateaubriand, and Lamartine. By the 1850's they had chosen new targets. Sainte-Beuve's explanation for this antagonism, like Gautier's, was that the French are born with a penchant for literary civil wars. The ancients always oppose the moderns, seldom realizing that they were once moderns themselves.[9] Looking back on the accomplishments of Romanticism, Sainte-Beuve singles out poetry as its greatest achievement. During the Restoration lyricism seemed to have flourished.

Après les premières années de tâtonnement et de légère incertitude, on vit se dessiner en tous sens, des tentatives nouvelles—en histoire, en philosophie, en critique, en art. La poésie eut de bonne heure sa place dans ce concours universel: elle sut se rajeunir et par le sentiment et par la forme. Elle aussi, à son tour, elle put produire des merveilles. (*C.L.*, XIV, 69)

Although the program which Romanticism had set for itself was too ambitious to be wholly accomplished, in the main a great deal was achieved, Sainte-Beuve conceded. Poetic language enjoyed a new freedom to develop. New sources of inspiration were found. In short, had Romantic poetry not existed, modern French literature would have been greatly improverished.[10] If lyricism was the strong point of Romanticism, its nostalgia and escapist tendencies were its weakness, in Sainte-Beuve's opinion. Although inspiration from the Middle Ages, the Orient, the primitive past, or idealized future added color to the Romantics' writings, and although authors presented their sources in a new light, these qualities betrayed a fundamental disquiet in the Romantic nature which set the writer against his times and served to bring on his downfall. (*C.L.*, XIV, 70) Ironically, Sainte-Beuve here turns against Romanticism

---

[9] Sainte-Beuve. *Oeuvres: Premiers Lundis, Portraits littéraires, Fin des Portraits littéraires, Portraits de femmes.* Texte présenté et annoté par Maxime Leroy. Ed. de la Pléiade. (Paris: Gallimard, 1951), II, 1094.

[10] "Mais étendons notre vue et songeons un peu à ce qu'a été la poésie lyrique moderne . . . et demandons-nous quelle figure nous ferions avec tant de richesses étrangères modernes, si nous n'avions pas eu notre poésie, cette même école tant ralliée. Vous vous en moquez à votre aise en famille, et pour la commodité de votre discours, le jour où vous entrez à l'Académie; mais devant l'Europe, supposez-la absente, quelle lacune!" (*C.L.*, XIV, 78)

its indictment of Neo-Classicism. In his opinion neither school was timely and thus both were failures. Each wasted creative energy in its denigration of the present and preference for the past. Each favored illusion over reality. The notable exception to this group, Balzac, whose writings were both timely and realistic, nevertheless gets no recognition for his immunity to the Romantic malady. In principle, it was the writer such as Balzac whom Sainte-Beuve claimed to admire most, the artist at peace with his epoch, who faithfully reproduced it. Having favored Realism over Romanticism, Sainte-Beuve's silence concerning Balzac's and Stendhal's importance in its development is strikingly unfair. Personal pique can be the only explanation.

In reviewing the history of the movement Sainte-Beuve points out that in less than fifty years its momentun had diminished considerably. Instead of marching forward, progressing, as it did especially during the period of the Restoration, Romanticism in the late 1840's dragged itself along, its members divided among themselves without the spirit of a group. Such an evolution seemed natural to the critic, for he believed that literary movements are destined to flower and fade as did Vigny and Lamartine. It was time for Romanticism to have a replacement, he remarked. (*Chat.*, I, 32) Doubtless Realism was his choice.

Interestingly Sainte-Beuve also viewed the great diversity of talent among the Romantics as a liability. He too compares the epoch to the Renaissance, but negatively. (*Por. cont.*, II, 424) He felt that unity was a prime virtue. Without it there could be only dilettantism. An age like the Renaissance had not yet found its way, in his opinion. Selectivity and maturity such as exhibited in the Age of Louis XIV had produced better works. The Romantics, with their desire to do all—poetry, drama, and novels—wasted much effort. Had Hugo been able to control his orchestra of talents, Sainte-Beuve concludes, the result would have been much more impressive. (*Por. cont.*, II, 328) Such a judgment seems unduly harsh.

Turning from Sainte-Beuve's general remarks on Romanticism to more specific statements on its individual authors, let us focus our attention on his reaction to their theories of aesthetic progress and to their claims to have accomplished it.

Mme de Staël was a true heroine for Sainte-Beuve, a woman of rare intelligence. He was impressed by her treatise on literature and theory of perfectibility. Sainte-Beuve did not accept all of her conclusions, however; for example he thought she had mistakenly preferred the Romans to the Greeks, supposedly for greater *sensibilité*, when the opposite seemed to be the case to him. In general, though, he found the treatise to contain much truth. (Chat., I, 68) It was the optimism of the author, her firm faith in the future of mankind, her fervent wish to see political and social stability and the establishment of liberty, in sum, her humanitarianism, which endeared her to Sainte-Beuve. Unfortunately her contemporaries did not recognize her fine qualities, and because she exaggerated her arguments to prove her point, they dismissed her as unreliable. (*Por. litt.*, I, 398) Had Mme de Staël been accepted, she could have exerted a beneficial influence on the development of the arts in the nineteenth century. She could have served as a nucleus around which the emerging Romantic Movement could have formed, Sainte-Beuve suggests. (Plé., II, 1132)

Sainte-Beuve stands out as an exception among the writers of his age for his interest in Mme de Staël's theory of perfectibility and more so for his fine understanding of its complex construction. Few writers of this period seemed concerned with her dream. Several reiterated her arguments, but without acknowledging their source. Sainte-Beuve, on the other hand, refers to her and her writings frequently. Perhaps because he did not know her personally, he could more fully enjoy her talents.

Sainte-Beuve seized the distinction which Mme de Staël had made in the application of her theory of perfectibility to the fine arts. In general, she had proclaimed it inapplicable, with the exception of poetry, which, having an intellectual basis, was able to progress as mankind increased in knowledge. Sainte-Beuve refers to this often-ignored detail, implying agreement with it.

Mme de Staël n'assujettit pas à la loi de perfectibilité les beaux-arts, ceux qui tiennent à l'imagination; mais elle croit au progrès, surtout dans les sciences, la philosophie, l'histoire même, et aussi, à certains égards, dans la poésie, qui, de tous les arts, étant celui qui se rattache le plus directement à la pensée, admet chez les modernes un accent plus profond de rêverie, de tristesse, et une analyse de passions inconnue aux anciens. (Plé., II, 1084)

Sainte-Beuve praised Chateaubriand for his originality, calling him the greatest writer of imagination in the nineteenth century. (*C.L.*, I, 452) The critic's estimation of Chateaubriand is exceedingly high because he thought of the author of *Le Génie* as a turning point in literature. Sainte-Beuve speaks of him as the first writer of the modern decadence. To have labeled the beginning of the Romantic era as the onset of decadence seems strange. This opinion comes of course from post-Romantic Sainte-Beuve who by the 1850's viewed Romanticism's dissatisfaction with the present as symptomatic of literary ill health.

Chateaubriand's merit lay in his ability as a magician of words. Sainte-Beuve felt that he had no rival in this capacity, having reintroduced lyricism into literature after a century of unpoetic, philosophical writings.

En France nul n'a mieux conçu et pratiqué cette magie des syllabes, cet assemblage, cet accord des mots heureux et beaux par eux-mêmes, que M. de Chateaubriand; et quoiqu'il l'ait fait avec préméditation, avec artifice, il y a tout lieu de l'en remercier comme du plus grand service rendu au goût, après l'excès de métaphysique et la débauche d'abstraction qui avait précédé. (*C.L.*, XIII, 169)

One can assume that Sainte-Beuve viewed as progress the achievements of this magician. The critic was struck by his skilful blending of inspiration from antiquity and the Middle Ages in *Le Génie*. (*Chat*. I, 91) He also recognized the invention of a new means of expression in literature in Chateaubriand's development of the sentiment of melancholic revery in *René*. (*C.L.*, XIV, 72) In fact, it is this work which Sainte-Beuve labels Chateaubriand's masterpiece. (*C.L.*, I, 452)

Hugo as judged by Sainte-Beuve was a superior poet and in this genre may have accomplished literary progress, but in drama he was a failure, in the novel, good but not outstandingly so. It is difficult to determine an honest appraisal of Hugo because Sainte-Beuve's public criticism of him was so full of hero worship in the early period, then as friendship waned, the reviews ceased, and the private comments became increasingly vitriolic. One can practically dismiss the critic's opinion as being too biased to be valuable in all but his statements on Hugo's poetry. In this instance he continually showed deep admiration. Since his appreciation did not falter despite the many upsets in his relationship with the poet, one can assume that it was sincere and profound.

In an early article on Hugo, the poet, Sainte-Beuve shows no hesitation in acknowledging his accomplishments as progress. The critic claims that it is the young Romantic who truly created the ode in France, that Ronsard's were mere preliminary studies of the genre. Written in 1829 the article is flawed by exaggeration.

> Victor Hugo, le premier peut-être depuis Pindare, et précisément parce qu'il n'a songé nullement à l'imiter, a conçu l'ode dans toute sa naïveté, et dans toute sa splendeur, et en a fait, non pas une oeuvre de cabinet, une étude ingénieuse et artificielle, mais un cri de passion, un chant solennel et inspiré. (Plé. I, 298)

Sainte-Beuve felt Hugo unrivalled in his political odes, e.g. "Ode à la colonne," and credits him with having invented a new kind, the imaginative ode. The young critic exclaimed: "Et là encore, on peut dire qu'il a passé par tous les progrès et qu'il les a épuisés." He cites as an example of this new poetry "Feu du ciel," "Mazeppa," and "Les Fantômes," from *Les Orientales*. He goes so far as to say that after Hugo no further progress in ode writing could possibly be made. (Plé. I, 299)

As a novelist Hugo most pleased Sainte-Beuve with his *Dernier jour d'un condamné*. The critic notes in it a penetrating analysis of sentiment which had no precedent in literature.

> Je ne [crois] pas qu'on ait encore analysé avec tant de profondeur et de précision des sentiments humains à la fois aussi intimes et aussi pontifs qu'en ce dernier roman de Victor Hugo; jamais les fibres les plus déliées et les plus vibrantes de l'âme n'ont été à ce point mises à nu et en relief; c'est comme une dissection au vif sur le cerveau d'un condamné. (Plé. I, 301)

In drama *Cromwell* was accepted by the young Sainte-Beuve as evidence of progress in art. In 1829 Sainte-Beuve felt that it indicated the correct route for drama to follow. The play had a double value. Primarily it was a work of art; secondly, a literary manifesto. Thus it doubly served aesthetic progress. (Plé. I, 273)

Few would agree with this generous appraisal today, it should be noted. These flattering views date from the height of friendship between Hugo and Sainte-Beuve.

Their enthusiasm should be balanced by later negative remarks. The private notebook, *Mes Poisons*, abounds with them, often caustic, personal diatribes labeling Hugo grotesque, absurd, a conceited fool. In contrast to the flattery earlier written on *Cromwell*, in this notebook Sainte-Beuve, thinking of the fiasco *Les Burgraves*, gleefully related that Hugo suffered no greater failure than in the drama. [11]

Sainte-Beuve was far from consistent in assigning rank to the members of the Romantic Movement. He once claimed to have avoided making a hierarchy, but he frequently was guilty of doing so. His estimation of Lamartine was high, perhaps because he considered him not really a Romantic but an independent figure, whose own development paralleled that of the Movement. (*C.L.*, XIV, 75) Lamartine, in his estimation, was second only to Chateaubriand as leader of the century's artistic revolution. (*Por. Litt.*, I, 310)

Sainte-Beuve credits Lamartine, as he did Chateaubriand and Hugo, with having produced a kind of poetry which displayed harmonies previously unknown in literature. Once singling him out as the poet par excellence of the century, he wrote that it was Lamartine "de qui date, en effet, le renouvellement de notre muse moderne . . . et par qui la lyre française a pour la première fois trouvé ces cordes nouvelles, inouïes, *inaudita prius*." (*Por. litt.*, III, 143–144) Poetically Lamartine contributed significantly to the progress of the arts.

It was Lamartine's flirtation with the idea of social prog-

---

[11] Sainte-Beuve. *Mes poisons, cahiers intimes inédits*. Publiés avec une introduction et des notes par Victor Giraud. (Paris: Librairie Plon, 1926), p. 47.

ress which most irritated Sainte-Beuve. The critic viewed this as an attempt on the poet's part to burden the muse with an inferior task. Beauty, not utopia, should be the goal of art, Sainte-Beuve insisted. Lamartine was wrong in trying to achieve both. "La Muse de poésie, tel que je le conçois," the critic wrote," est si à part et si au-dessus de ces choses, qui même, quand elles semblent immenses aux contemporains, ne sont que des choses d'un jour." (*Chat.*, I, 242) Art must not become too timely or it will be forgotten with the events which inspired it, Sainte-Beuve warned, modifying his earlier stand.

Vigny is credited with having added a new elegance to poetry. Even after the wonderful creations of Chateaubriand and Lamartine, his works seemed strange and new. Lyrically Vigny is unsurpassed, as evidenced by his "Eloa." "C'est éblouissant de ton, de touche, et d'une magnificence élégante que la poésie française n'avait point connue jusqu'alors." (*N.L.*, VI, 411)

Vigny's sympathy for the idea of progress received no more approbation from the critic than did Lamartine's. Sainte-Beuve was amused, however, by Vigny's attitude. Typically the poet was only half committed to the doctrine, Sainte-Beuve felt. He was too much a fatalist to be a true utopian. "Il regrettait de l'ordre ancien plus de choses encore qu'il n'en espérait de l'ordre nouveau, il voulait et il ne voulait pas." (*N.L.*, VI, 427)

Sainte-Beuve admired Gautier for his contribution to literary progress by his development of art criticism. Gautier was a true innovator because he was able to criticize art as a painter as well as a writer. Diderot and Stendhal, admirable critics that they were, always viewed their subjects as outsiders would, uninitiated into the secrets of the craft. (*N.L.*, VI, 314–315) It was the unique association of artists and writers in the Romantic Movement which made Gautier's contribution possible. By the time the young Théophile had joined the group, literature and painting were well allied. Painter and author shared the secrets of each other's techniques and when possible attempted to transfer them to their own disciplines. The influence of this reciprocity was seen in the establishment of two important reviews which helped to elevate the public's artistic taste—*L'Artiste* and *La Gazette des Beaux-Arts*. (*N.L.*, VI, 316–317)

Gautier stands alone in literary history because of his verbal portraits. How unfortunate for us moderns, Sainte-Beuve complains, that the ancients had no such writer to record for posterity their works of art. Paintings may last but a short time, whereas these sensitive word-pictures can be observed indefinitely.

> Imaginez ce que ce serait si un Pausanius, un Pline, avait fait pour les tableaux des anciens exactement ce que Théophile Gautier fait aujourd'hui pour les nôtres: les érudits seraient dispensés de tant conjecturer sur ce qu'ils ne savent pas bien. On ne connaît plus les tableaux grecs; il faut les deviner. (*N.L.*, VI, 319)

In trying to depict verbally what others had done with colors and lines Gautier was forced to extend his vocabulary, adding innumerable terms of art. Some of these words, those which were not too technical, have won a permanent place in literature. Gautier has performed the invaluable service of giving articulation to man's sentiments on art which previously were clumsily expressed.

> Il suffit pour son honneur . . . qu'il ait rendu impossibles après lui les descriptions vagues et ternes dont on se contentait auparavant. Une beauté *incomparable, merveilleuse, ineffable, extraordinaire, incroyable*, toutes ces qualifications indécises et commodes, si chères au grand siècle, à Mlle de Scudéry et à son admirateur, M. Cousin, ne sont plus de mise aujourd'hui. Le mot *indicible* n'est plus français depuis ce nouveau maître en fait de vocabulaire a su tout dire. (*N.L.*, VI, 329)

The four remaining authors studied in this work—Stendhal, Balzac, Musset, and Baudelaire—were not appreciated by Sainte-Beuve, and thus elicited no acknowledgment that they, too, had contributed to the progress of literature during the nineteenth century. André Billy in his *Sainte-Beuve, sa vie et son temps* pleads the critic's defense on the grounds that the personalities of these authors so irritated Sainte-Beuve that they obscured the value of their works for him. Billy goes so far as to claim that Sainte-Beuve was more a moralist than a critic or aesthetician. [12]

Sainte-Beuve himself attempted to explain his aversion to several of his contemporaries in an article published in 1845. He then noted that over the years he had changed position in relation to the Romantics, having begun as their comrade, then later disengaging himself from their influence, becoming their observer and judge. Disentangled from close personal relationships with them, he was freer to detect their faults.

> On peut par là marquer les deux temps de ma manière critique, si j'ose bien en parler ainsi; dans le premier, j'interprète, j'explique, je professe les poètes devant le public, et je suis tout occupé à les faire valoir. Je deviens leur avocat, leur secrétaire, ou encore leur héraut d'armes, comme je me suis vanté et de l'être souvent. Dans le second temps, ce point gagné, je me retourne vers eux, je me fais en partie public, et je les juge. (*Por. cont.*, I, 3)

The above explanation was intended for public consumption. A more forthright statement is found in *Mes Poisons*:

> Il me devient impossible d'écrire sur les principaux auteurs du temps; j'en suis depuis longtemps à juger, non plus leurs ouvrages, mais leur personne même, et à tâcher d'en saisir le dernier mot. Ce genre d'observation touche de trop près à l'homme pour être imprimé de notre vivant. (p. 127)

Diagnosis of Nineteenth-Century Literary Ills

Sainte-Beuve was not particularly optimistic in his appraisal of the present state of affairs in literature or in predicting its future development. His cynicism and lack of commitment to the principles of any one school increased with the passing of the years, marking the end of his career in great contrast with his earlier optimism and sense of alignment with emerging Romanticism. Sainte-Beuve more and more took on the appearance of a crotchety old man, dissatisfied with his long and busy life, who in the twilight years reviewed his life, remembering the faults of his associates, trying to have the last

---

[12] André Billy. (Paris: Flammarion, éditeur, 1952), I, 122.

word in old arguments and wishing to avenge himself for every slight. He gives the impression that the nineteenth century was a more irritating age in which to live. Many of Sainte-Beuve's criticisms of the times reflect the opinions of the other authors studied here. Yet the critic's are more acrid. The repetition of his complaints throughout his articles leads one to conclude that Sainte-Beuve was more obsessed with his era's failings than were his contemporaries.

Sainte-Beuve was not tempted by a belief in the perfectibility of mankind. Rather he spoke of human folly as a constant factor throughout the ages. In a fit of depression he wrote in 1843 that his era seemed an exception to this rule, for folly was more rampant, man more stupid than ever. (*Por. cont*, II, 327)

The main reason for the early nineteenth-century's literary failure was, in Sainte-Beuve's opinion, the conceit inherent in the Romantic temperament. The critic's term for this trait, to him the most irritating of all the flaws of the Romantics, was *fatuité*, meaning self-complacency as well as conceit. Sainte-Beuve traced its origin to Lord Byron, the arch-Romantic, the super-egotistical. (*Por. cont.*, II, 329) Vanity had prompted the Romantics to assume that all their utterances were perfect in form and content. Hence they had refused to labor over their works, polishing rough ideas into lasting form.

> Le principal défaut des artistes d'aujourd'hui, peintres ou poètes, c'est de prendre l'intention pour le fait, de croire qu'il leur suffit d'avoir pensé une belle chose pour que cette chose paraisse belle; au lieu de se donner la peine de réaliser l'idéal de leur conception, ils nous en jettent le fantôme. (*Por. cont.*, III, 512)

How much better it would have been to have lived in a less pretentious age, Sainte-Beuve must have mused, uncluttered by Hugos and Balzacs. Oh, to have had more masterpieces and less promise of them. Such was not his luck.

> Prenez des noms, je ne m'en charge pas, mais essayez. C'est d'un pompeux, ou d'un pimpant, ou d'un négligé, ou d'un discret, ou d'un libertin affectés. Oh! qu'on me rende la race de ces honnêtes gens de talent qui faisaient tout bonnement de leur mieux, avec naturel, travail et sincérité. (*Por. cont.*, II, 330)

The conceit of the second-generation Romantics had as a by-product greed—greed for glory and for money. The literature which was produced with these goals in mind was labeled by the critic, "Industrial Literature." It was a product designed for a market, intended to earn a profit. Art was of little concern to its mercenary creators.

Industrial literature had always existed, Sainte-Beuve admits, but never to the extent that it did after the Revolution of 1830. From that date on, authors seemed more open in seeking remuneration. They did not hesitate to fix a price on their talent. Of course, Sainte-Beuve had in mind Balzac as the epitome of the *littérateur industriel*. Because of the novelist's activities in the "Société des gens de lettres," a union whose purpose was to protect and enhance the material well-being of its writer-members, he further lost the critic's respect. Balzac went too far in assigning monetary value to each member's talent. His behavior was both ungentlemanly and unliterary.

> Sa lettre [de Balzac] sur la propriété littéraire . . . ne tend à rien moins qu'à proposer au Gouvernement d'acheter les oeuvres des *dix ou douze maréchaux de France*, à commencer par celles de l'auteur lui-même qui s'évalue à *deux millions*, si j'ai bien compris. Vous imaginez-vous le Gouvernement désintéressant l'auteur de la *Physiologie du mariage*, afin de la mieux répandre, et débitant les *Contes drôlatiques* comme on vend du papier timbré? (*Por. cont.*, II, 469)

Literary industrialism was an outgrowth of democracy, a concept perhaps acceptable on a political level, but not on an artistic one, Sainte-Beuve maintained. The masses now required a literature for their level. If a new work did not meet their standards, inferior to those of good art, its author was condemned. Everyman demanded a voice in literary criticism. He had replaced the censor in decreeing what should and should not be produced. The result of this extension of democracy into the arts proved disastrous, Sainte-Beuve declared. Only specialists, aesthetic aristocrats, like himself, should be allowed to judge artistic creations. Sainte-Beuve, like other Romantics, did not like competition from the man in the street. (*Por. cont.*, II, 454)

259

Industrial literature was responsible for immoral works as well, Sainte-Beuve felt. Writers knew that sensationalism and tawdry subjects sold better than moral, less scintillating ones. Eager to earn a profit they indulged the depravity of their readers.

> La fatuité combinée à la cupidité, à l'industrialisme, au besoin d'exploiter fructeusement les mauvais penchants du public, a produit, dans les oeuvres d'imagination et dans le roman, un raffinement d'immoralité et de dépravation qui devient un fait de plus en plus quotidien et caractéristique, une plaie ignoble et livide qui chaque matin s'étend. (*Por. cont.*, II, 330)

"Classical Literature,"
Sainte-Beuve's Formula for Progress

These gross faults of present day writers convinced Sainte-Beuve that "classical literature" alone was worthy of esteem. Without it there could be no progress in art. "Classical literature," as Sainte-Beuve defined it, borrowing a great deal from Goethe, is literature which enjoys a healthy outlook, one which is in accord with its epoch, content with its social cadre and political institutions. Quite obviously Romanticism was not at peace with its age—neither was Sainte-Beuve for that matter. Forced to live in an era which galled them, Romantic writers were unable to create a lasting, harmonious work, Sainte-Beuve thought. Whatever merits their creations may contain, their disquiet distracted from their overall value.

> Les littératures romantiques, qui sont surtout de coup de main et d'aventure, ont leurs mérites, leurs exploits, leur rôle brillant, mais en dehors des cadres, elles sont à cheval sur deux ou trois époques, jamais établies en plein dans une seule, inquiètes, chercheuses, excentriques de leur nature, ou très en avant ou très en arrière, volontiers ailleurs,—errantes. (*C.L.*, XV, 369–370)

The classicist in his contentment is not immune from sadness, pain, or suffering, the traits emphasized by the Romantic, but he controls them, not the other way round, realizing that beauty must be tranquil. Agony and frustration are not allowed to dominate his works. (C.L., XV, 370)

There is a long tradition of classical literature, dating from antiquity. In France it has flourished during the reign of Louis XIV when there was unity among writers, a singleness of purpose in art. Men of that time were proud of their epoch and its accomplishments, quite the opposite of present-day writers. The eighteenth century destroyed the tradition by its preference for the individual to the group, for the eccentric to the normal. It paved the way for the cult of abnormality in the nineteenth century. In doing so classicism disappeared from art. Into the vacuum came decadence.

> La vraie décadence, dans une littérature brillante et qui compte encore des talents puissants, prend sa source dans le désaccord qu'il y a entre l'inspiration véritable et le résultat apparent dans le manque d'harmonie et de vérité au sein des plus beaux ouvrages. (*Chat.*, I, 103)

Chateaubriand serves as an example of the century's decline. His romantic qualities—his nostalgia for the past, the exotic—were decadent in nature. *Atala*, his masterpiece, signals the corruption of literature. Its source of inspiration should have been nineteenth-century France, not Homer, the Bible, and the American wilderness.

> L'inconvénient, c'est à avoir à chercher des beautés simples ou grandioses en y remontant avec effort, plutôt que de les rencontrer directement et de première venue: mais cet inconvénient à peu près inévitable, devient un des caractères inhérents à toutes les secondes et troisièmes époques; et c'est pour cela que nous ne sommes pas en 1800 à l'aurore d'un grand siècle, mais seulement au début de la plus brillante des périodes de déclin. (*Chat.*, I, 200)

Even Romanticism's return to nature, counted by some as its principal progress, is dismissed by Sainte-Beuve as a second-rate accomplishment. The ancients were much more successful in rendering nature, he felt, in direct contrast with Chateaubriand, for they did not have to overcome artificiality first.

> C'est que les Anciens n'ont pas eu à faire comme les Modernes, qui sont partis de l'abstrait et du factice social pour revenir au naturel, et qui ont en tout à reconquérir en ce genre. Il a fallu faire violence aux habitudes de salon pour reprendre pied, pas à pas, dans la

nature! Il a fallu (à la lettre) sortir de l'Hôtel de Rambouillet pour découvrir le Mont-Blanc et même la vallée de Montmorency. (*Chat.* I, 243)

Neither was Romanticism's claim of timeliness proof of progress, Sainte-Beuve believed. Basically, the Romantics could never be timely, when they were at odds with their era, a contradiction somehow they never explained. Their boasts of having created a drama suitable for the times was proved false by the revival of Classical theatre in the 1840's, showing the public's preference for simplicity and freshness to Romantic complexity and bombast. (Plé., I, 759)

In drama the Greeks have remained unsurpassed in Sainte-Beuve's estimation. Only *Athalie* and *Polyeucte* can be considered rivals to the works of the ancients. The Greeks achieved a beauty and austerity in their plays which are statuesque. Because of this their dramas have stood over the centuries as unique and immortal. Modern tragedy, Classical as well as Romantic, will not enjoy the same fate. It is too emotional, too attached to sentiment. It is framed by society, marked by a specific era. It has suffered the influence of Christianity, encouraging a schizophrenia in its characters. While others have named these same qualities as proof of modern drama's superiority over antiquity's, Sainte-Beuve draws the opposite conclusions. He admits that modern drama has a kind of beauty which is different from the past's, but he does not think it superior. Modern drama is like a finished painting. Greek drama resembles a statue. Interestingly Sainte-Beuve prefers the statue. (Plé. I, 765)

Despite the melancholic nature of the preceding statements, Sainte-Beuve did believe artistic progress possible. He longed for a return of the classical age, to him the literary paradise. With the reestablishment of its doctrines, eternal art would flourish once again. The promise of great works would be fulfilled.

Sainte-Beuve's theory of progress is essentially one of progress by addition, rather than by replacement. His respect for the ancients was too great to allow him to think them inferior to the moderns. He recognized the fact, however, that the ancients were incomplete and needed to be supplanted by more recent artists. Whenever an addition to the existing core of artistic creations occurred, this should be placed alongside its predecessors, extending the breadth of aesthetic achievement. All great works of art, literary ones in particular, have fallen within the limits of the classical tradition, Sainte-Beuve believed. No great writer, not even Shakespeare, has escaped its confines. (*C.L.*, XV, 366) To insure the continuance of great works and great authors the hallowed tradition must be re-established, overcoming the Romantics' resistance to it.

The classical author, by Sainte-Beuve's definition, is the one who makes progress in art. The true classicist enriches the human mind by augmenting the treasury of human knowledge and/or accomplishments. He is the writer who has discovered a moral truth or eternal passion, when others have felt that all was known. The true classicist extends the boundaries of art by his discoveries and innovations.

Contrary to the Romantics' view of him, the true classicist is not limited by either roles or models. He obeys only his individual genius. There is no one classical style to be followed, but a style for each author. Working in total freedom, the writer remains classical by the quality of his work. (*C.L.*, III, 42)

In agreement with the Romantics, the true classicist abhors imitation. If maintaining the tradition meant simply repetition of the past, then all writers would be Homers or Racines, depending on one's preference. Such an idea is, of course, ludicrous. Furthermore, it smacks of artisanry, not artistry.

Croire qu'en imitant certaines qualités de pureté, de sobriété, de correction et d'élégance, indépendamment du caractère même et de la flamme, on deviendra classique, c'est croire qu'après Racine père, il y a lieu à Racine fils; rôle inestimable et triste, ce qui est le pire en poésie. (*C.L.*, III, 49)

By being himself, by adding to the storehouse of knowledge in his own particular way, each new classicist carries art forward one step. In this sense there is progress in art. The classical tradition being open-ended, man can look forward to continuous aesthetic advance.

Sainte-Beuve's belief is necessarily an eclectic one, for narrowness of any sort would rule out progress beyond a preferred period as does the prejudice of those who feel either Homer or Racine unequalled. Demanding only that each new work have the same fine qualities which characterize the monuments of the past, Sainte-Beuve dreams of a Pantheon of great writers of all sorts who, by fulfilling the condition of adding to the literary treasure, can be called classical.

> Le Temple du goût, je le crois, est à refaire; mais en le rebâtissant, il s'agit simplement de l'agrandir, et qu'il devienne le Panthéon de tous les nobles humains, de tous ceux qui ont accru pour une part notable et durable la somme des jouissances et des titres de l'esprit. (*C.L.*, III, 50)

In Sainte-Beuve's imagined Pantheon there is no rank. The moderns stand beside the ancients as equals. Each man is noted for his unique contribution, his own particular progress, but on the whole his works are not valued over those of another. (*C.L.*, III, 51–53)

The time has come for the appearance of another classical writer, Sainte-Beuve announced in the 1860s. The poetic promise of the early nineteenth century has been unfulfilled. Disciples have proved inferior to masters, they have been imitators, not innovators. The new poet will doubtless achieve literary progress, Sainte-Beuve believed, for he now has total freedom in which to work. He has no restrictions on language or his source of inspiration. He can run the gamut from the simplicity of the *trouvères* to the hardiness of the moderns, from the grandeur of the "Chanson de Roland" to the lyricism of Musset. The richest tradition now exists on which the new poet can build.

> Votre palette est la plus riche, la plus diverse, la plus variée; vous n'avez qu'à puiser au gré de vos inspirations, suivant votre habileté et votre audace; mais vous ne confondrez rien, vous unirez tout; vous fondrez tout à la flamme de votre génie; vous remettez chaque chose à son point dans la trame du bel art, ô grand poète qui naîtrez! (*Por. litt.*, III, 186)

By virtue of the richness of the background on which the new poet will build, his accomplishments should be considerable, but in the matter of talent or genius, he will not be more gifted than the great poets of the past. Genius is a constant factor, Sainte-Beuve maintained. In this area there is no progress. Progress occurs only by use of an ever-increasingly rich tradition by men of roughly equal talent. (*C.L.*, XV, 371)

In the history of literature it was the writer who built upon the accomplishments of the past whom Sainte-Beuve admired the most. Those who combine the best of several traditions, adding to them innovations of their own, ranked highest in his estimation. Dante was such an author. He superimposed medieval Christian thought on a background of pagan classical tradition. In addition, he created a new literary type in the character of Beatrice. By synthesis and invention Dante in his *Commedia* furthered the progress of art. Racine is also admired by the critic for his combination of the Biblical and the Hellenic. *Athalie* displays the best of both traditions. (*C.L.*, XV, 361, 365)

Sainte-Beuve's theory of literary progress is far from startling. Its conservative claims reflect the character of the critic who preferred the *juste milieu* to extremes. That Sainte-Beuve believed artistic progress possible at all is in some ways surprising, for his preferences in literature lay in the past, not the present. One can only conclude that it is remarkable that the bitterly disillusioned Sainte-Beuve of the 1860s still held to the hope of future literary triumphs when, in his opinion, the century has begun so awkwardly. Pro-classical and pro-ancient that he was, Sainte-Beuve was also a modern. His faith in the eternity of art rivals that of Perrault.

> Les destinées de l'art ne sont pas un accident qu'un autre accident supprime; elles vont reprendre leur cours selon une pente nouvelle, et se creuser un autre lit à travers la société plus magnifique et plus fertile. (*Por. litt.*, I, 395)

265

Chapter Thirteen

Conclusion

The concept of progress, human and aesthetic, debated since the time of the ancient Greeks and Romans, and particularly from the Renaissance to the Revolution in France, continued to evoke interest among French writers of the first half of the nineteenth century.[1] During the Romantic Era, the leading authors of the day sought to determine the nature and extent of man's progress in all his endeavors and especially in his literature. Their opinions on progress often differ from those expressed by earlier debaters. Less certain of either the inevitability or the continuous nature of progress than the seventeenth or eighteenth-century proponents of the doctrine, Romantic writers considered the theory with suspicion and reservation. While not totally abandoning the belief in perfectibility, either of mankind or his art, they qualified the concept, thinking progress to be possible instead of inevitable, sporadic rather than continuous.

As the Romantics differed from their predecessors, they

---

[1] Portions of this chapter, entitled "French Romantics on Aesthetic Progress," were presented before the Pacific Northwest Council on Foreign Languages and Literatures (PNCFL), Edmonton, Alberta, Canada, May 1982.

also disagreed among themselves about the nature and extent of progress in the history of mankind. One finds a variance of opinion ranging from extreme optimism, as in the case of Mme de Staël, to extreme pessimism, Musset's for example, on the question of human and artistic perfectibility—a divergence easily understood when one considers that it is the opinions of highly individualistic authors under study here and that external events, which to some degree conditioned their thinking, were dissimilar for first and second-generation Romantics.

With such divergence in mind then, can one expect to extract a "Romantic Theory of Progress"? Yes, but only to a degree. There are points of agreement which can be totalled to produce a Romantic definition generally acceptable to most contributors, but such a definition is seriously limited. It is more precise to speak of the "Romantics' Theories of Progress," for their discussion was most varied and rich. Instead of conformity or unity, as one might expect from a seventeenth-century mind, one finds in the nineteenth century a mentality which is diverse, if not contradictory, nuanced, and complex. And as a result, the nineteenth-century approach to the question of progress appears more sophisticated and mature than the comparatively simpler and more naïve attitude of earlier partisans of progress. Thus there had been not only an evolution in point of view, but also a maturation in thought since the time of a Du Bellay, Perrault, or Condorcet. As a negative result, however, idealism often gave way to cynicism.

Two factors were perhaps responsible for this change in attitude. First, the Romantics profited from hindsight. Because the theory of progress had been thoroughly discussed for at least three hundred years, it was well formulated and explored. Thus the follies of earlier and less cautious protagonists, who had not yet been intimidated by history's harsh lessons, could be avoided. Secondly, the Romantics brought to the debate an aesthetic sensitivity and curiosity which was without parallel. Their religion of art and cult of the artist caused them to defend the theory of aesthetic progress in an unprecedented manner.

Romantics on Human Progress

Two kinds of progress have been considered here: human and aesthetic. They are, of course, inextricably bound to each other, for literature and the arts being human creations also enjoy the benefits of human advance. Social-minded Romantics were particularly aware of the relationship. Hugo, for example, believed that the arts progressed with humanity, for a more cultivated and better educated public required better works. The Romantics' delineation of human progress was far from uniform. Whereas material, technical, and scientific progress were recognized as well as intellectual advance (i.e., the accumulation of knowledge, not increased genius), moral and social progress proved to be more controversial ideas. Indeed more authors thought man had regressed morally—Stendhal, Musset, and Sainte-Beuve, for example. More kind were Gautier and Baudelaire, who believed mankind to be no better, if no worse.

Social progress was a most divisive issue. Many Romantics believed in it fervently and worked to accomplish it. Others scoffed at the hope of man creating utopia. Mme de Staël, Hugo, Vigny, Lamartine, and Balzac all thought society perfectible and themselves responsible for contributing to its perfection. Mme de Staël believed human perfectibility to be inevitable and indefinite. Man need only wish to progress to do so. The writer was to aid mankind by publishing enlightened treatises designed to correct ills, destroy prejudices, and spread wisdom. Like a benevolent *philosophe* the modern writer was to tutor his less informed brothers in the ways of goodness and truth. Hugo agreed that society was perfectible and that it needed special help to attain its goal. He believed the poet, being divinely inspired, thus more enlightened and intuitive than ordinary man, best suited to guide mankind toward utopia. Hugo likened the poet-leader to a modern Prometheus, for he was to direct mankind from darkness to light.

Whereas Mme de Staël and Hugo unquestionably accepted the task of hastening the perfection of society, Vigny and Lamartine noted the difficulties of the undertaking. The poet, they pointed out, was not always accepted by his brothers as the god-sent leader of mankind and indeed was frequently rejected and persecuted by the masses because of his uniqueness. They warned that the poet's role in society was dual in nature. He was both a messiah and a martyr. Yet, regardless of the sacrifice or persecution involved, neither Vigny nor Lamartine considered relieving the poet of his important mission. Less altruistic writers disagreed. Musset, who did not believe in progress, pointed out that art and morality were entirely separate spheres, which he claimed were unrelated. Beauty, not Truth, was the artist's quest. Propaganda only denatured art. Equally emphatic were Gautier and Baudelaire who rejected Hugo's plea of "art for progress" and embraced instead the philosophy of "art for art."

The rejection of the alliance between art and progress by some Romantics is understandable. First of all, disclaiming social responsibility was a kind of self-defense. Musset, Gautier, and Baudelaire all wished to protect themselves from the hostility of the average man toward the artist. They could not envision martyring themselves unnecessarily for unappreciative humanity.

The Romantics' view of the relationship between artist and public, while varying from paternalism to scorn, was nevertheless founded on a common theory. All Romantics believed in the superiority of the artist, an idea derived from Rousseau, which in turn had come from Plato. Rousseau, like Plato, thought the artist to be morally and aesthetically superior to his fellow man. Both agreed that the price of this gift was social conscience. While Hugo and others accepted both components of the theory, Gautier and Baudelaire rejected the moral aspect and clung more fervently to the aesthetic one.

In the Romantic myth of the artist there was also considerable snobbery. Even charitable Hugo did not think himself the equal of the humanity he was sent to lead. Therefore, uncharitable writers such as Gautier and Baudelaire drew even sharper lines of distinction between themselves and the masses. Gautier thought the artist to be endowed with a sixth sense, aesthetic sensitivity, which elevated him as far above ordinary man as man was above the animals. Baudelaire praised the *sui generis*, the originality of each artist. Sainte-Beuve echoed the idea, describing the artist as that rare being who possessed "une monade unique et individuelle." In all these distinctions there was an assumption of aristocracy, founded on talent, not money, stimulated by the growing disgust of these writers with the leveling processes of the century. Democracy and industrialism were prime targets of their wrath. Equality, they believed, had meant the lowering of standards to a base common denominator. As a result the public was now an indistinguishably mediocre mass. Industrial growth had led to the rise of the bourgeoisie whose money grew more powerful every day. Set apart from the mediocre and materialistic public was the unique and spiritual artist, the isolated superior being.

Romantics on Progress in Literature and the Other Fine Arts

Since the Romantics were highly conscious of their elite status, their pride often led them to conclude that literature was progressing during the nineteenth century because of their own contributions. The Romantic ego played no small part in the formulation of theories of aesthetic advance.

Of the many theories proposed by the Romantics to explain the nature of literary progress, two proved to be more universally acceptable. The first was that because of greater realism modern literature was superior to the works of earlier eras. The second was that contemporary writings, reflective of an advanced civilization, were more complex, more complete, and thus better than the partial and simple literary creations of the past.

The first theory of literary progress through greater realism appeared under many guises. Some Romantics asserted that recent works were more psychological than earlier ones and thus expressed greater understanding of human nature. Both Mme de Staël and Chateaubriand recognized an "interiorization" of literature since the time of the Greeks, meaning that writers' emphasis had changed from primary concern with external events—description—to increased interest in interior motives or passions—analysis. Mme de Staël credited man's increased knowledge of himself and the universe, brought about through continued intellectual progress, for this advance. Chateaubriand thought Christianity responsible for the improvement. Because of the religion's doctrines modern man suffered a kind of schizophrenia, he noted, his soul torn between the forces of good and evil. Due to a highly developed conscience, modern man was more interested than his pagan forebears in explanations, not merely descriptions, of his actions. Musset even agreed with Chateaubriand. He contrasted Sophoclean and Cornelian tragedy, calling one "exterior," the other "interior." Christianity was responsible for this change for the better, he believed.

The increased role of psychology in modern literature inevitably led to the discovery of sentiments previously overlooked by earlier writers less concerned with man's soul. Mme de Staël, Chateaubriand, Gautier, and Baudelaire all pointed to melancholy, which they believed to be a peculiarly modern emotion, whose inclusion in literature had increased the aesthetic quality of recent works. Mme de Staël called the new emotion *douleur*; Chateaubriand *le vague des passions* or *mal du siècle*; Baudelaire spleen. Essentially it was a similar malaise, a feeling of being out of sorts with the times, at odds with the rest of humanity.

Modern writers' attention to romantic love was also heralded as a discovery made possible through new psychological insight which had broadened the aesthetic spectrum. Knowing the human heart better, recent writers now portrayed many nuances of love, particularly the tender and delicate, and offered explanations for the lovers' behavior which earlier writers had either ignored or not noticed. Because of this heightened sensitivity many modern works were considered superior to the colder and cruder writings of the past.

Mme de Staël preferred love to the other "new" sentiments discovered and exploited by her contemporaries, but even she grew weary of its monopoly of novelists' attention. She then advised the depiction of other emotions in the novel,

271

more suitable for older people, such as hate and ambition, to broaden the aesthetic horizon. Her advice was soon followed. Stendhal and Balzac sought out new emotions and new characters, depicting ambition, jealousy, and avarice not only of noble persons, but of bourgeois and peasants as well. The Romantics' quest for realism was not limited to the interior side of man, his passions, but was applied to his exterior or milieu, as well. Descriptions of things as well as explanations of thoughts preoccupied modern writers. Thus they came to surpass the ancients who had once been thought superior in this aspect. Stendhal advised that novels be more realistic when he suggested that the novel should be a mirror traveling along a highway. Balzac concurred and scrupulously depicted decors, giving attention to details overlooked by previous writers. Not only in the novel but in other genres as well writers sought more realism. Chateaubriand criticized the ancients for their lack of descriptive poetry, which he explained was due to their preoccupation with mythology. The ancients, he noted, viewed Neptune, not the sea, and consequently did not see nature but symbols. With Christianity's destruction of the pagan point of view, modern writers' eyes were opened to the wonders of the physical world, and they began to write of landscapes and storms and their new sense of communion with nature.

Hugo saw the incorporation of realism into the drama as evidence of literary progress. By depicting the grotesque as well as the sublime, drama now gave a total and more realistic view of life. Aesthetic potential had doubled, he contended, and the juxtaposition of the two poles of beauty had intensified the positive one. Baudelaire furthered Hugo's attempt at total reality by his inclusion of the ugly rendered beautiful in verse. Gautier applauded both writers' innovations as progress.

Stendhal, believing increased realism heightened the emotional impact of all works of literature, displayed a typically Romantic attitude. He, like Hugo, Musset, and Baudelaire, equated the pleasure works gave with their quality. Because Romantic works moved the reader more, they were better than the more restrained and less cathartic works of Classicism, he contended.

The second and equally important general Romantic theory of literary progress was that because of recent works' greater complexity and completeness, they were superior to earlier ones. Often this theory was expressed in terms of synthesis. Individual authors again gave varying examples of the phenomenon; nevertheless, they viewed the marriage of heretofore separated aesthetic endeavors as a means of progress. This theory, as well as the previous one, calling for more realism, will continue to appeal to other nineteenth-century writers long after the demise of Romanticism.

Hugo's *drame* was of course a synthesis—a combination of lyric, epic, and dramatic genres. It contained the best qualities of all three, the playwright believed, and thus was greater than any component genre. Musset thought Hugo had not gone far enough in his quest for totality in art, however, and suggested that to Hugo's *drame*, representative of Romantic drama, Classical drama, typified by the tragedies of Corneille and Racine, be grafted to create a new and better whole. Chateaubriand also wished to see a synthesis of Classicism and Romanticism. He wished for a blending of the Christian-Classical tradition of the Age of Louis XIV and the experimental attitude of nineteenth-century Romanticism. Balzac regretted the division of literature into that of "ideas" and "images" and called for a new, total literature which he named "eclectic." Baudelaire took Balzac to task, for he warned that mere eclecticism, the assemblage of varying parts, did not produce a harmonious work, and thus true synthesis was necessary to insure that the whole was greater than the sum of its parts. Interestingly Baudelaire's theory of *correspondances* is also reflective of the Romantic desire for synthesis. Baudelaire sought reciprocal aesthetic responses as well as stimuli. By hearing painting and seeing music, he more fully enjoyed art.

Gautier praised the reciprocity of the arts, thinking the intermingling of poetry and painting, *les transpositions d'art*, mutually beneficial. He wished to see the barriers between art forms removed so that the total work could be achieved. Preceding Wagner, he envisioned the perfect masterpiece, a *Gesamtkunstwerk*, a kind of opera which would excel verbally and graphically as well as tonally.

Sainte-Beuve was less specific in his desire for synthesis, not singling out any particular genre or discipline to be merged. He believed, however, that all aesthetic progress was the result of synthesis, the grafting of new material to existing stock. By adding to the treasure of past masterpieces, modern artists/writers continued the progress of art/literature.

The Romantics' desire for synthesis was coupled with their search for greater complexity in art, for they believed the new richness and variety of contemporary creations to be proof of aesthetic progress. Chateaubriand had early in the century formulated the law that art progressed as it moved from the simple to the complex. The ancients, he had noted, were simpler and more natural in their art. With the advance of civilization, life became more complicated and less natural. Modern writers, stymied by the richness of their environment found that they could not depict everything and were forced to choose only relevant aspects. They then created unnatural forms which surpassed the natural in beauty and complexity. The artificiality of civilization was thus reflected in literature. Chateaubriand labeled this process *le beau idéal*, the art of choosing and hiding.

Other writers were equally impressed by the increased artificiality of modern art and literature, which it will be remembered had been condemned by Rousseau as morally harmful. Gautier and Baudelaire particularly praised the increase of artifice and ornament as signs of improvement in the arts. Indeed Baudelaire's defense of *l'art décadent* was on the grounds that because of its greater variety, richness, and complexity, it was superior to earlier and less sophisticated artistic expressions. Balzac also believed nineteenth-century art greater than any preceding era's, for the present was grander than the past, and art reflected the era's grandeur. Things were both bigger and better in the nineteenth century. In addition, modern civilization was more varied and complex, which allowed for the addition of hundreds of types of new beauty, new situations, and new characters to be incorporated by art and literature.

Literary progress was thus the result of additions and innovations of modern, and especially contemporary, writers, according to the Romantics. By filling literary lacunae and by correcting the mistakes of past authors, the Romantics were achieving progress. To correct and to extend the accomplishments of the past, one had to do differently from the past. Thus imitation, or continuance of the old, had to be substituted by innovation, or creation of the new.

The preference for innovation instead of imitation predates Romanticism by at least two hundred years, for the moderns during the *Querelle des Anciens et des Modernes* had rejected Du Bellay's suggestion that to equal the ancients one must imitate them. The Saint-Sorlins, Perraults, and Fontenelles, who opted for superiority, not mere equality, encouraged their contemporaries to do what the ancients would do if alive today. Sainte-Beuve gave the same advice two centuries later. He believed that contemporaries, because they were alive, could possibly improve upon the quality of the art they had inherited from the past, whereas the ancient greats, being dead, could correct none of their mistakes.

Innovation requires absolute freedom. Rules and models must be avoided or imitation soon recurs. Hugo was perhaps the leading spokesman for artistic freedom under Romanticism. He denied that art had boundaries or limits. Thus its progress could be eternal. Balzac envisioned the great artist as pioneer, the one who forged ahead of the crowd, seeking new fields of conquest. He called the artist who made progress the man who "dared to dare."

Both Hugo and Balzac believed freedom necessary to language as well as literature. Hugo boasted of putting "un bonnet rouge sur le vieux dictionnaire," of having extended the ideals of the political revolution to the artistic one. There were no longer unacceptable words, he contended; the writer was now free to choose his vocabulary unrestrictedly. Balzac profited from Hugo's triumph and enlarged his vocabulary to depict his characters more realistically. Gautier's boast of having transformed the dictionary into a palette was further evidence that Hugo's example was admired and continued by his contemporaries.

Freedom within existing genres was soon coupled with freedom to create new ones. The Romantics pointed to the novel, modernity's creation, as the product of such freedom and evidence of literary progress. Stendhal went as far as to say that the novel, because of its freshness, represented the only means of significant literary progress in the nineteenth century, because innovation and progress within the traditional genres had been exhausted. Hugo agreed that the novel afforded an excellent opportunity to achieve literary progress, but he did not feel it was the only means. Characteristically Hugo sought both human and aesthetic progress by means of the novel, hoping to improve social conditions through his message as well as to achieve literary progress through the quality of his work. Balzac especially saw the novel as the means of surpassing all previous literary endeavors. He believed the novel to be unique, for it alone was thoroughly modern and synthetic. The novel combined comedy and tragedy, the lyric, epic, and dramatic. It, too, was capable of addressing itself to man's social and moral problems. Balzac ardently believed that the novel, and particularly his own, has produced great literary progress.

The drama likewise expected to show evidence of aesthetic advance. Hugo's new *drame,* by combining the lyric, epic, and dramatic, as well as synthesizing comedy and tragedy, and by juxtaposing the sublime and grotesque, was thought without equal.

By cherishing freedom and preferring innovation to imitation the Romantics were seeking timeliness in art. They wished to be modern, avant-garde, not traditional or antiquated. Believing beauty to be relative, i.e., never created in a definitive form, the Romantics thought nineteenth-century beauty to be equal, if not superior, to other expressions of beauty in previous eras. In addition, they believed that by creating a type of beauty especially adapted to the needs of the times, it would be more pleasing, more moving, and thus superior. The relevance of works to the era counted heavily in the Romantics' opinion toward determining their value.

The discussion of relative versus absolute beauty and its corollary, timely versus timeless beauty, was not original with the Romantics. Plato's theory of ideal archetypes, resurrected by French Renaissance poets, expressed much the same ideas. Like their sixteenth-century counterparts many Romantic poets recognized both aspects of beauty, the eternal and the temporal, and hoped to surpass others in their partial depiction of Ideal Beauty which existed only in the celestial spheres. The Romantics also took note of the dangers of too much insistence on timeliness. They sought to maintain the fine distinction which separates the timely from the faddish, for they did not wish to be relegated to the past as outdated writers, as they unhesitatingly had done with their predecessors. The value of timelessness was not underestimated by such modernists as Stendhal, Musset, Gautier, or Baudelaire.

The cult of modernity, nurtured by most Romantics, was perhaps best expressed by Balzac and Baudelaire. Balzac bragged of having no debts to the past. He had begun anew. Baudelaire's championing of *le beau moderne*, a type of beauty heretofore nonexistent, was another expression of timeliness.

Modernity as an aesthetic religion is of course a product of the eternal theory of the ages of civilization, begun by the Greeks and repeated by seventeenth and eighteenth-century quarrelers. The Romantics, however, seemed unsure of their century's age, with Hugo, Vigny, and Lamartine thinking the era to be virile and second-generation Romantics such as Gautier, Baudelaire, and Sainte-Beuve believing it to be in decline. The difference in optimism is striking. All agreed that an adult literature was now needed for a mature civilization. Earlier and more adolescent civilizations needed less sophisticated art. Baudelaire's favored *art décadent* was meant for the twilight of civilization. It abounded in artifice, ornament, variety, and complexity just as the age it reflected. Not only was such literature different from earlier varieties, Baudelaire insisted, but it was also superior.

Not all Romantics were content with their own era, and

some continued to long for a more perfect past, just as the ancient Greeks and Romans had wished for a return to the Golden Age. Musset particularly was guilty of this nostalgia, condemned by Vigny and Lamartine as wasteful. Gautier and Sainte-Beuve, fellow Hellenists, also looked wistfully to the past glories of earliest civilization. Stendhal also grumbled about the inadequacies of the nineteenth century. Renaissance Italy, however, not ancient Greece or Rome, appealed to him. Sainte-Beuve took all the Romantics to task for their longing for either the past or the far-distant. He diagnosed their malcontent as an illness, a symptom of a decadent age. Of all the Romantics it was Sainte-Beuve, however, who suffered most from this malady.

Another theory repeated during the Romantic discussion of progress besides that of the Golden Age was that of the Cycles of History. Vigny, Lamartine, and Sainte-Beuve all thought man and art cyclically progressed and declined. Vigny and Lamartine expressed their belief in terms of the flowering and fading of literary movements, which when harvested fertilized the soil for succeeding generations. Although each member of the cycle was short-lived, it was superior to its predecessor because of the richer background which had produced it, they believed.

A third old, but not ancient, idea survived during the Romantic debate—the belief that art, being different in nature from science, lay outside the scheme of progress. Hugo had noted that scientific advance annuls the accomplishments of the past, proving them either wrong or insufficient, whereas innovations in art do not lessen the quality of older, less innovative works. Baudelaire condemned the term *progress* generally because he associated it with technology and materialism. He thought the word too scientific to be applied to the spiritual realms of art. Both denigrators of the term also recognized that artistic progress was a possibility. They concluded that it did not void what came before but complemented it. This compromise definition, more readily accepted by the other Romantics, became the pervading distinction of artistic progress from scientific progress during the early nineteenth century.

While the Romantics were ultimately optimistic about the status of the arts and literature during their times, they did note regressions and faults which they felt diminished aesthetic quality. Again expressive of the intense individuality of the Romantic authors, one man's complaint was often another's claim to progress.

Mythology was often criticized as harmful to literature on the grounds that it was an artificial and foreign point of view. Mme de Staël, Chateaubriand, Balzac, and Baudelaire were especially hostile toward the ancient myths, if for varying reasons. On the contrary, Musset thought them more poetic than the Christian legend and that their loss to literature would mean a depreciation of its value. The devil's advocate in many aesthetic issues, Musset also attacked the era's fondness for realism which he felt lessened the role of the imaginative in art. Hugo's grotesque, he argued, was sheer ugliness. Art should reproduce beauty, he warned, not indiscriminately portray surroundings. Gautier as well as Musset resisted the Christianization of modern literature, if not favoring the return to the use of the pagan myths. Both authors believed art and religion to be separate spheres which suffered when combined. Musset's attack on realism was echoed by Baudelaire, who although favoring Hugo's incorporation of the grotesque in art, did not believe that art should unthinkingly reproduce reality. The artist must exaggerate, add and omit, he suggested. Imagination, not memory, was the more important trait of the true creator.

Despite the Romantics' criticisms of their age, they were generally proud of its literary triumphs. Many referred to their era as a second Renaissance, which they believed to be more glorious than the first. Mme de Staël had predicted the oncoming rebirth, thinking it would be the result of the progress of intellectual poetry. Hugo believed that he and his colleagues were greatly responsible for its arrival because of their lyrical accomplishments. Vigny and Lamartine also spoke proudly of the new Renaissance, the Romantic Era, when not only poetry, but all the fine arts had reached new heights of achievement. Gautier concurred that the times were similar to the Renaissance, but he believed that the Elizabethan age was more appropriate for comparison than fifteenth-century Italy, for Shakespeare was the Romantics' source of inspiration, not rediscovered Homer or Virgil. Sainte-Beuve alone likened the nineteenth century to the sixteenth negatively. He thought the two Renaissances too diffuse in talent, too eclectic in taste to equal the more uniform and harmonious Age of Louis XIV.

Concluding Remarks: The Unending Quarrel

The idea of progress was vigorously championed in the first half of the nineteenth century in France. Some thought man nearing utopia, others believed the fine arts, especially literature, to be approaching perfection. Differences of opinion abounded on the nature and rate of both man's and the arts' progress, nevertheless optimism prevailed over pessimism.

Concerning aesthetic progress, the Romantics concluded that it was different from scientific advance, for it did not void what had come before, but complemented it. In addition, artistic progress was thought to be sporadic, not continuous, and possible, not inevitable. It was generally defined as an extension of artistic activity, the result of innovation which made modern works more complete than their predecessors. The original creator, the one who achieved progress in the arts, was thought to be most like Balzac's pioneer or Hugo's genius, at the forefront of aesthetic activity.

Resistance to the association of the words *progress* and *art* existed among the Romantics as it does today. The myth of the artist as a unique being, his masterpieces as a unique phenomenon, so encouraged by the Romantics, entrenched such reluctance. Nevertheless, even the Romantics came to believe the fine arts, at least capable of progressing, if not destined to do so. As the individual creator adds however minutely to their existing treasury, progress is achieved.

A contemporary of the authors studied in this essay, a lexicographer for the *Dictionnaire Larousse du XIXe Siècle,* while recognizing the limitations of the theory and the strong objections to it, nevertheless proposed a compromise explanation of artistic progress which sums up the attitude of most Romantics. Holding the progress of knowledge responsible for the ensuing aesthetic advance, he wrote in the 1860's:

De toutes les branches de l'activité humaine, celles qui paraissent être les plus réfractaires au progrès sont les lettres, la poésie et les arts. . . . D'autre part notre temps a produit des formes littéraires nouvelles, le drame, le roman, et fait du journal un admirable engin intellectuel. Quelques-uns des poètes modernes peuvent aller de pair avec les plus grands de tous les âges. Admettons que, de notre temps, l'architecture, la sculpture, la peinture, la poésie même, si l'on veut, soient inférieures à ce qu'elles étaient dans l'antiquité et à l'époque de la Renaissance, ne pourrait-on dire que les mêmes arts, servant à exprimer un degré plus élevé de pensée et d'âme, sont par là même supérieurs. . . . Sur des pensers nouveaux faisons des vers antiques, écrivait André Chénier. Que les vers ne puissent être plus beaux qu'ils ont été, soit; si, au mérite d'aussi beaux vers, se joint le mérite de *pensers nouveaux* et plus nobles, ou plus profonds, ou plus vastes, plus dignes de l'homme devenu supérieur, n'est-ce pas là un progrés?[2]

A more recent observer of the Romantic Era shares this anonymous writer's optimism. Philippe Van Tieghem in *Le Romantisme français* unhesitatingly calls the accomplishments of that movement progress. His conviction equalled theirs, that literary progress was possible because the Romantics themselves had accomplished it.

Nos poètes romantiques ne sont plus seulement plus touchants, plus émus que leurs prédécesseurs; ce sont de *meilleurs* poètes, d'un art plus achevé. La prose n'est pas seulement un instrument, elle est par elle-même un objet d'art, souple, coloré, nuancé, riche en résonances. C'est ce progrès incontestable de la notion d'art qui fut l'apport le plus considérable du Romantisme littéraire; il ne constitue pas une révolution mais un perfectionnement en même temps qu'un enrichissement.[3]

---

[2] "Progrès", *Le Grand Dictionnaire Universel du XIXe Siècle.* Ed. Pierre Larousse. (Paris: Administration du G.D.U., 1866).

[3] (Paris: Presses Universitaires de France, 1944), p. 126.

Van Tieghem, unlike the lexicographer, recognized the truly Romantic contribution to the discussion of literary progress, the movement's cult of the artist and of art, its heightened aesthetic sensitivity. Like Gautier, Balzac, and Baudelaire, Van Tieghem believed nineteenth-century literature, reflective of the complexity, artifice, and sophistication of the age, represented an advance over the simpler, less nuanced works of earlier eras.

As we have seen, the Romantic discussion of progress was not without precedent and, it must be noted, has not been without successors. In principle, the time period of the debate could be extended to the present, for its issues continue to interest students of literature and the fine arts as they did seventeenth and eighteenth-century *querelleurs* as well as the Romantics.

Since the Romantic Era many prominent French writers have employed the arguments of former debaters of progress. One finds rich material on the subject in the correspondences of Flaubert and Taine, the art criticism of Zola, and the essays of Valéry. To sample just two of the many statements to come from post-Romantic writers, those of Proust and Sartre, one sees that the struggle of innovation over imitation, the search for a new, complete literature, expressed by the Perraults as well as the Baudelaires, has never subsided.

Proust speaks of the perpetual rivalry of novelty and tradition in reference to Bergotte, the novelist friend of the young Marcel. Meditating upon his diminishing esteem for Bergotte's works, which for many years he thought without rival, and his growing admiration for those of a more modern and difficult writer, Marcel concludes that the pattern of the new replacing the old is a general one applicable to literature. Referring to the basic questions of the debate on progress, he doubts the distinction commonly held that science alone is capable of progress while art stands forever still. Believing each artist to find a new rapport between things, he concludes that succeeding discoveries could well create a chain of artistic progress. In "Le Côté des Guermantes" the narrator suggests:

Celui qui avait remplacé pour moi Bergotte me lassait non par l'incohérence mais par la nouveauté, parfaitement cohérente, de rapports que je n'avais pas l'habitude de suivre. . . . Et j'arrivais à me demander s'il y avait quelque vérité en cette distinction que nous faisons toujours entre l'art, qui n'est pas plus avancé qu'au temps d'Homère, et la science aux progrès continus. Peut-être l'art ressemblait-il au contraire en cela à la science; chaque nouvel écrivain original me semblait en progrès sur celui qui l'avait précédé; et qui me disait que dans vingt ans, quand je saurais accompagner sans fatigue le nouveau d'aujourd'hui, un autre ne surviendrait pas devant qui l'actuel filerait rejoindre Bergotte.[4]

Sartre also makes use of the Romantics' arguments on progress in his defense of a *littérature engagée* against the attack of the supporters of a *littérature pure*.

Que si l'on considère les sujets comme des problèmes toujours ouverts, comme des sollicitations, des attentes, on comprendra que l'art ne perd rien à l'engagement; au contraire, de même que la physique soumet aux mathématiciens des problèmes nouveaux qui les obligent à produire un symbolisme neuf, de même que les exigences toujours neuves du social ou de la métaphysique engagent l'artiste à trouver une langue neuve et des techniques nouvelles. Si nous n'écrivons plus comme au XVIIe siècle, c'est bien que la langue de Racine et de Saint-Evremond ne se prête pas à parler des locomotives ou du prolétariat. Après cela, les puristes nous interdiront peut-être d'écrire sur les locomotives. Mais l'art n'a jamais été côté des puristes.[5]

The circle is unbroken. There are always new moderns to oppose recent ancients. Innovation constantly struggles against imitation. Sartre's call for timeliness is centuries old.

---

[4] *A la recherche du temps perdu*. Ed. de la Pléiade. (Paris: Gallimard, 1954), II, 238.
[5] "Qu'est-ce que la littérature?", *Situations II*. (Paris: Gallimard, 1948), p. 76.

stuðia humanitatis

PUBLISHED VOLUMES

Louis Marcello La Favia, *Benvenuto Rambaldi da Imola: Dantista.* xii–188 pp. US $9.25.

John O'Connor, *Balzac's Soluble Fish.* xii–252 pp. US $14.25.

Carlos García, *La desordenada codicia,* edición crítica de Giulio Massano. xii–220 pp. US $11.50.

Everett W. Hesse, *Interpretando la Comedia.* xii–184 pp. US $10.00.

Lewis Kamm, *The Object in Zola's* Rougon-Macquart. xii–160 pp. US $9.25.

Ann Bugliani, *Women and the Feminine Principle in the Works of Paul Claudel.* xii–144 pp. US $9.25.

Charlotte Frankel Gerrard, *Montherlant and Suicide.* xvi–72 pp. US $5.00.

The Two Hesperias. Literary Studies in Honor of Joseph G. Fucilla. Edited by Americo Bugliani. xx–372 pp. US $30.00.

Jean J. Smoot, *A Comparison of Plays by John M. Synge and Federico García Lorca: The Poets and Time.* xiii–220 pp. US $13.00.

Laclos. Critical Approaches to Les Liaisons dangereuses. Ed. Lloyd R. Free. xii–300 pp. US $17.00.

Julia Conaway Bondanella, *Petrarch's Visions and their Renaissance Analogues.* xii–120 pp. US $7.00.

Vincenzo Tripodi, *Studi su Foscolo e Stern.* xii–216 pp. US $13.00.

GENARO J. PÉREZ, *Formalist Elements in the Novels of Juan Goytisolo.* xii–216 pp. US $12.50.

SARA MARIA ADLER, *Calvino: The Writer as Fablemaker.* xviii–164 pp. US $11.50.

LOPE DE VEGA, *El amor enamorado*, critical edition of John B. Wooldridge, Jr. xvi–236 pp. US $13.00.

NANCY DERSOFI, *Arcadia and the Stage: A Study of the Theater of Angelo Beolco* (called *Ruzante*). xii–180 pp. US $10.00

JOHN A. FREY, *The Aesthetics of the ROUGON-MACQUART.* xvi–356 pp. US $20.00.

CHESTER W. OBUCHOWSKI, *Mars on Trial: War as Seen by French Writers of the Twentieth Century.* xiv–320 pp. US $20.00.

JEREMY T. MEDINA, *Spanish Realism: Theory and Practice of a Concept in the Nineteenth Century.* xviii–374 pp. US $17.50.

MAUDA BREGOLI-RUSSO, *Boiardo Lirico.* viii–204 pp. US $11.00.

ROBERT H. MILLER, ed. *Sir John Harington: A Supplie or Addicion to the Catalogue of Bishops to the Yeare 1608.* xii–214 pp. US $13.50.

NICOLÁS E. ÁLVAREZ, *La obra literaria de Jorge Mañach.* vii–279 pp. US $13.00.

MARIO ASTE, *La narrativa di Luigi Pirandello: Dalle novelle al romanzo "Uno, Nessuno, e Centomila."* xvi–200 pp. US $11.00.

MECHTHILD CRANSTON, *Orion Resurgent: René Char, Poet of Presence.* xxiv–376 pp. US $22.50.

FRANK A. DOMÍNGUEZ, *The Medieval Argonautica.* viii–122 pp. US $10.50.

EVERETT HESSE, *New Perspectives on Comedia Criticism.* xix–174 pp. US $14.00.

ANTHONY A. CICCONE, *The Comedy of Language: Four Farces by Molière.* xii–144 $12.00.

ANTONIO PLANELLS, *Cortázar: Metafísica y erotismo.* xvi–220 pp. US $10.00.

MARY LEE BRETZ, *La evolución novelística de Pío Baroja.* viii–476 pp. US $22.50.

Romance Literary Studies: Homage to Harvey L. Johnson, ed. Marie A. Wellington and Martha O'Nan. xxxvii–185 pp. US $15.00.

GEORGE E. MCSPADDEN, *Don Quijote and the Spanish Prologues*, volume I. vi–114 pp. US $17.00.

Studies in Honor of Gerald E. Wade, edited by Sylvia Bowman, Bruno M. Damiani, Janet W. Díaz, E. Michael Gerli, Everett Hesse, John E. Keller, Luis Leal and Russell P. Sebold. xii–244 pp. US $20.00.

LOIS ANN RUSSELL, *Robert Challe: A Utopian Voice in the Early Enlightenment*. xiii–164 pp. US $12.50.

CRAIG WALLACE BARROW, *Montage in James Joyce's* ULYSSES. xiii–218 pp. US $16.50.

MARIA ELISA CIAVARELLI, *La fuerza de la sangre en la literatura del Siglo de Oro*. xii–274 pp. US $17.00.

JUAN MARÍA COROMINAS, *Castiglione y La Araucana: Estudio de una Influencia*. viii–139 pp. US $14.00.

KENNETH BROWN, *Anastasio Pantaleón de Ribera (1600–1629) Ingenioso Miembro de la República Literaria Española*. xix–420 pp. US $18.50.

JOHN STEVEN GEARY, *Formulaic Diction in the* Poema de Fernán González *and the* Mocedades de Rodrigo. xv–180 pp. US $15.50.

HARRIET K. GREIF, *Historia de nacimientos: The Poetry of Emilio Prados*. xi–399 pp. US $18.00.

El cancionero del Bachiller Jhoan López, edición crítica de Rosalind Gabin. lvi–362 pp. US $30.00.

VICTOR STRANDBERG, *Religious Psychology in American Literature*. xi–237 pp. US $17.50.

M. AMELIA KLENKE, O.P., *Chrétien de Troyes and "Le Conte del Graal": A Study of Sources and Symbolism*. xvii–88 pp. US $11.50.

MARINA SCORDILIS BROWNLEE, *The Poetics of Literary Theory: Lope de Vega's* Novelas a Marcia Leonarda *and Their Cervantine Context*. x–182 pp. US $16.50.

NATALIE NESBITT WOODLAND, *The Satirical Edge of Truth in "The Ring and the Book."* ix–166 pp. US $17.00.

JOSEPH BARBARINO, *The Latin and Romance Intervocalic Stops: A Quantitative and Comparative Study*. xi–153 pp. US $16.50.

SANDRA FORBES GERHARD, *"Don Quixote" and the Shelton Translation: A Stylistic Analysis*. viii–166 pp. US $16.00.

EVERETT W. HESSE, *Essays on Spanish Letters of the Golden Age*. xii–208 pp. US $16.50.

VALERIE D. GREENBERG, *Literature and Sensibilities in the Weimar Era: Short Stories in the "Neue Rundschau."* Preface by Eugene H. Falk. xiii–289 pp. US $18.00.

ANDREA PERRUCCI, *Shepherds' Song (La Cantata dei Pastori)*. English version by Miriam and Nello D'Aponte. xix–80 pp. US $11.50.

MARY JO MURATORE, *The Evolution of the Cornelian Heroine*. v–153 pp. US $17.50.

FERNANDO RIELO, *Teoría del Quijote*. xix–201 pp. US $17.00.

GALEOTTO DEL CARRETTO, *Li sei contenti e La Sofonisba*, edizione e commento di Mauda Bregoli Russo. viii–256 pp. US $16.50.

BIRUTÉ CIPLIJAUSKAITÉ, *Los noventayochistas y la historia*. vii–213 pp. US $16.00.

EDITH TOEGEL, *Emily Dickinson and Annette von Droste-Hülshoff: Poets as Women*. vii–109 pp. US $11.50.

DENNIS M. KRATZ, *Mocking Epic*. xv–171 pp. US $12.50.

EVERETT W. HESSE, *Theology, Sex and the Comedia and Other Essays*. xvii–129 pp. US $14.50.

HELÍ HERNÁNDEZ, *Antecedentes italianos de la novela picaresca española: estudio lingüístico-literario*. x–155 pp. US $14.50.

ANTONY VAN BEYSTERVELDT, *Amadís, Esplandián, Calisto: historia de un linaje adulterado*. xv–276 pp. US $24.50.

ROUBEN C. CHOLAKIAN, *The "Moi" in the Middle Distance: A Study of the Narrative Voice in Rabelais*. vii–132 pp. US $16.50.

JUAN DE MENA, *Coplas de los Siete Pecados Mortales* and First Continuation, Volume I. Edition, Study and Notes by Gladys M. Rivera. xi–212 pp. US $22.50.

JAMES DONALD FOGELQUIST, *El Amadís y el género de la historia fingida*. x–253 pp. US $21.50.

EGLA MORALES BLOUIN, *El ciervo y la fuente: mito y folklore del agua en la lírica tradicional*. x–316 pp. US $22.50.

La pícara Justina. Edición de Bruno Mario Damiani. vii–492 pp. US $33.50.

Red Flags, Black Flags: Critical Essays on the Literature of the Spanish Civil War. Ed. John Beals Romeiser. xxxiv–256 pp. US $21.50.

RAQUEL CHANG-RODRÍGUEZ, *Violencia y subversión en la prosa colonial hispanoamericana*. xv–132 pp. US $18.50.

DAVID C. LEONARD AND SARA M. PUTZELL, *Perspectives on Nineteenth-Century Heroism: Essays from the 1981 Conference of the Southeastern Studies Association*. xvi–164 pp. US $20.00.

La Discontenta and La Pythia, edition with introduction and notes by Nicholas A. De Mara. vii–214 pp. US $17.00.

CALDERÓN DE LA BARCA, *The Prodigal Magician,* translated and edited by Bruce W. Wardropper. vii–250 pp. US $20.00.

JOHN R. BURT, *Selected Themes and Icons from Medieval Spanish Literature: Of Beards, Shoes, Cucumbers and Leprosy.* xi–111 pp. US $16.50.

ALAN FRANK KEELE, *The Apocalyptic Vision: A Thematic Exploration of Postwar German Literature.* vii–129 pp. US $19.00.

ARIÉ SERPER, *Huon de Saint-Quentin: Poète satirique et lyrique.* Etude historique et édition de textes. v–135 pp. US $20.00.

ROBERT COOGAN, *Babylon on the Rhone: A Translation of Letters of Dante, Petrarch, and Catherine of Siena on the Avignon Papacy.* x–126 pp. US $19.50.

LAWRENCE H. KLIBBE, *Lorca's "Impresiones y paisajes": The Young Artist.* xi–165 pp. US $18.00.

NANCY D'ANTUONO, *Boccaccio's "Novelle" in the Theater of Lope de Vega.* xiv–190 pp. US $21.50.

BEVERLY WEST, *Epic, Folk, and Christian Traditions in the "Poema de Fernán González."* v–174 pp. US $18.50.

ERASMO GABRIELE GERATO, *Guido Gustavo Gozzano: A Literary Interpretation.* xii–126 pp. US $19.50.

JOAN CAMMARATA, *Mythological Themes in the Works of Garcilaso de la Vega.* xiv–168 pp. US $21.50.

ROBERT A. DETWEILER AND SARA M. PUTZELL-KORAB, eds. *Crisis in the Humanities.* xxi–217 pp. US $19.50.

MALCOLM K. READ, *The Birth and Death of Language: Spanish Literature and Linguistics: 1300–1700.* xii–213 pp. US $25.50.

TERRY SMILEY DOCK, *Woman in the* Encyclopédie: *A Compendium.* xii–179 pp. US $18.59

DARLENE J. SADLIER, *Imagery and Theme in the Poetry of Cecília Meireles: A Study of "Mar Absoluto."* 1–126 pp. US $19.59

ELWOOD HARTMAN, *French Romantics on Progress: Human and Aesthetic.* xiv–283 pp. US $26.50

FORTHCOMING PUBLICATIONS
HELMUT HATZFELD, *Essais sur la littérature flamboyante.*

ALONSO ORTIZ, *Diálogo sobre la educación del Príncipe Don Juan, hijo de los Reyes Católicos*. Introducción y versión de Giovanni Maria Bertini.

Novelistas femeninas de la postguerra española, ed. Janet W. Díaz.

ALBERT H. LE MAY, *The Experimental Verse Theater of Valle-Inclán*.

Le Gai Savoir: Essays in Linguistics, Philology, and Criticism. Dedicated to the Memory of Manfred Sandmann. Edited by Mechthild Cranston.

MIMI GISOLFI D'APONTE, *Teatro religioso e rituale della penisola Sorrentina e la Costiera Amalfitana*.

CORDELL W. BLACK. *Corneille's Denouements: Text and Conversion*.

Pedro Antonio de Alarcon: Obras Olvidadas. Edición de Cyrus DeCoster.